井上雄彦

Takehiko Inoue

EVERY ONCE IN A WHILE I FEEL MY AGE. I MISS AN EASY BASKET OR WHATEVER... IT SADDENS ME TO KNOW THAT IT'S ONLY GOING TO GET WORSE AS THE YEARS PASS. I'M JUST AN AMATEUR. CAN YOU IMAGINE WHAT THAT FEELS LIKE FOR A PRO?

AT THE SAME TIME I BEGAN PONDERING THE ISSUE OF RETIREMENT, MICHAEL JORDAN ANNOUNCED HIS. HE'S LEAVING THE COURT BEFORE HE STARTS TO LOSE HIS EDGE.

Takehiko Inoue's *Slam Dunk* is one of the most popular manga of all time, having sold over 100 million copies worldwide. He followed that series up with two titles lauded by critics and fans alike—*Vagabond*, a fictional account of the life of Miyamoto Musashi, and *Real*, a manga about wheelchair basketball.

SLAM DUNK
Vol. 16: SURVIVAL GAME

SHONEN JUMP Manga Edition

STORY AND ART BY TAKEHIKO INOUE

English Adaptation/Kelly Sue DeConnick
Translation/Joe Yamazaki
Touch-up Art & Lettering/James Gaubatz
Cover & Graphic Design/Sean Lee, Matt Hinrichs
Editor/Mike Montesa

Published by VIZ Media, LLC
P.O. Box 77010
San Francisco, CA 94107

10 9 8 7 6 5 4 3
First printing, June 2011
Third printing, July 2017

PARENTAL ADVISORY
SLAM DUNK is rated T for Teen and is recommended
for ages 13 and up. This volume contains realistic
violence and crude humor.
ratings.viz.com

SLAM DUNK

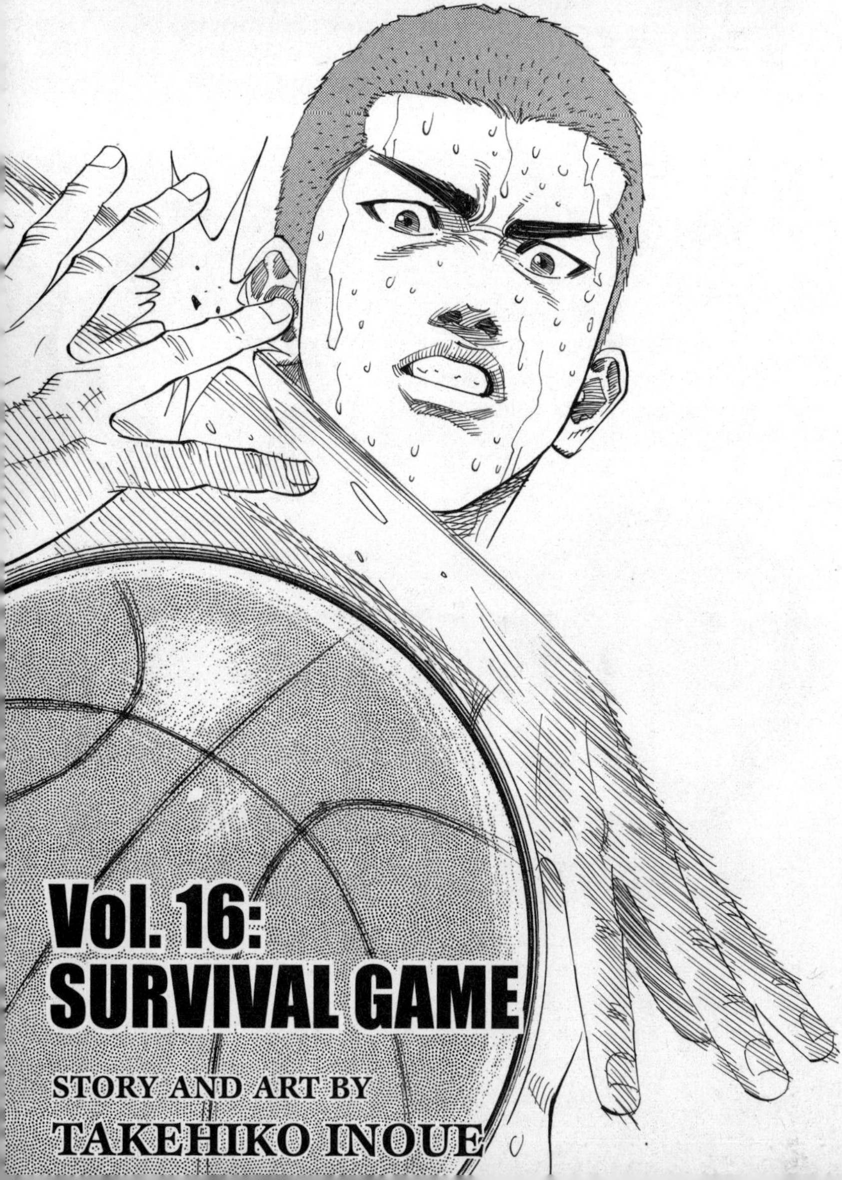

Vol. 16: SURVIVAL GAME

STORY AND ART BY

TAKEHIKO INOUE

Character Introduction

Hanamichi Sakuragi
A first-year at Shohoku High School, Sakuragi is in love with Haruko Akagi.

Haruko Akagi
Also a first-year at Shohoku, Takenori Akagi's little sister has a crush on Kaede Rukawa.

Takenori Akagi
A third-year and the basketball team's captain, Akagi has an intense passion for his sport.

Kaede Rukawa
The object of Haruko's affection (and that of many of Shohoku's female students!), this first-year has been a star player since junior high.

Fukuda

Sendoh

Ryota Miyagi
A problem child with
a thing for Ayako.

Ayako
Basketball Team
Manager

Hisashi Mitsui
An MVP during
junior high.

Our Story Thus Far

Hanamichi Sakuragi is rejected by close to 50 girls during his three years in junior high. He joins the basketball team to get closer to his beloved Haruko Akagi, but the constant fundamental drills cause him endless frustration.

After a good showing in their first exhibition, the team sets its sights on Nationals and ex-problem-child Ryota Miyagi reclaims his position as Point Guard. Not long after Miyagi's return, Hisashi Mitsui—a junior-high-MVP-turned-gang-thug—finds he too misses the game and rejoins the team.

Despite a valiant attempt, Shohoku loses to Kainan in a very close game. Shohoku has two more games to play in the tournament, and if they want to stay alive they have to win them both! Sakuragi's got talent but his inexperience is his downfall. Realizing this, Sakuragi renews his commitment to the team after a fight with Rukawa. He shaves his head and sets himself to making 500 practice shots a day!

Vol. 16:
SURVIVAL GAME

Table of Contents

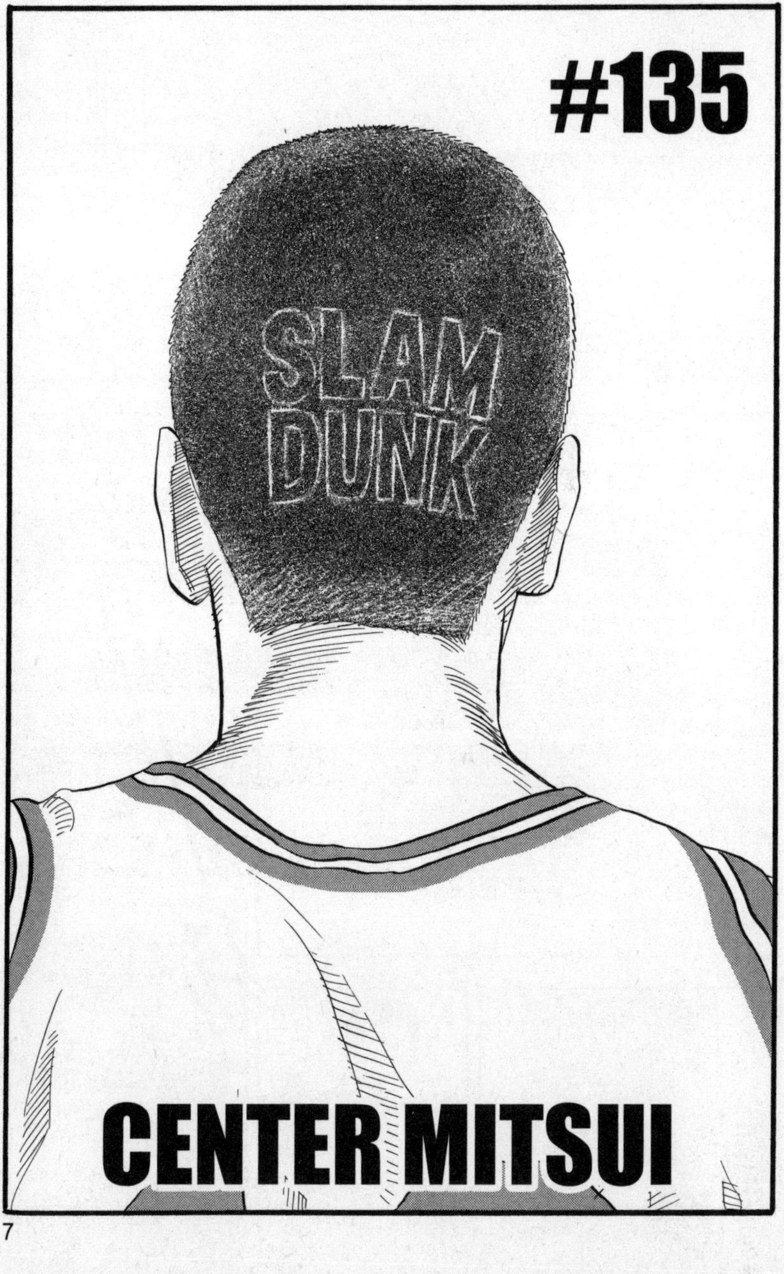
#135
SLAM
DUNK
CENTER MITSUI

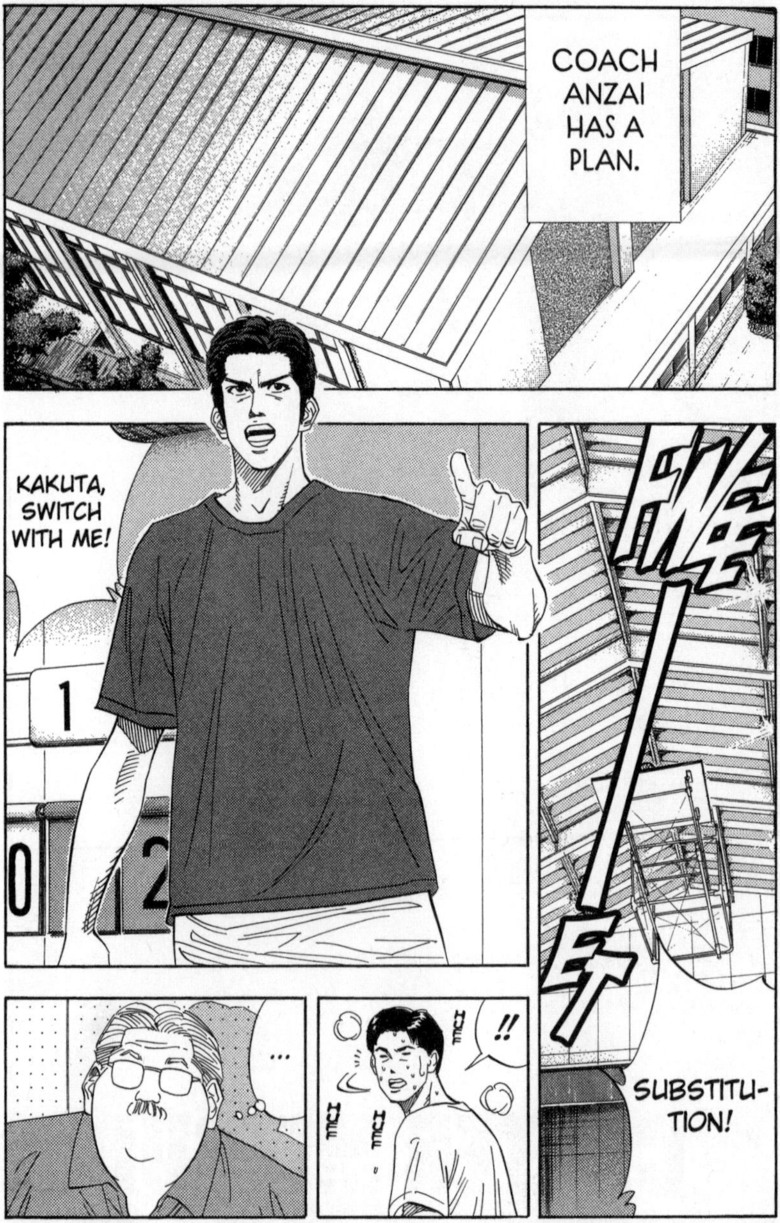
COACH ANZAI HAS A PLAN.
FWE—ET
SUBSTITU-TION!
KAKUTA, SWITCH WITH ME!
!!
HUFF
HUFF
HUFF
...

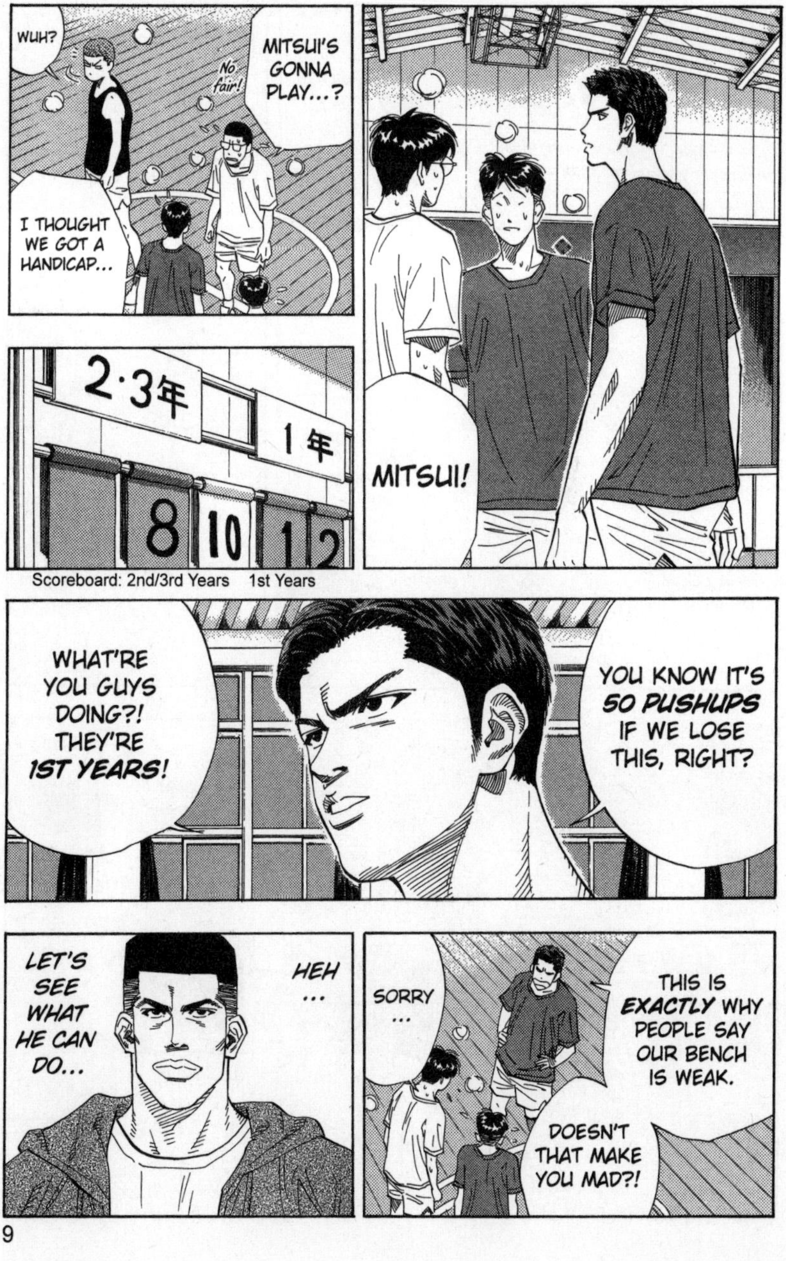
MITSUI!
MITSUI'S GONNA PLAY...?
No fair!
WUH?
I THOUGHT WE GOT A HANDICAP...
2·3年
1年
8 10 1 2
Scoreboard: 2nd/3rd Years 1st Years
YOU KNOW IT'S **50 PUSHUPS** IF WE LOSE THIS, RIGHT?
WHAT'RE YOU GUYS DOING?! THEY'RE **1ST YEARS**!
THIS IS **EXACTLY** WHY PEOPLE SAY OUR BENCH IS WEAK.
SORRY...
DOESN'T THAT MAKE YOU MAD?!
HEH...
LET'S SEE WHAT HE CAN DO...

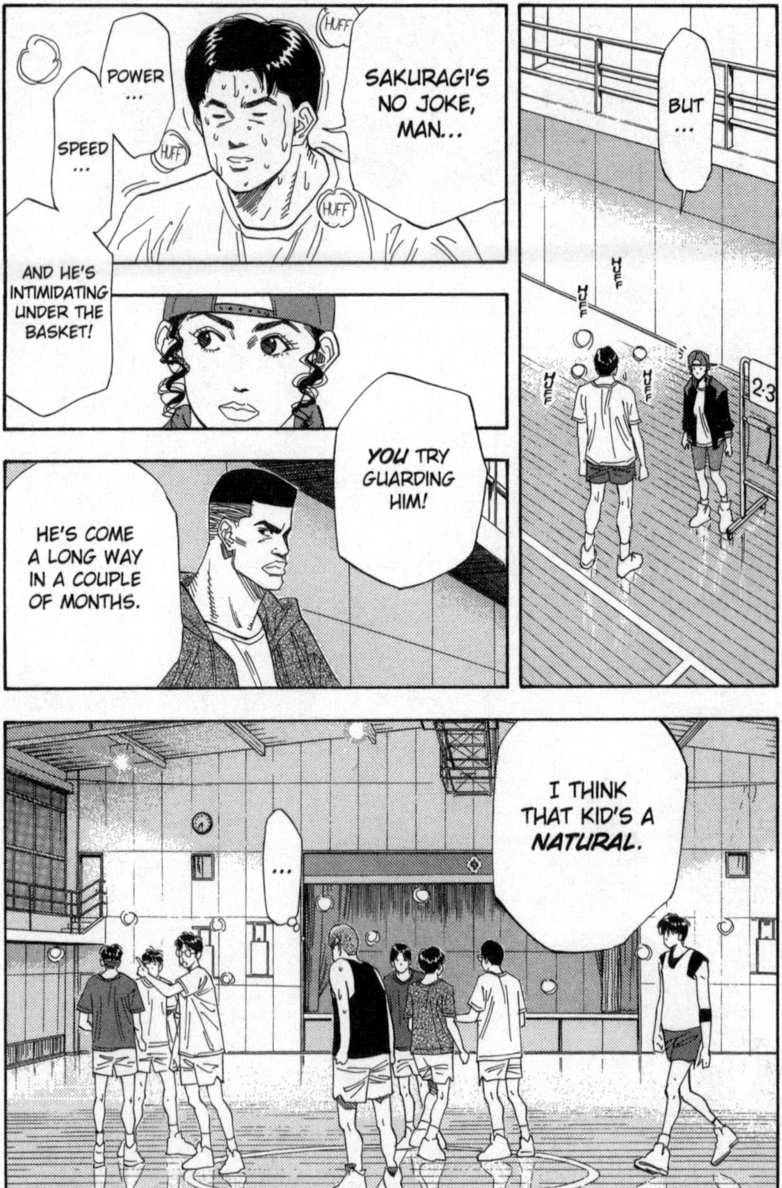
BUT ...
HUFF
HUFF
HUFF
HUFF
HUFF
SAKURAGI'S NO JOKE, MAN...
HUFF
POWER ...
HUFF
SPEED ...
AND HE'S INTIMIDATING UNDER THE BASKET!
YOU TRY GUARDING HIM!
HE'S COME A LONG WAY IN A COUPLE OF MONTHS.
I THINK THAT KID'S A *NATURAL*.
...

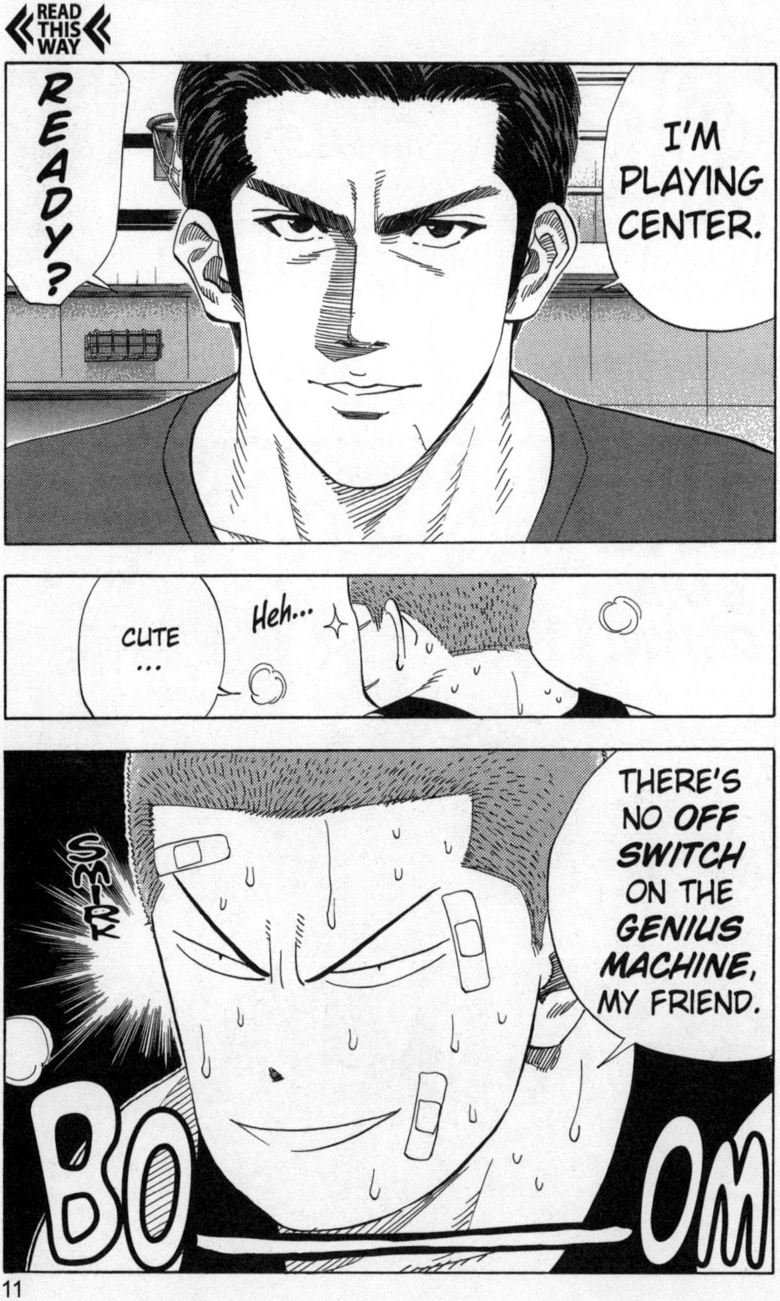
READ THIS WAY
I'M PLAYING CENTER.
READY?
Heh...
CUTE ...
THERE'S NO *OFF SWITCH* ON THE *GENIUS MACHINE*, MY FRIEND.
SMIRK
BOOM

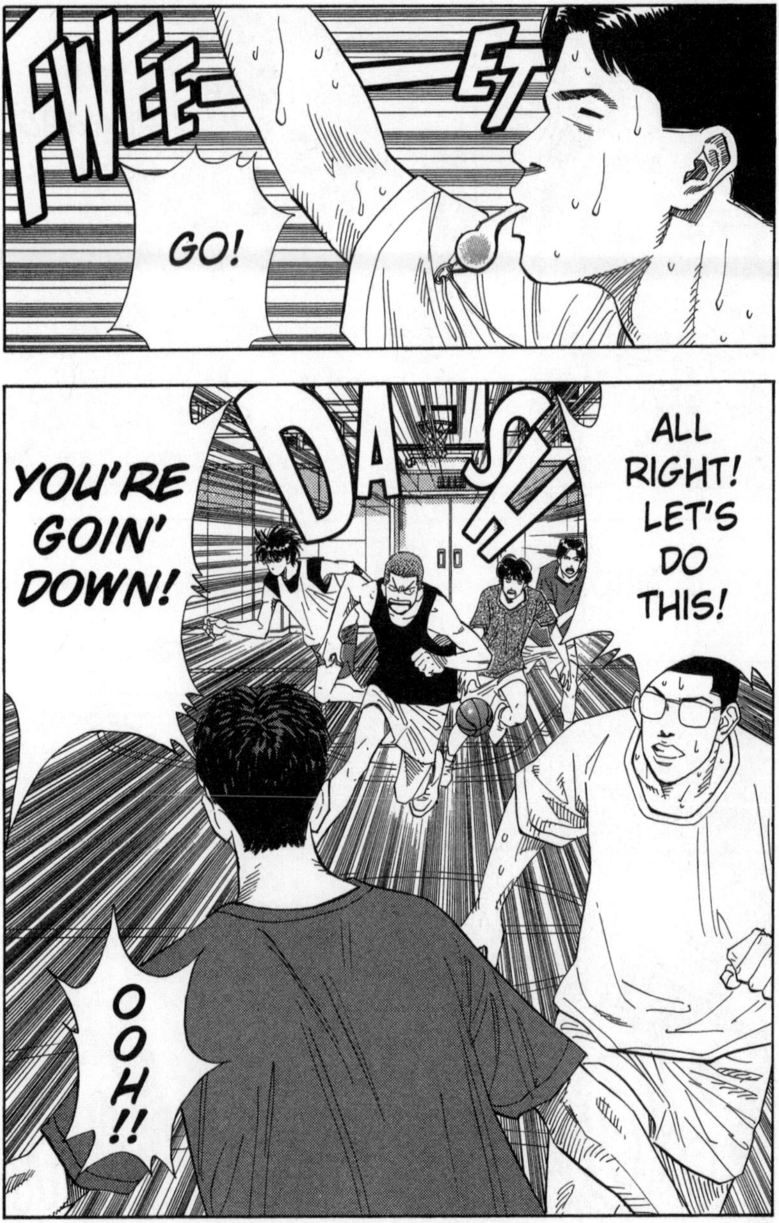
FWEE-ET
GO!
ALL RIGHT! LET'S DO THIS!
DASH
YOU'RE GOIN' DOWN!
OOH!!

READ THIS WAY

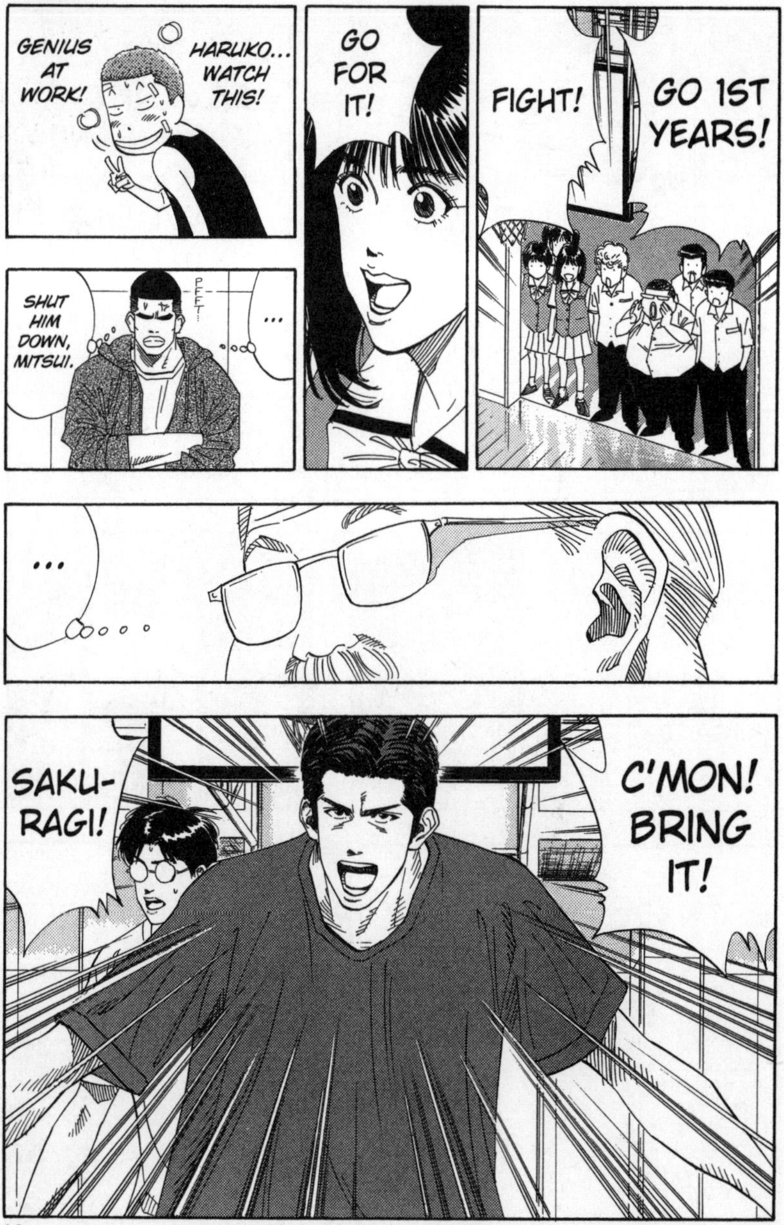
GO 1ST YEARS!
FIGHT!
GO FOR IT!
HARUKO... WATCH THIS!
GENIUS AT WORK!
...
PFFT
SHUT HIM DOWN, MITSUI.
...
C'MON! BRING IT!
SAKU-RAGI!

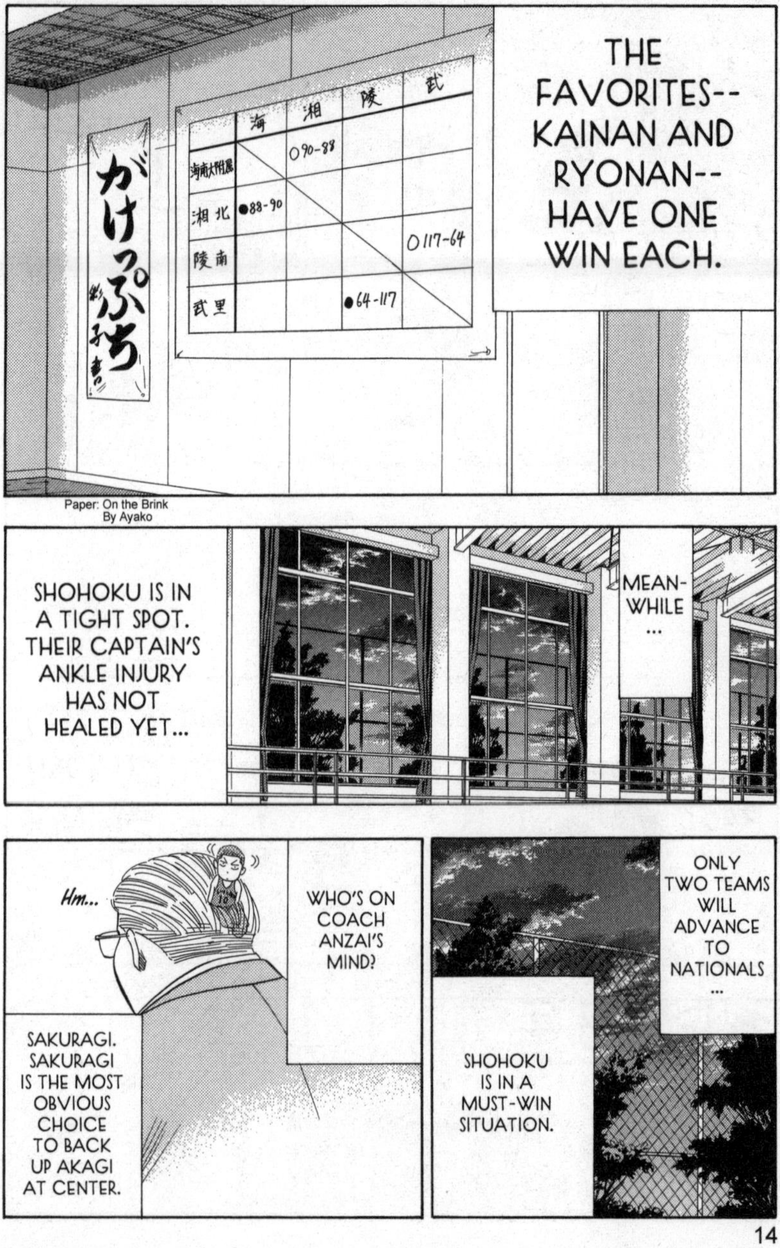
THE FAVORITES--KAINAN AND RYONAN--HAVE ONE WIN EACH.
海 湘 陵 武
海南大附属
湘北
陵南
武里
○90-88
●88-90
○117-64
●64-117
がけっぷち
彩子書
MEAN-WHILE...
SHOHOKU IS IN A TIGHT SPOT. THEIR CAPTAIN'S ANKLE INJURY HAS NOT HEALED YET...
ONLY TWO TEAMS WILL ADVANCE TO NATIONALS...
SHOHOKU IS IN A MUST-WIN SITUATION.
WHO'S ON COACH ANZAI'S MIND?
Hm...
SAKURAGI. SAKURAGI IS THE MOST OBVIOUS CHOICE TO BACK UP AKAGI AT CENTER.
Paper: On the Brink
By Ayako

READ THIS WAY

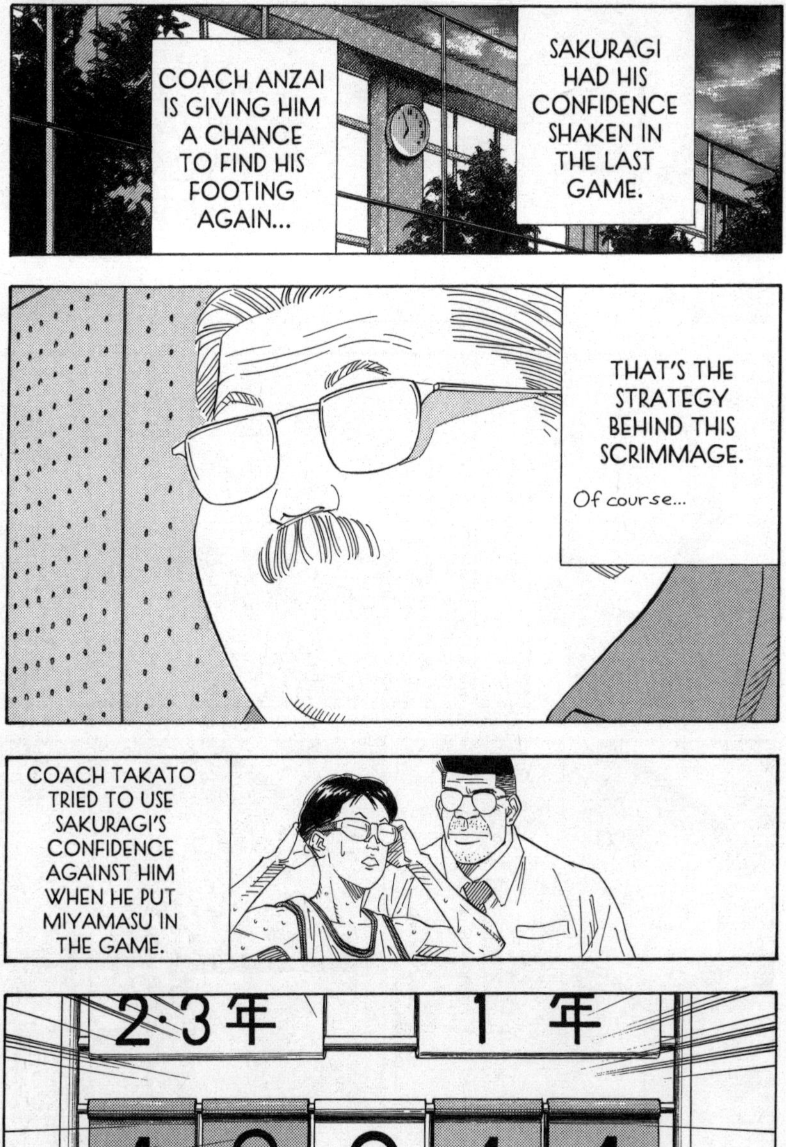

SAKURAGI HAD HIS CONFIDENCE SHAKEN IN THE LAST GAME.
COACH ANZAI IS GIVING HIM A CHANCE TO FIND HIS FOOTING AGAIN...
THAT'S THE STRATEGY BEHIND THIS SCRIMMAGE.
Of course...
COACH TAKATO TRIED TO USE SAKURAGI'S CONFIDENCE AGAINST HIM WHEN HE PUT MIYAMASU IN THE GAME.
2·3年
1年
1 8 6 1 4

Scoreboard: 2nd/3rd Years 1st Years

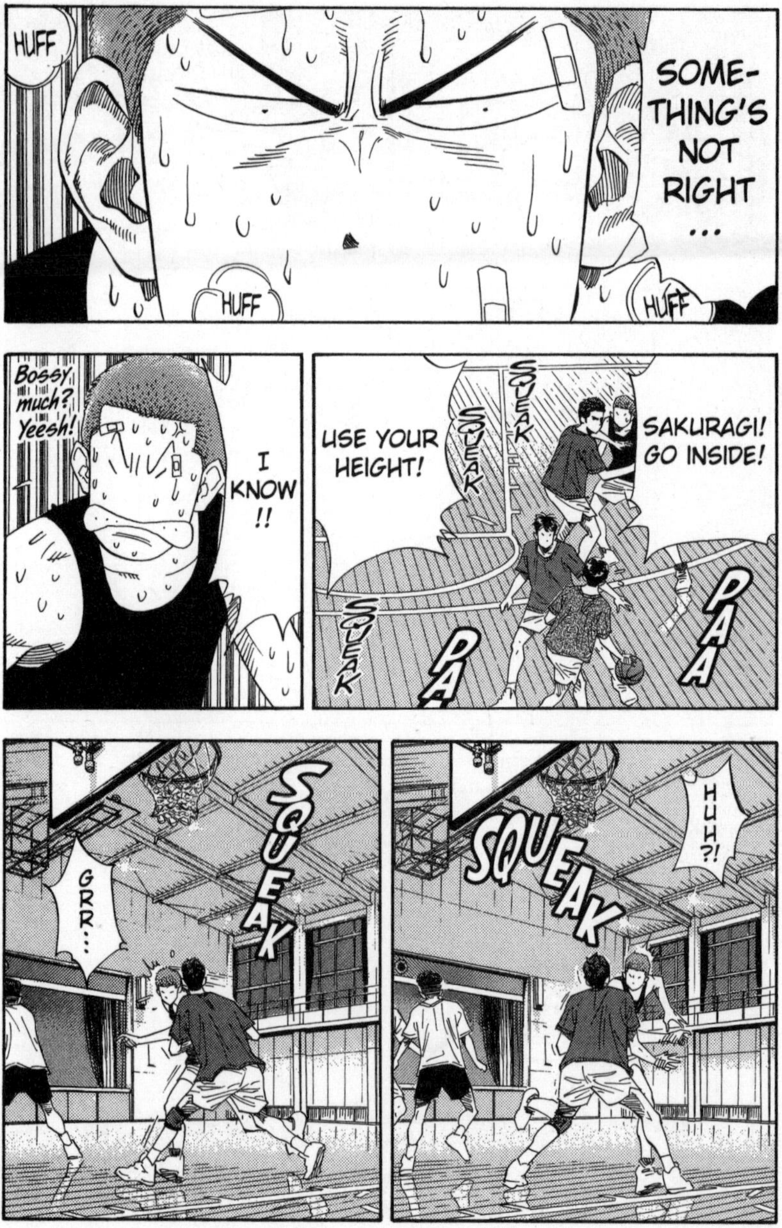
SOME-THING'S NOT RIGHT...
HUFF
HUFF
HUFF
SAKURAGI! GO INSIDE!
SQUEAK
SQUEAK
USE YOUR HEIGHT!
PAA
PA
SQUEAK
I KNOW!!
Bossy much? Yeesh!
HUH?!
SQUEAK
SQUEAK
GRR...

READ THIS WAY

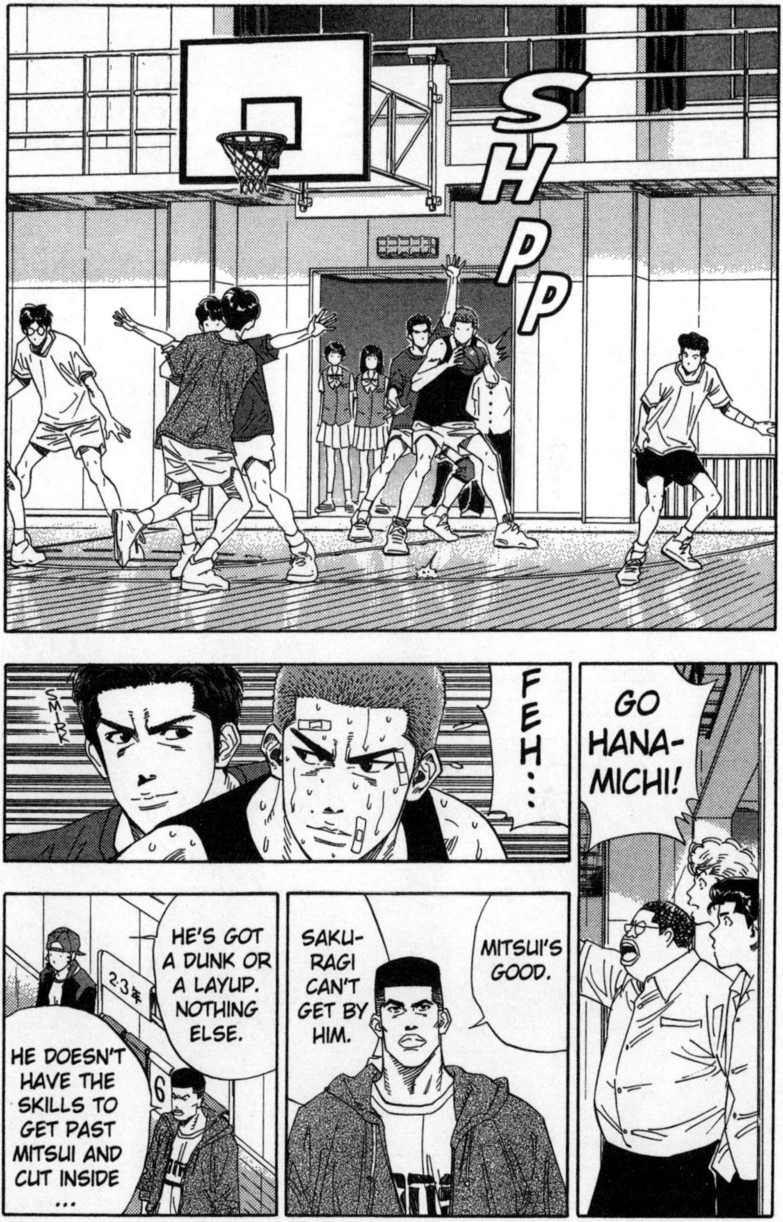
SHPP
GO HANA-MICHI!
FEH...
SMIRK
MITSUI'S GOOD.
SAKU-RAGI CAN'T GET BY HIM.
HE'S GOT A DUNK OR A LAYUP. NOTHING ELSE.
HE DOESN'T HAVE THE SKILLS TO GET PAST MITSUI AND CUT INSIDE ...

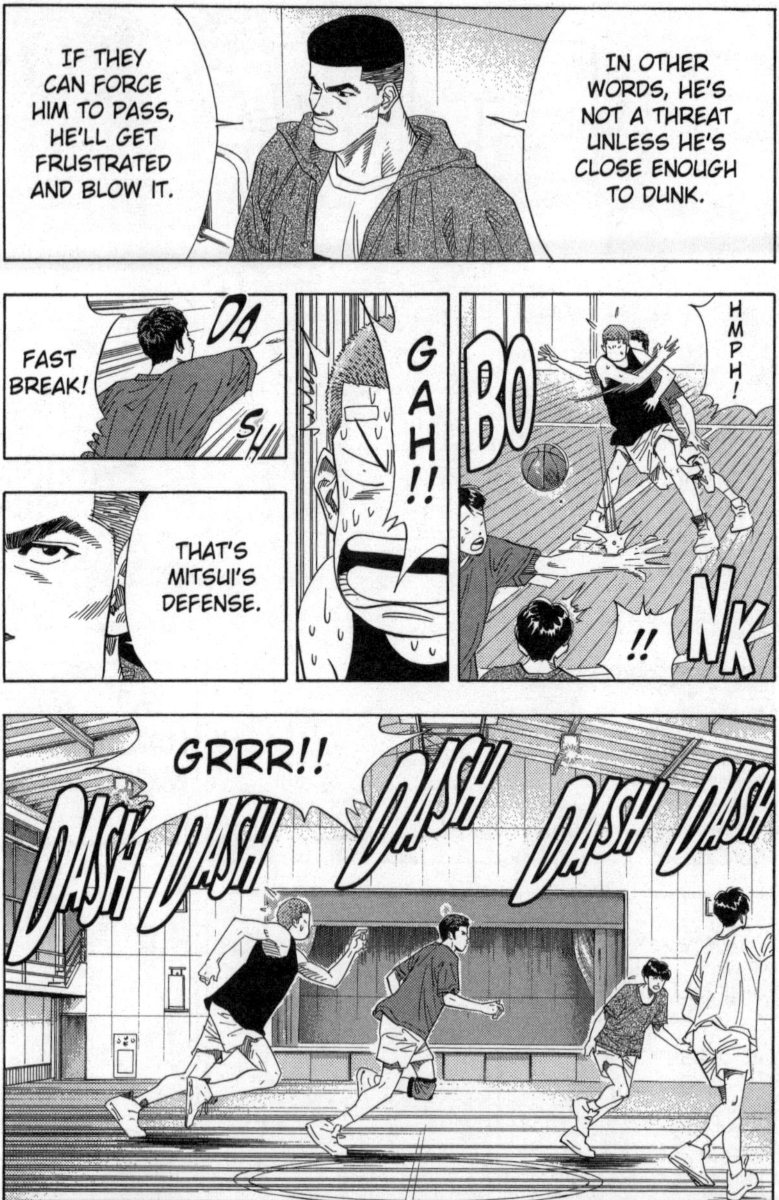
IN OTHER WORDS, HE'S NOT A THREAT UNLESS HE'S CLOSE ENOUGH TO DUNK.
IF THEY CAN FORCE HIM TO PASS, HE'LL GET FRUSTRATED AND BLOW IT.
HMPH!
BO
NK
!!
GAH!!
DA
SH
FAST BREAK!
THAT'S MITSUI'S DEFENSE.
GRRR!!
DASH
DASH
DASH
DASH
DASH
DASH

READ THIS WAY

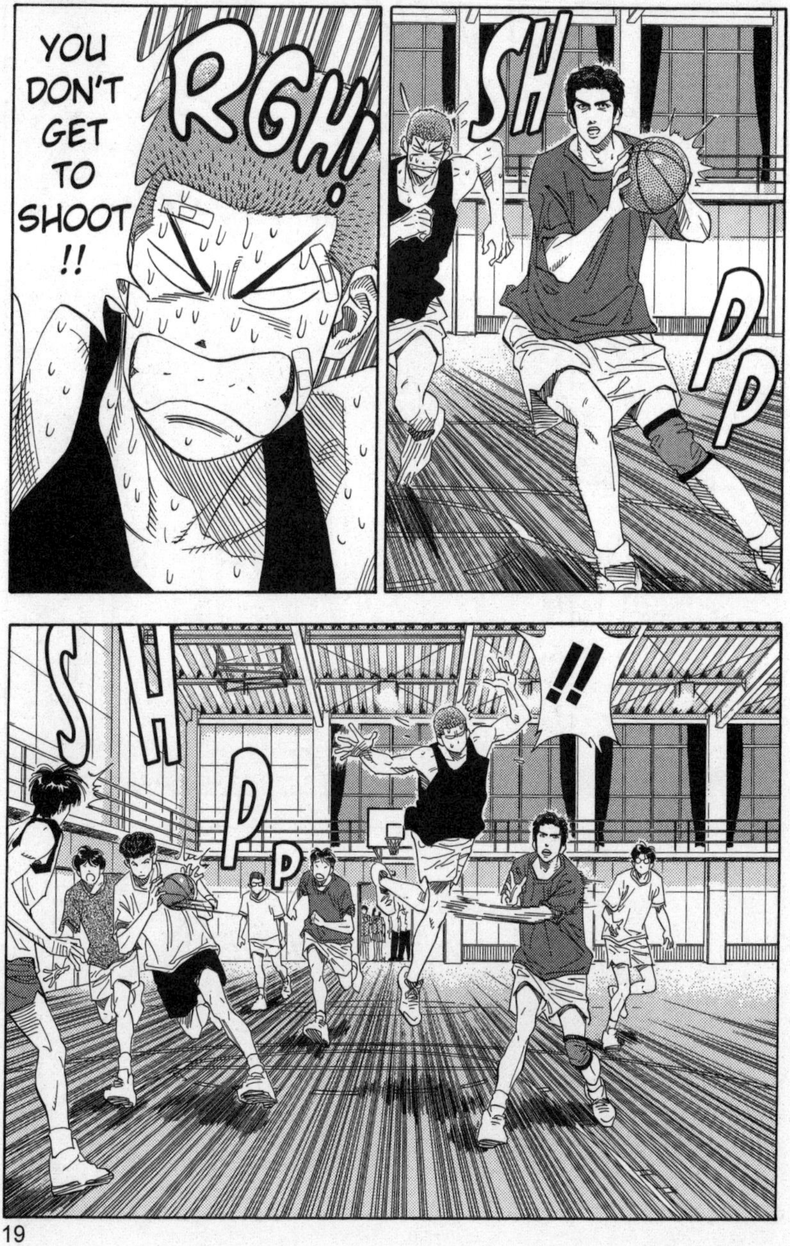
SH
PP
RGH!
YOU DON'T GET TO SHOOT !!
!!
SH
PP

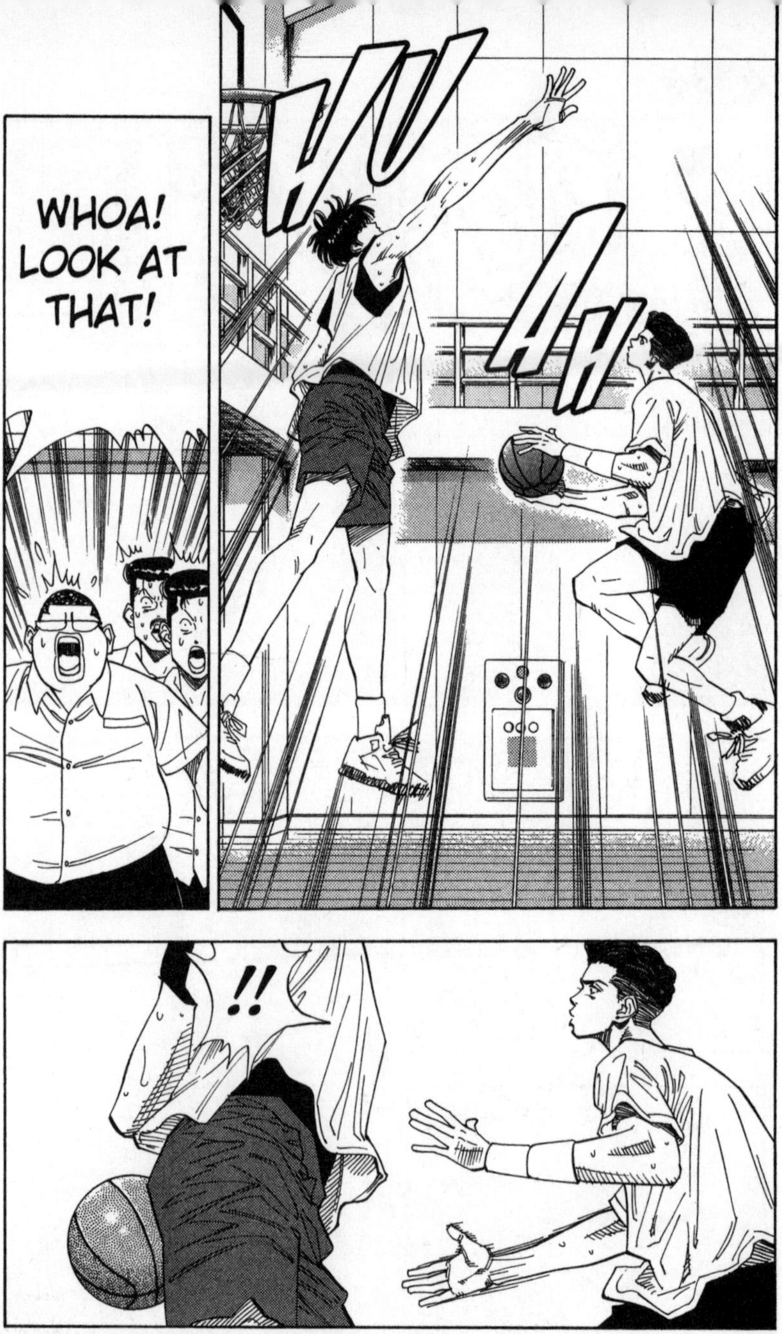
WHOA! LOOK AT THAT!
!!

READ THIS WAY

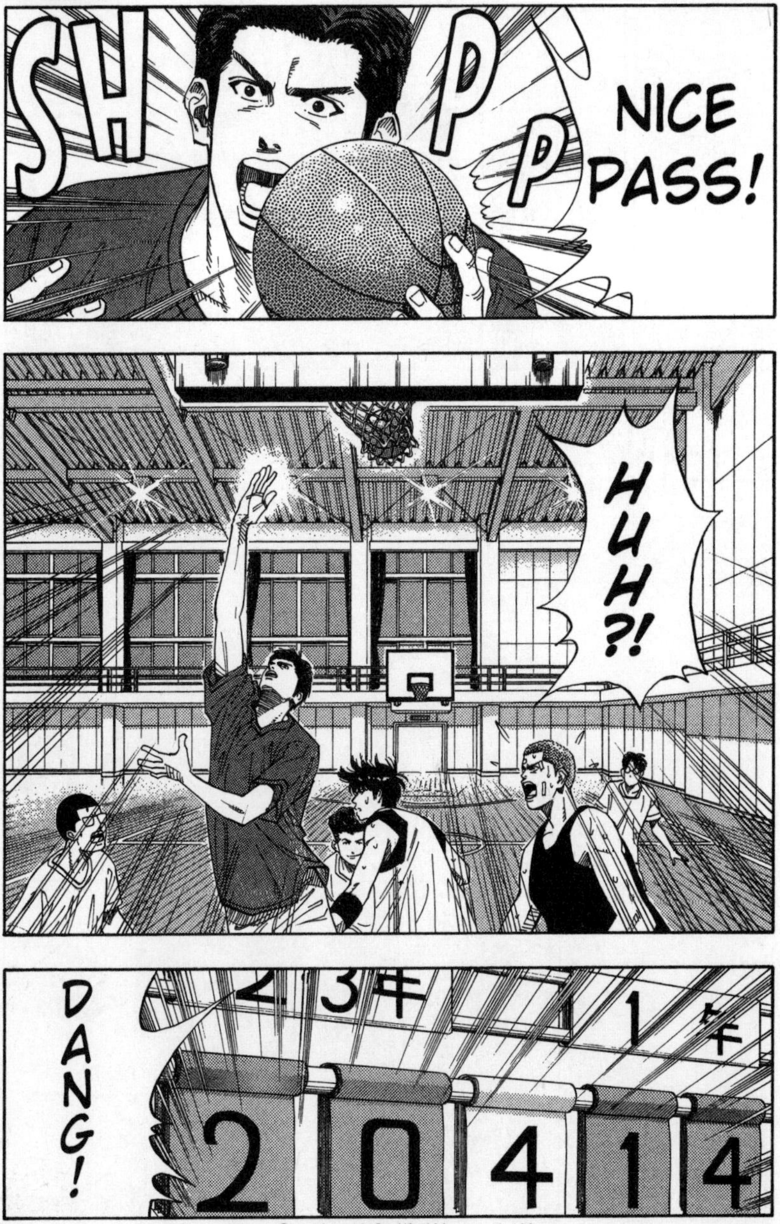
NICE PASS!
P P
SH
HUH?!
2 3年
1年
DANG!
2 0 4 1 4

Scoreboard: 2nd/3rd Years 1st Years

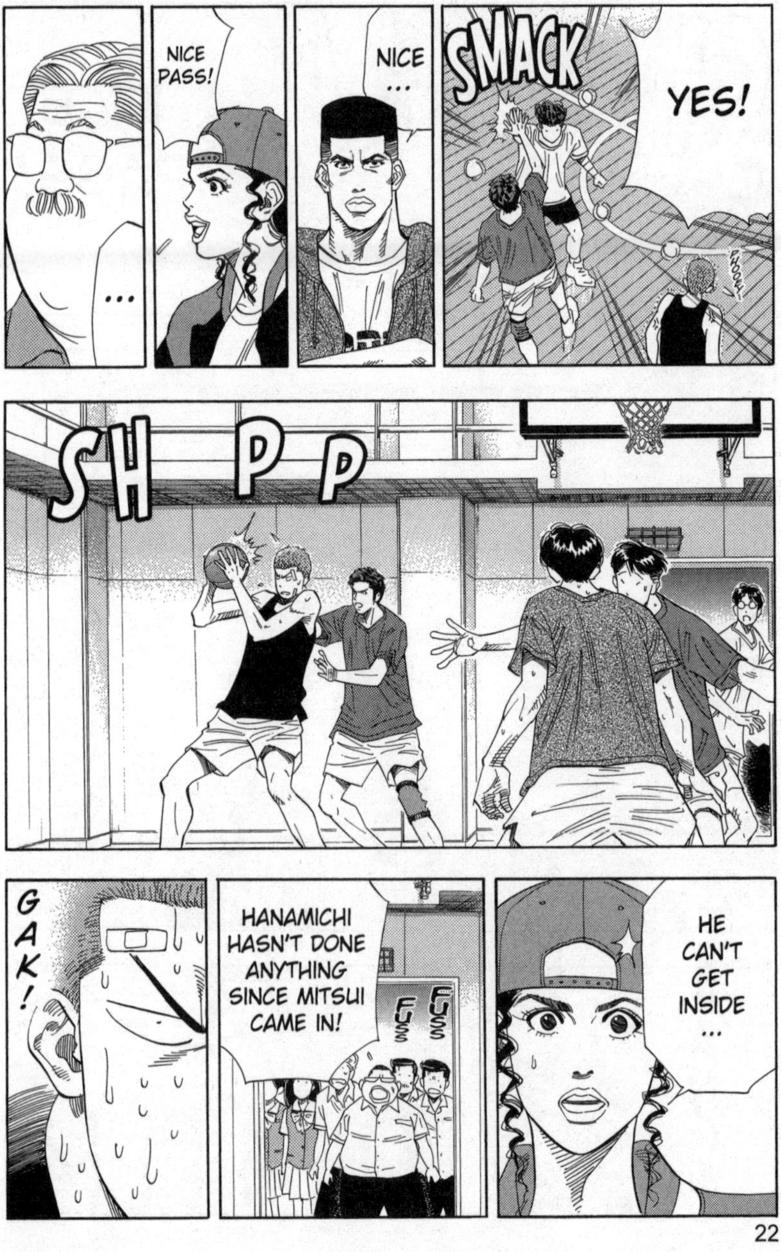
SMACK
YES!
PHOOF!
NICE ...
NICE PASS!
...
SHPP
HE CAN'T GET INSIDE ...
HANAMICHI HASN'T DONE ANYTHING SINCE MITSUI CAME IN!
FUSS FUSS
GAK!

READ THIS WAY

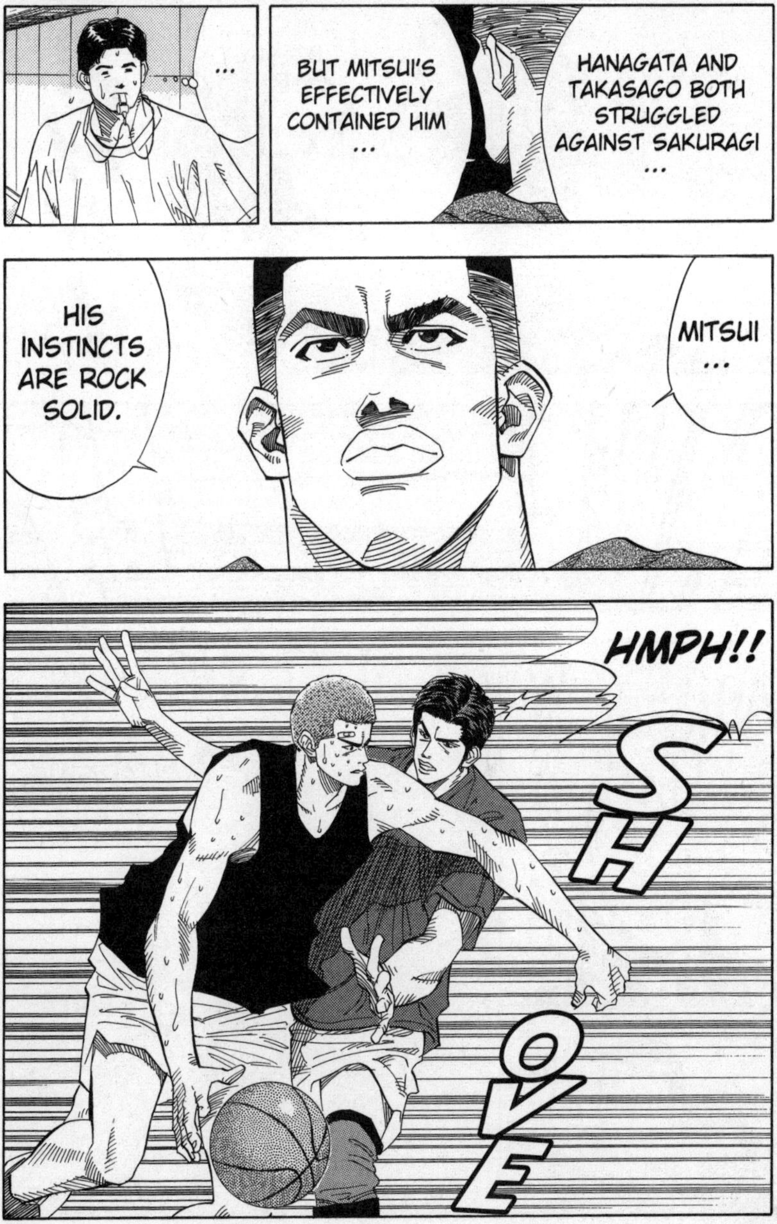

HANAGATA AND TAKASAGO BOTH STRUGGLED AGAINST SAKURAGI ...
BUT MITSUI'S EFFECTIVELY CONTAINED HIM ...
...
MITSUI ...
HIS INSTINCTS ARE ROCK SOLID.
HMPH!!
SHOVE

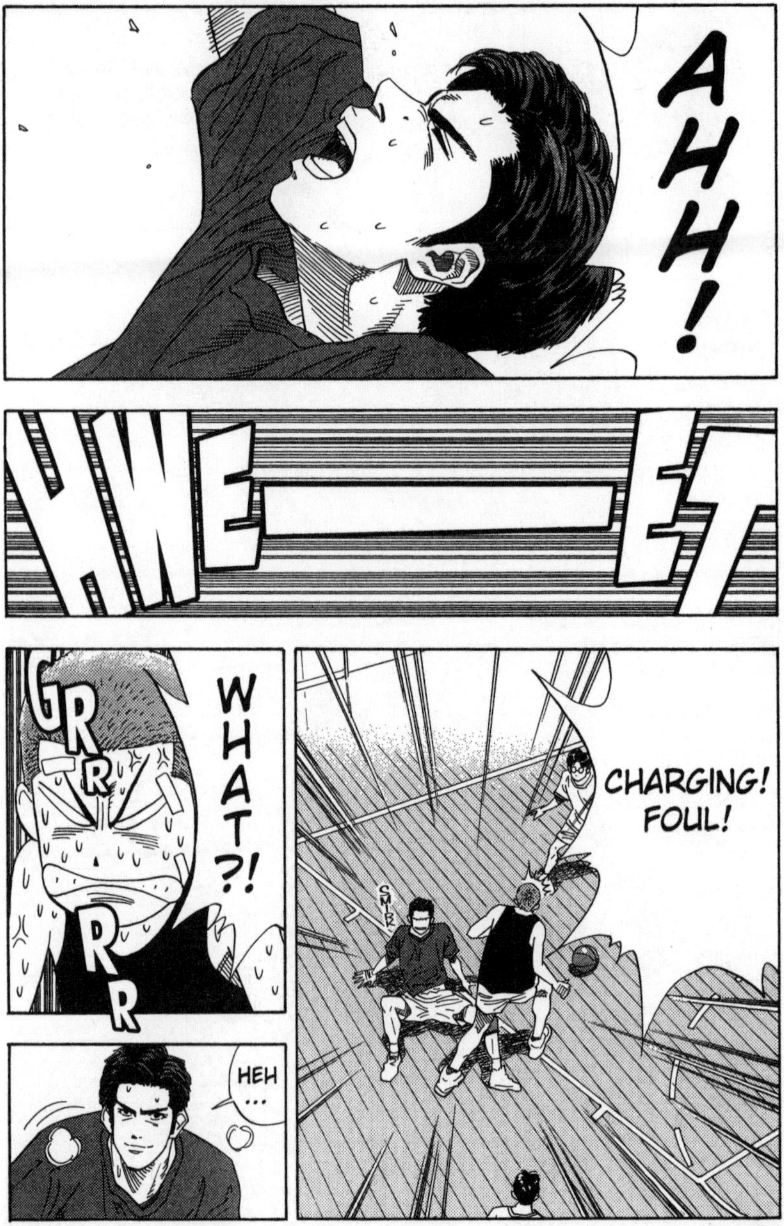
AHH!
HWE—ET
CHARGING! FOUL!
WHAT?!
GRRRR
HEH...

READ THIS WAY

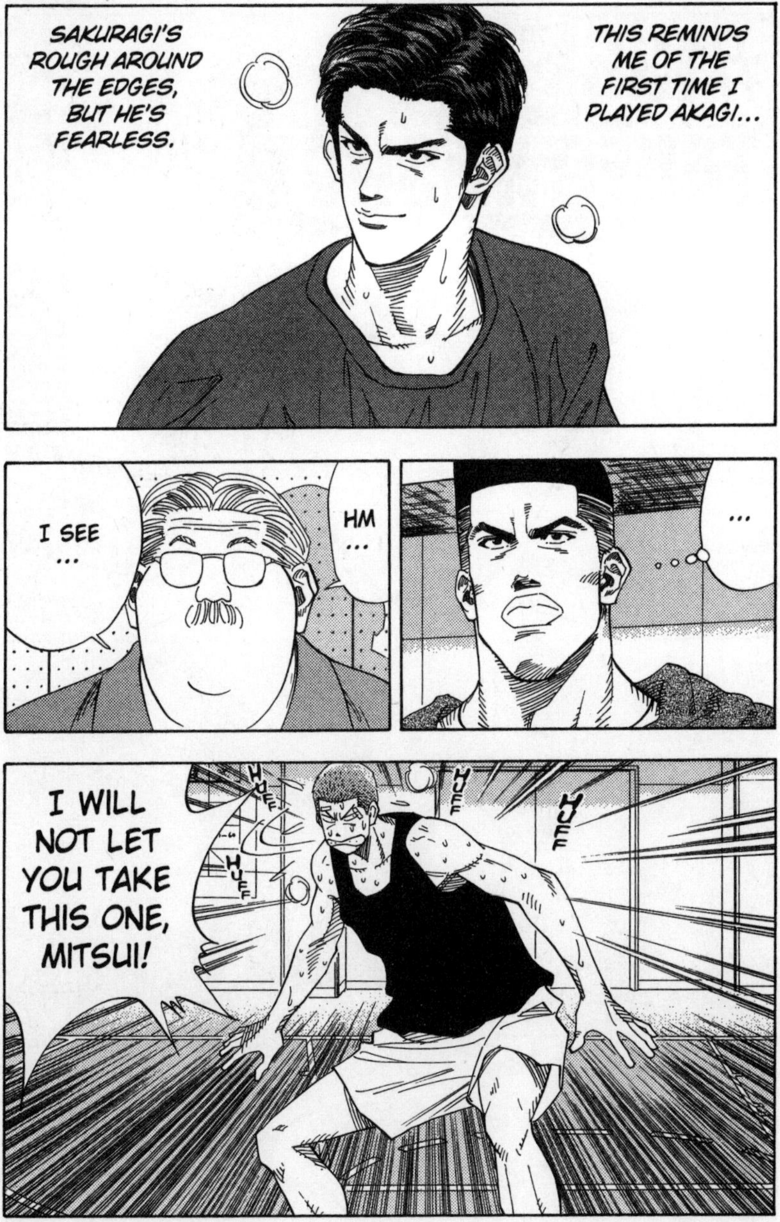
THIS REMINDS ME OF THE FIRST TIME I PLAYED AKAGI...
SAKURAGI'S ROUGH AROUND THE EDGES, BUT HE'S FEARLESS.
...
HM ...
I SEE ...
HUFF
HUFF
HUFF
HUFF
I WILL NOT LET YOU TAKE THIS ONE, MITSUI!

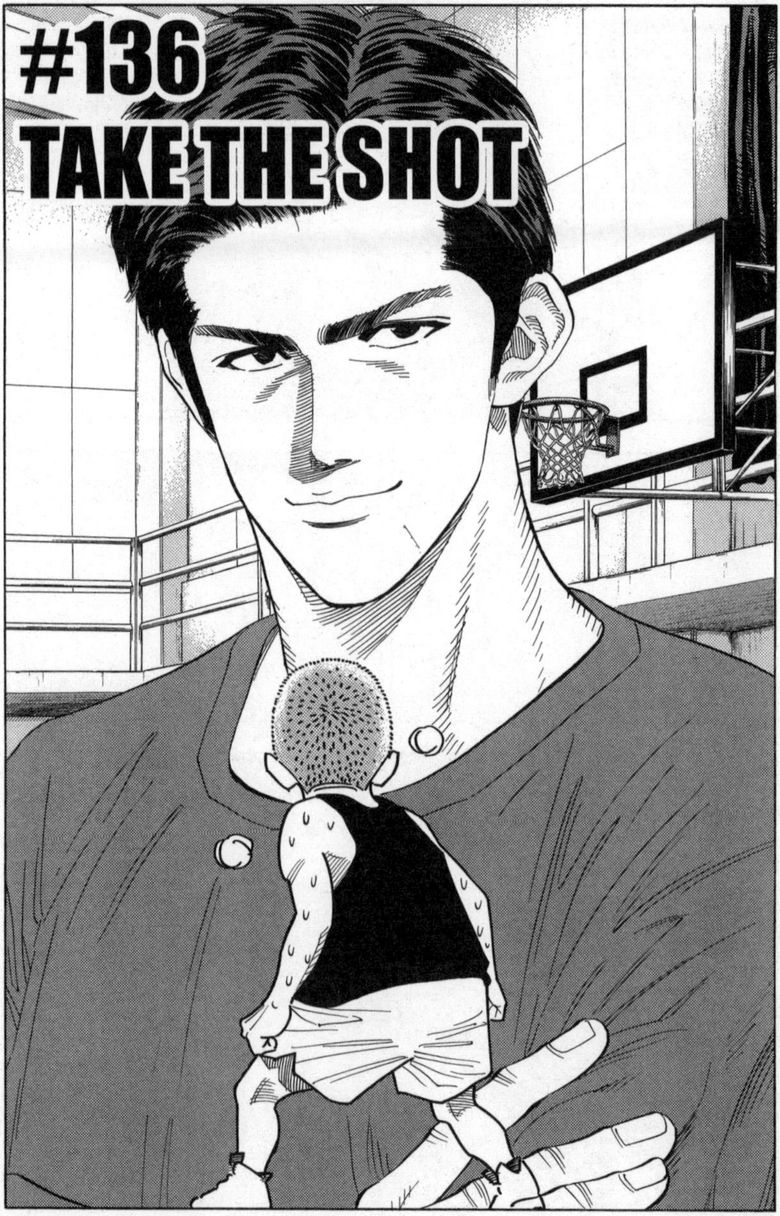
#136
TAKE THE SHOT

READ THIS WAY

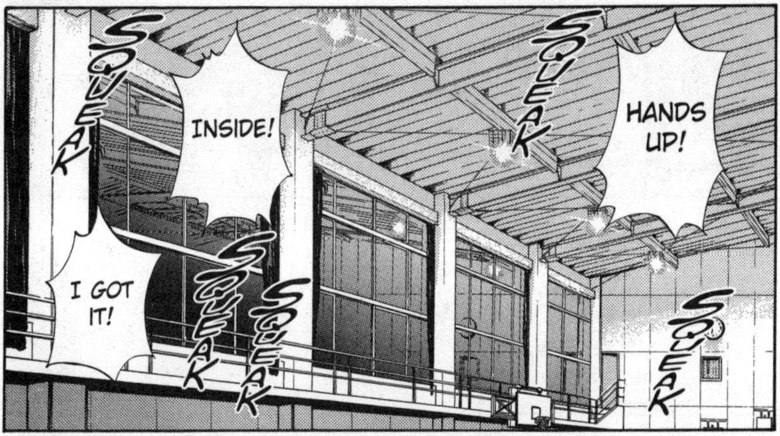
HANDS UP!
SQUEAK
SQUEAK
INSIDE!
SQUEAK
SQUEAK
SQUEAK
I GOT IT!

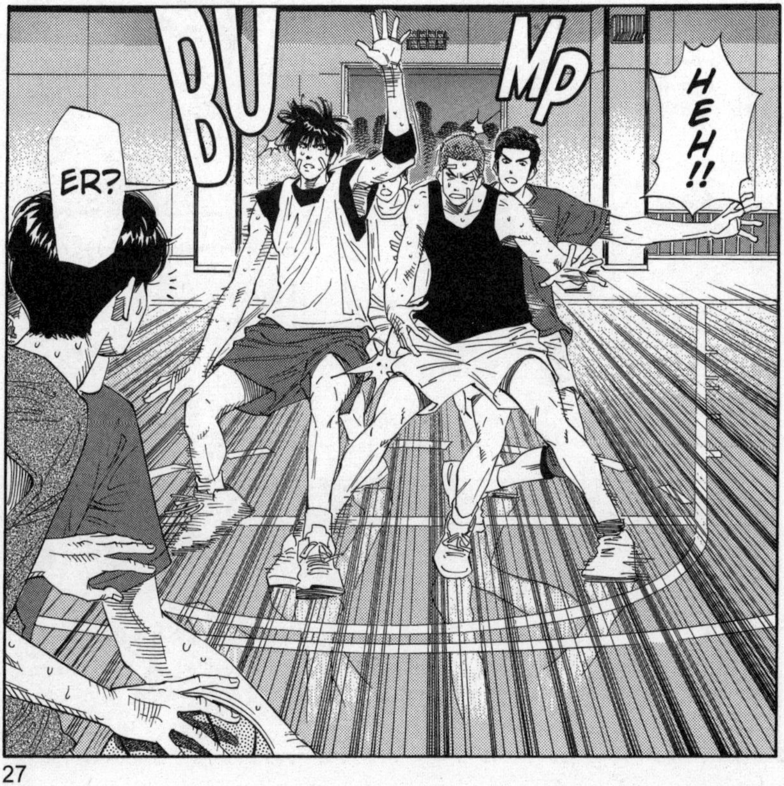
HEH!!
BUMP
ER?

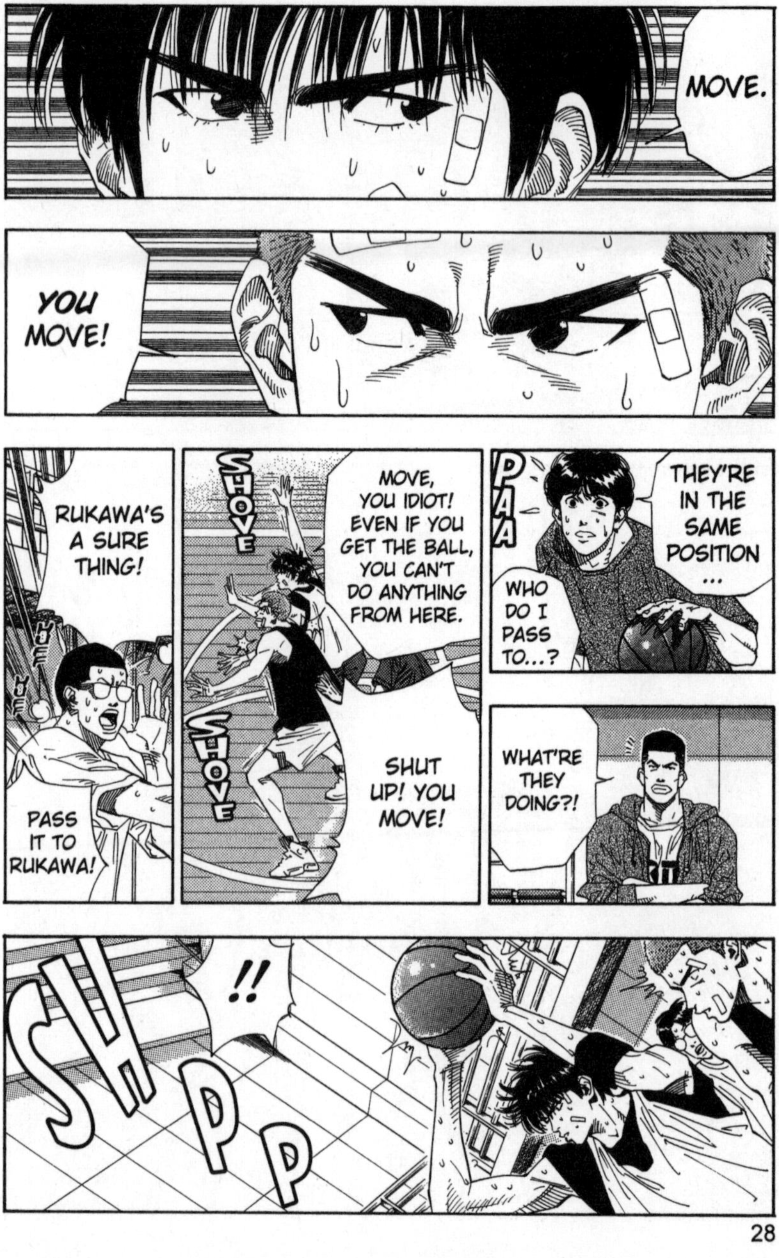
MOVE.
YOU MOVE!
THEY'RE IN THE SAME POSITION...
PAA
WHO DO I PASS TO...?
WHAT'RE THEY DOING?!
MOVE, YOU IDIOT! EVEN IF YOU GET THE BALL, YOU CAN'T DO ANYTHING FROM HERE.
SHOVE
SHUT UP! YOU MOVE!
SHOVE
RUKAWA'S A SURE THING!
PASS IT TO RUKAWA!
!!
SHPP

READ THIS WAY

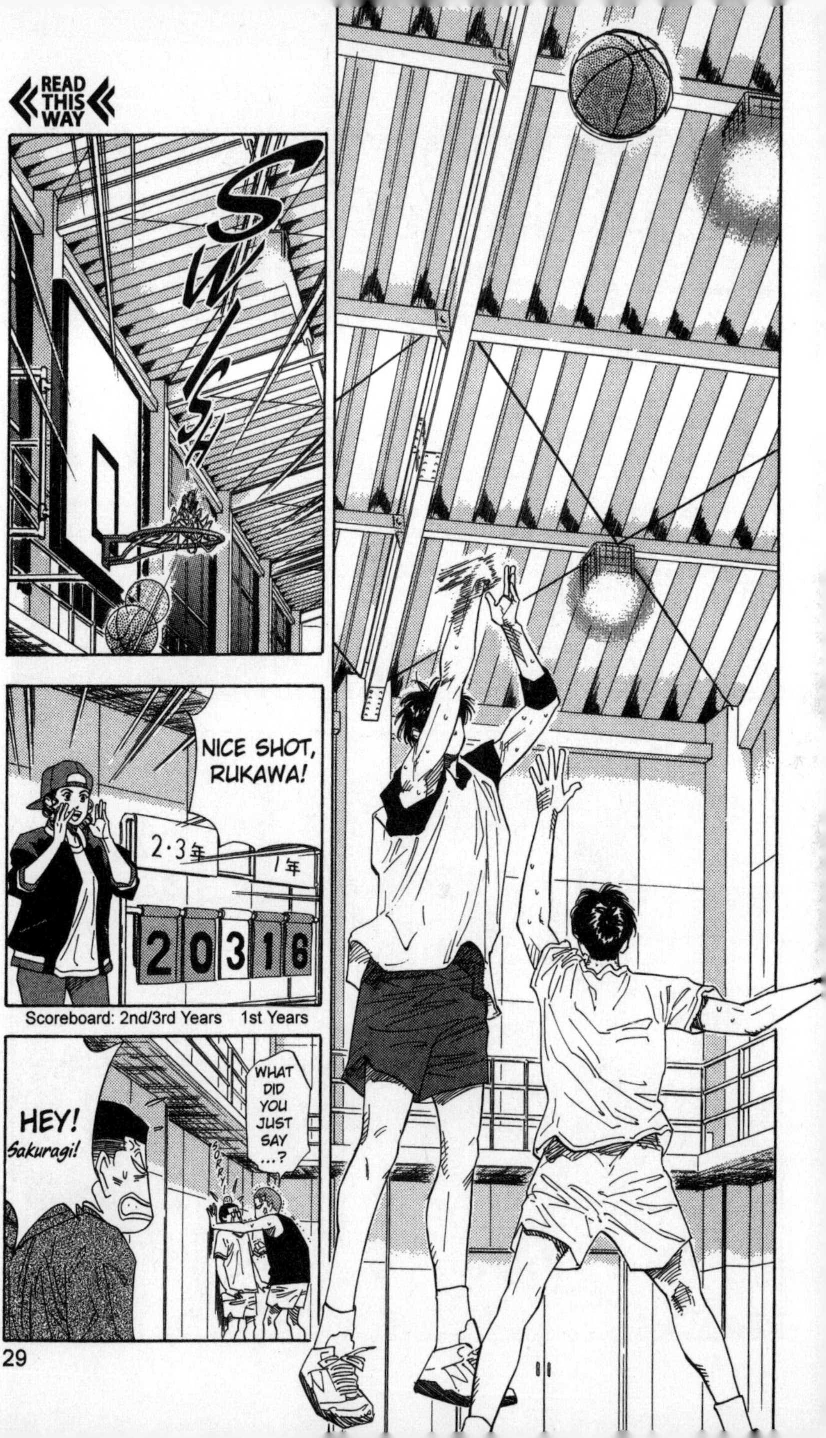
SWISH
NICE SHOT, RUKAWA!
2·3年
1年
20316
HEY! Sakuragi!
WHAT DID YOU JUST SAY ...?
SORRY!

Scoreboard: 2nd/3rd Years 1st Years

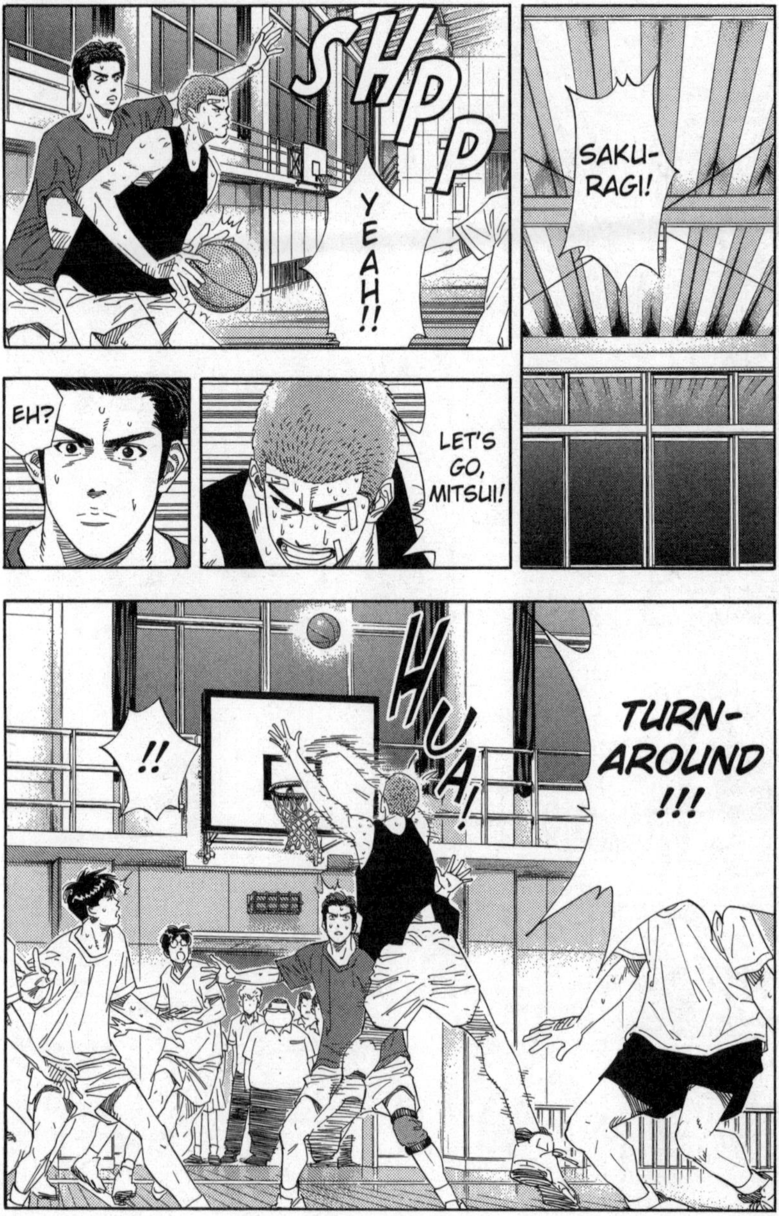
SAKU-RAGI!
SHPP
YEAH!!
LET'S GO, MITSUI!
EH?
TURN-AROUND!!!
HUA!
!!

READ THIS WAY

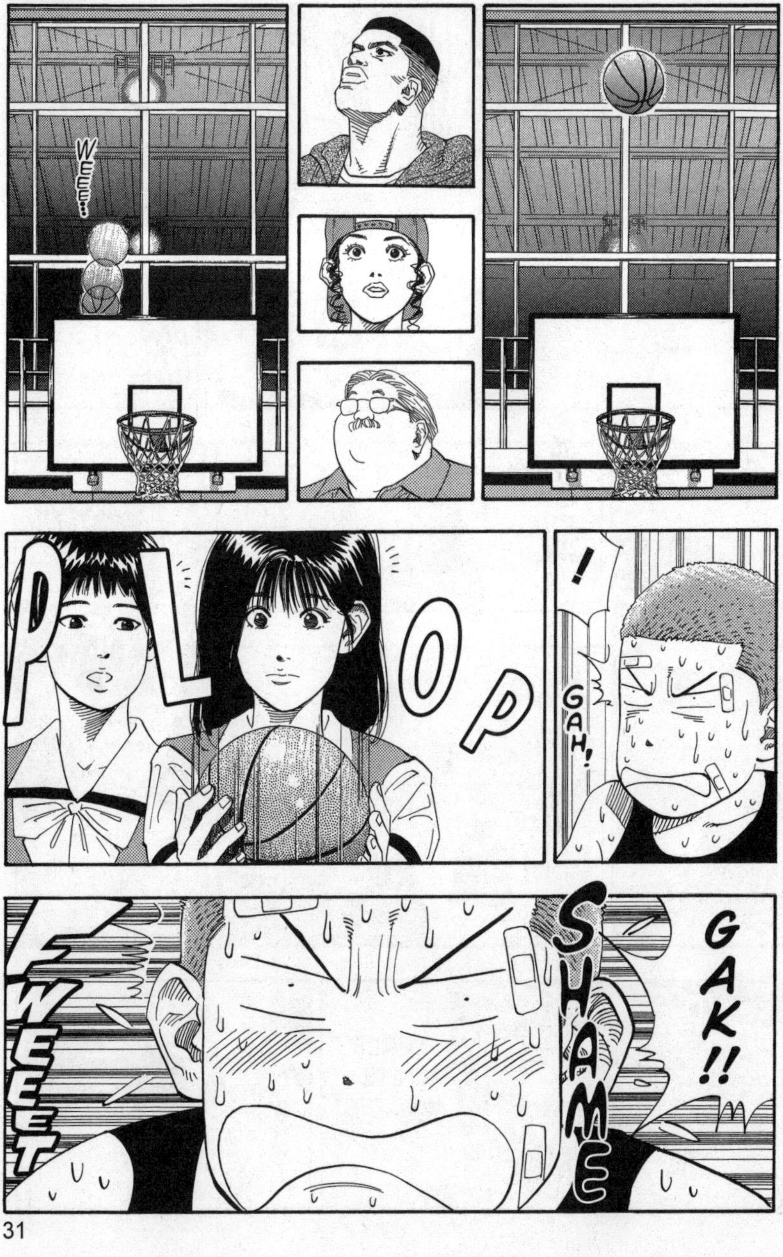
WEEE...
!
GAH!
PLOP
GAK!!
SHAME
FWEEET

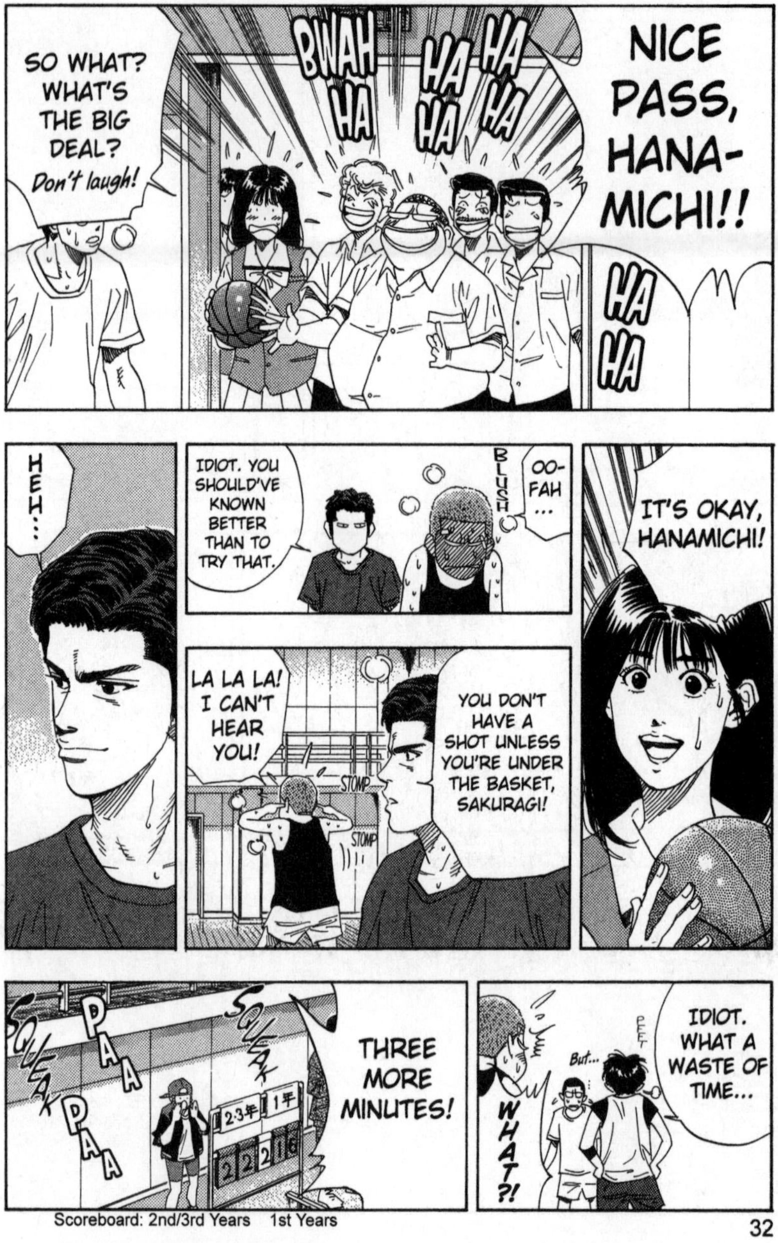
NICE PASS, HANAMICHI!!
HA HA HA
HA HA HA
BWAH HA
HA HA
SO WHAT? WHAT'S THE BIG DEAL? Don't laugh!
IT'S OKAY, HANAMICHI!
OO-FAH...
BLUSH
IDIOT. YOU SHOULD'VE KNOWN BETTER THAN TO TRY THAT.
YOU DON'T HAVE A SHOT UNLESS YOU'RE UNDER THE BASKET, SAKURAGI!
STOMP
STOMP
LA LA LA! I CAN'T HEAR YOU!
HEH...
IDIOT. WHAT A WASTE OF TIME...
PEET
But...
WHAT?!
THREE MORE MINUTES!
SQUEAK
PAA PAA
SQUEAK
PAA PAA
2·3年 1年
22 16
Scoreboard: 2nd/3rd Years 1st Years

READ THIS WAY

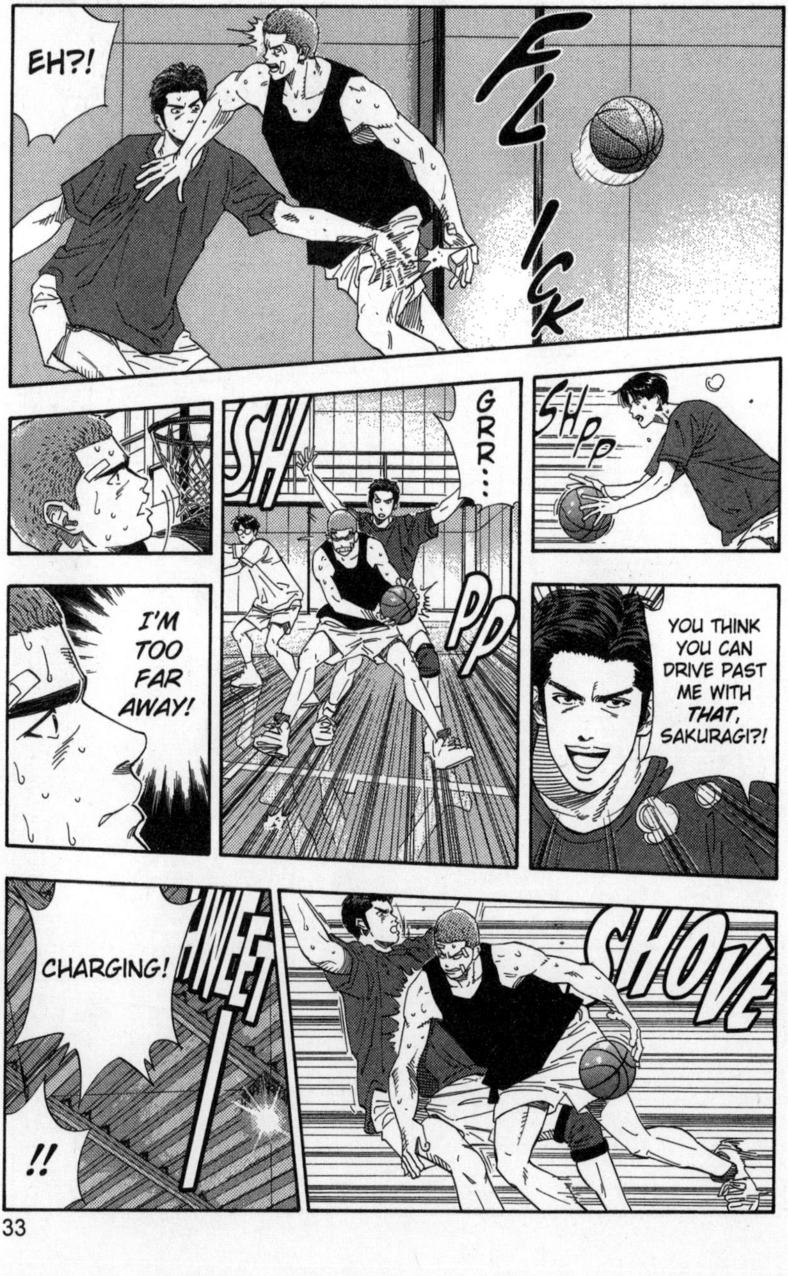
FLICK
EH?!
SHPP
YOU THINK YOU CAN DRIVE PAST ME WITH *THAT*, SAKURAGI?!
SH
GRR...
PP
I'M TOO FAR AWAY!
SHOVE
WEET
CHARGING!
!!

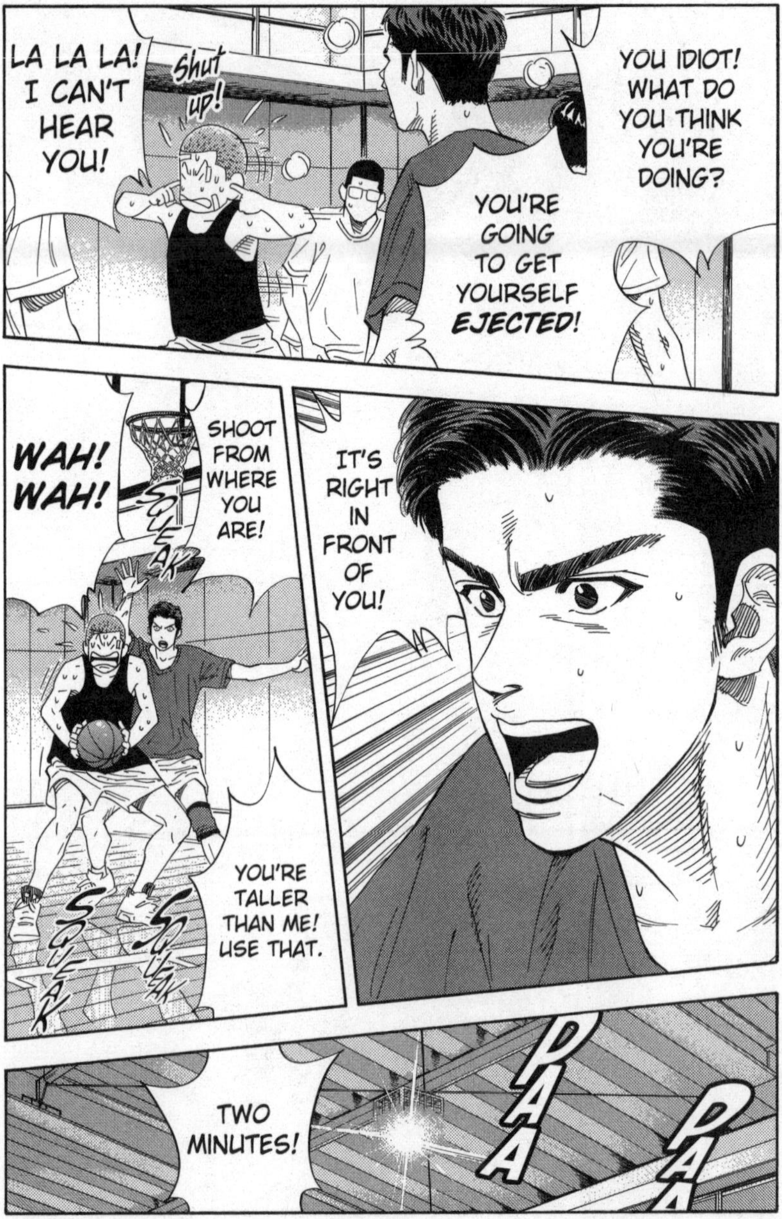
YOU IDIOT! WHAT DO YOU THINK YOU'RE DOING?
YOU'RE GOING TO GET YOURSELF *EJECTED*!
Shut up!
LA LA LA! I CAN'T HEAR YOU!
IT'S RIGHT IN FRONT OF YOU!
SHOOT FROM WHERE YOU ARE!
WAH! WAH!
SQUEAK
YOU'RE TALLER THAN ME! USE THAT.
SQUEAK
SQUEAK
PAAA
PAA
TWO MINUTES!

READ THIS WAY

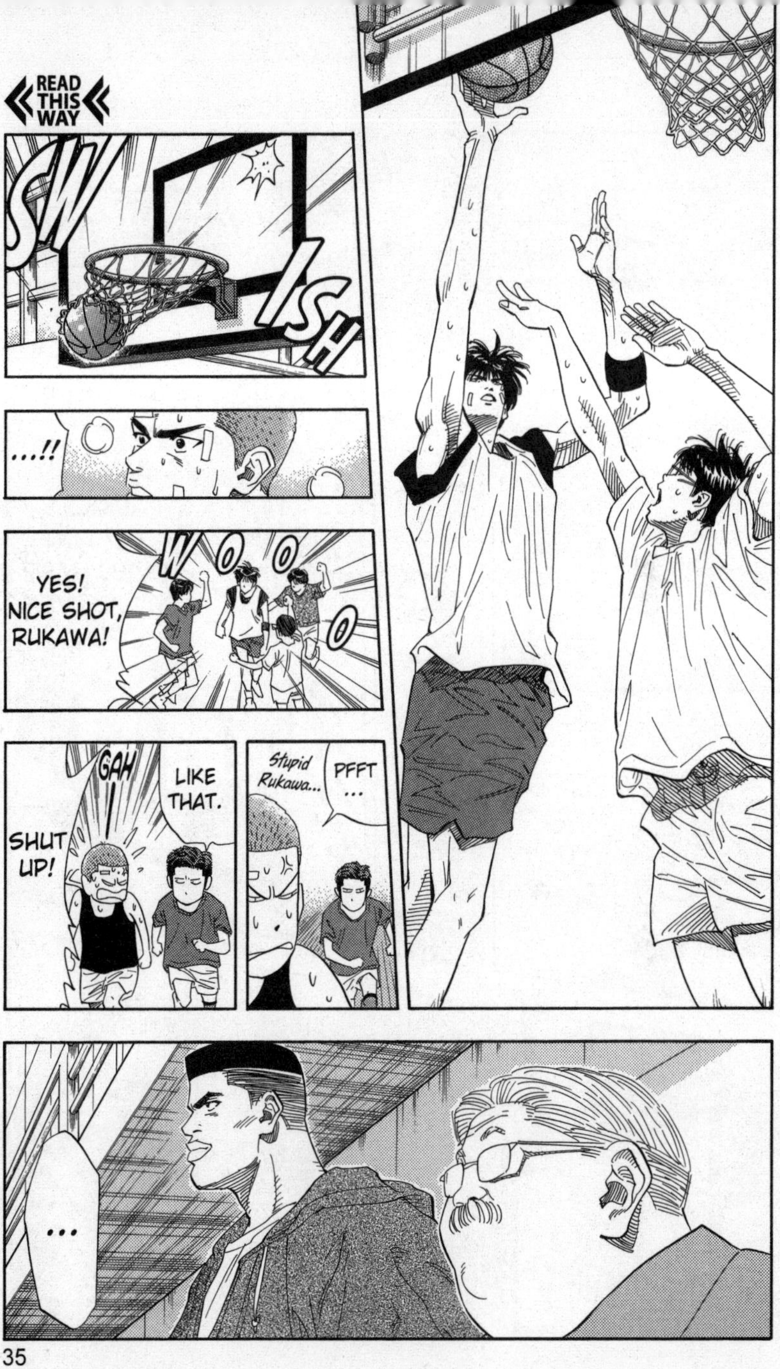
SWISH
...!!
WOOOO
YES! NICE SHOT, RUKAWA!
PFFT ...
Stupid Rukawa...
LIKE THAT.
GAH
SHUT UP!
...

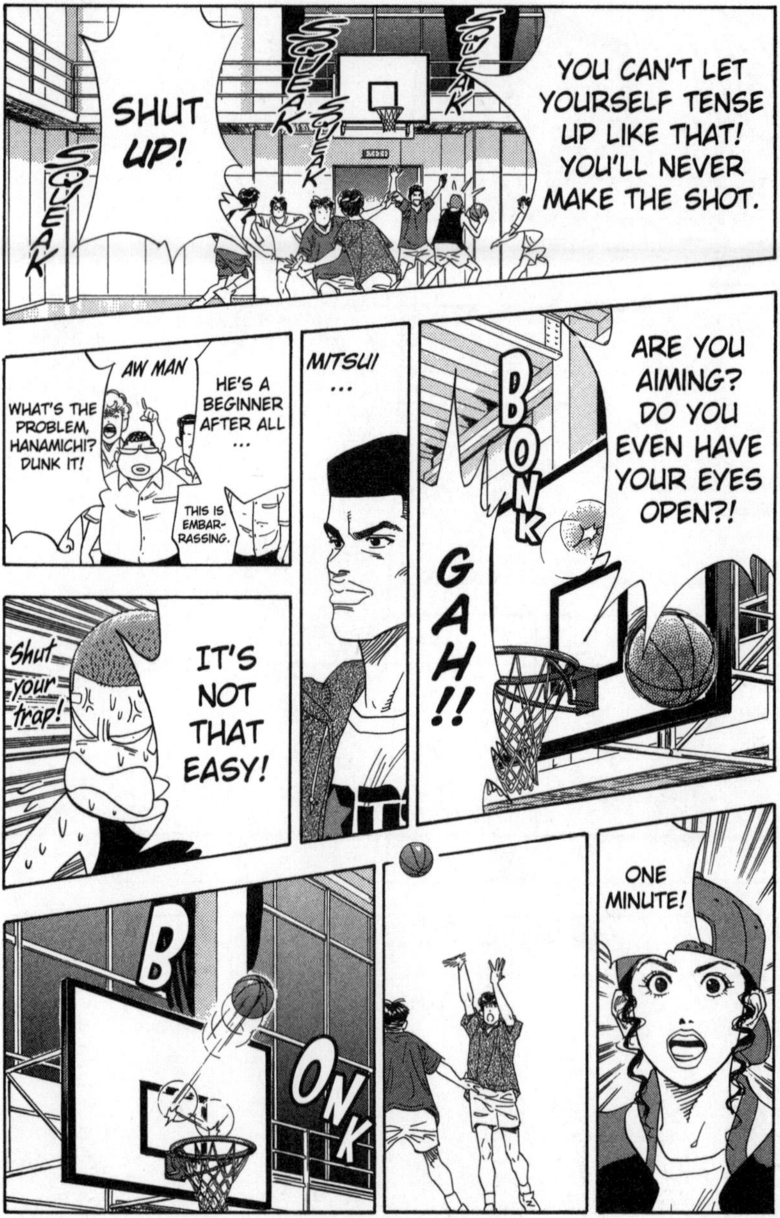
YOU CAN'T LET YOURSELF TENSE UP LIKE THAT! YOU'LL NEVER MAKE THE SHOT.
SQUEAK
SQUEAK
SQUEAK
SQUEAK
SHUT UP!
ARE YOU AIMING? DO YOU EVEN HAVE YOUR EYES OPEN?!
BONK
GAH!!
MITSUI ...
HE'S A BEGINNER AFTER ALL ...
AW MAN
WHAT'S THE PROBLEM, HANAMICHI? DUNK IT!
THIS IS EMBARRASSING.
IT'S NOT THAT EASY!
Shut your trap!
ONE MINUTE!
BONK

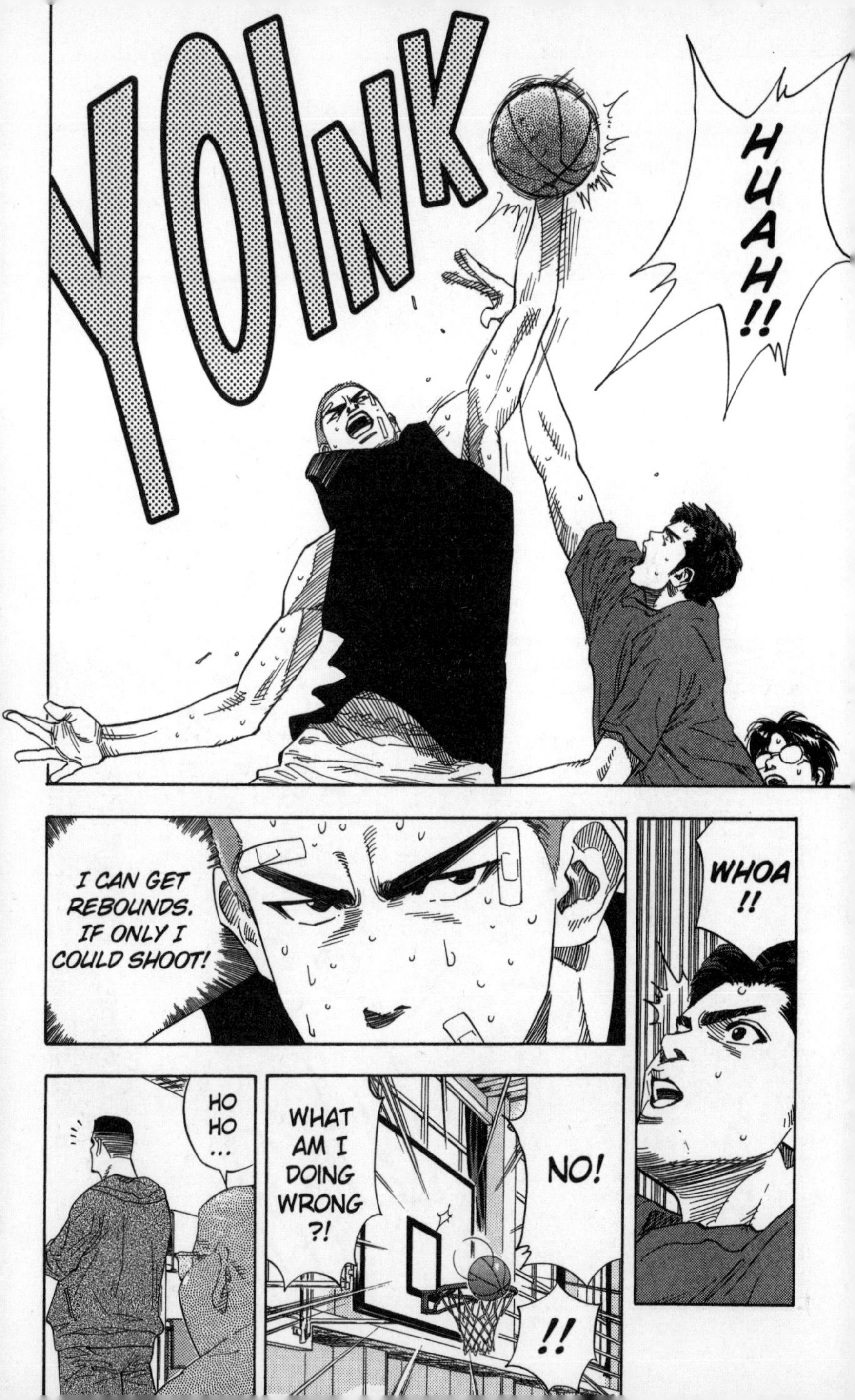
HUAH!!
YOINK
WHOA !!
I CAN GET REBOUNDS. IF ONLY I COULD SHOOT!
WHAT AM I DOING WRONG ?!
NO!
!!
HO HO ...

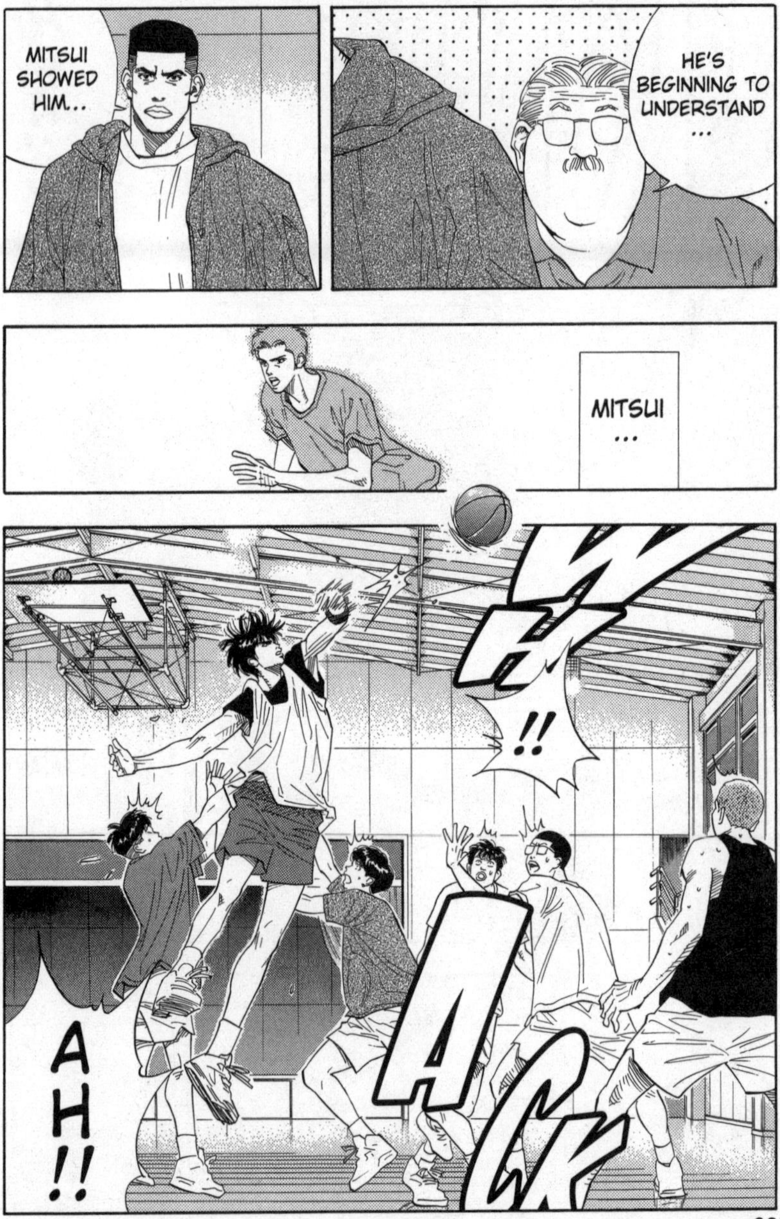
HE'S BEGINNING TO UNDERSTAND ...
MITSUI SHOWED HIM...
MITSUI ...
WHACK
!!
AH!!

READ THIS WAY

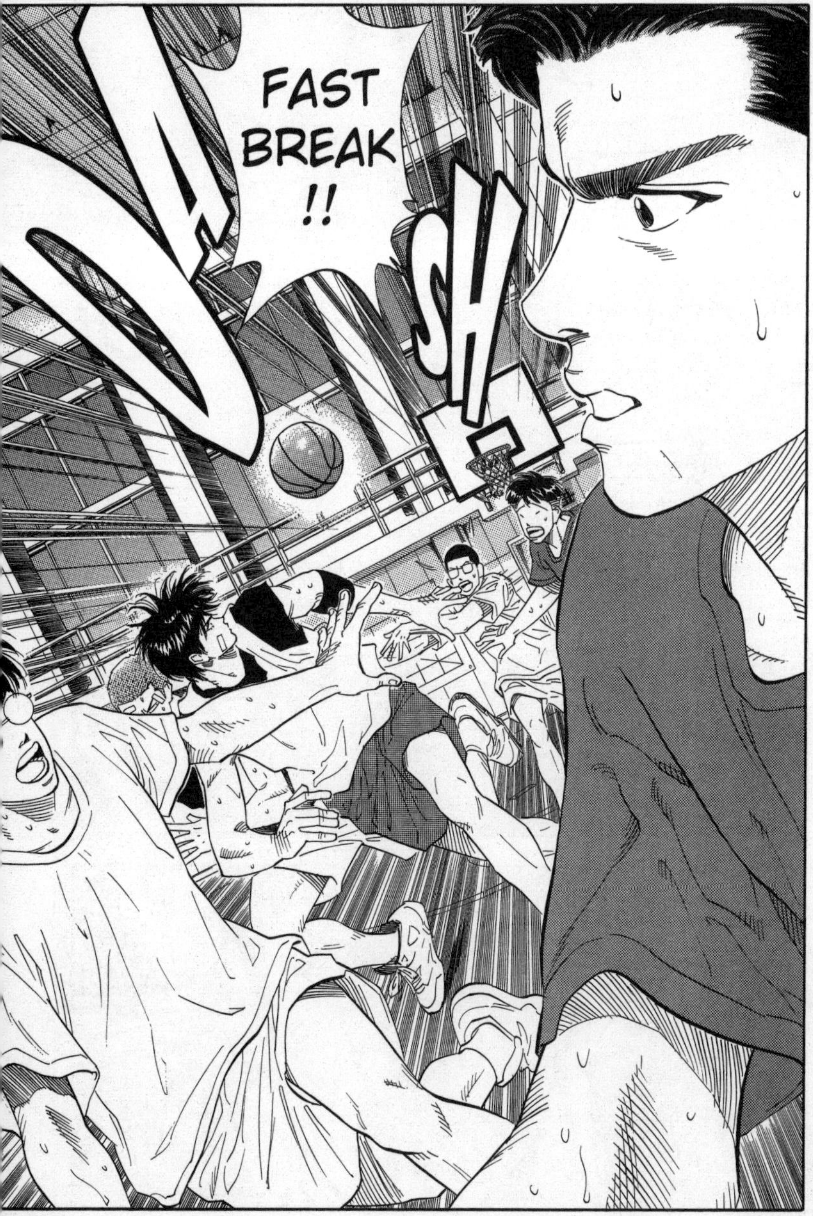
FAST BREAK !!
SH!

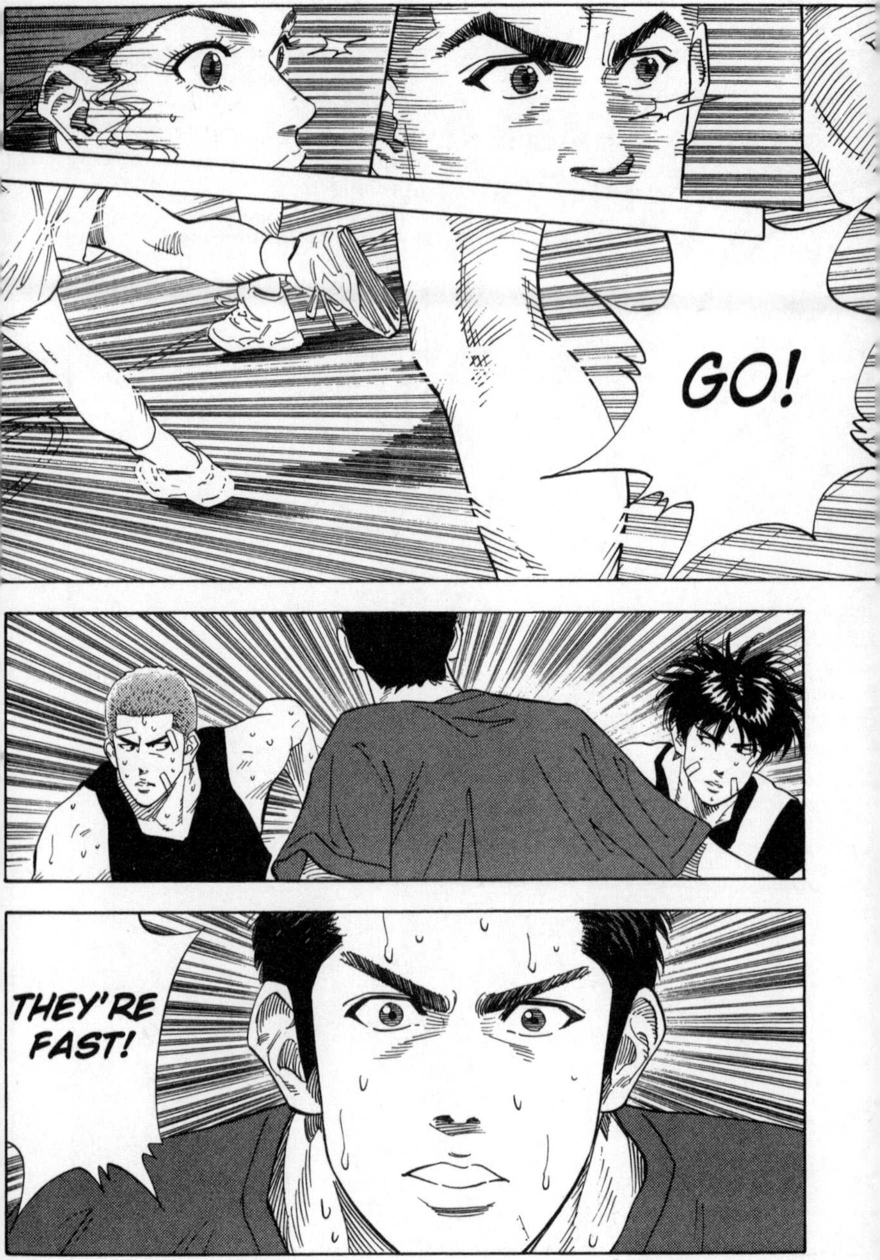
GO!
THEY'RE FAST!

READ THIS WAY

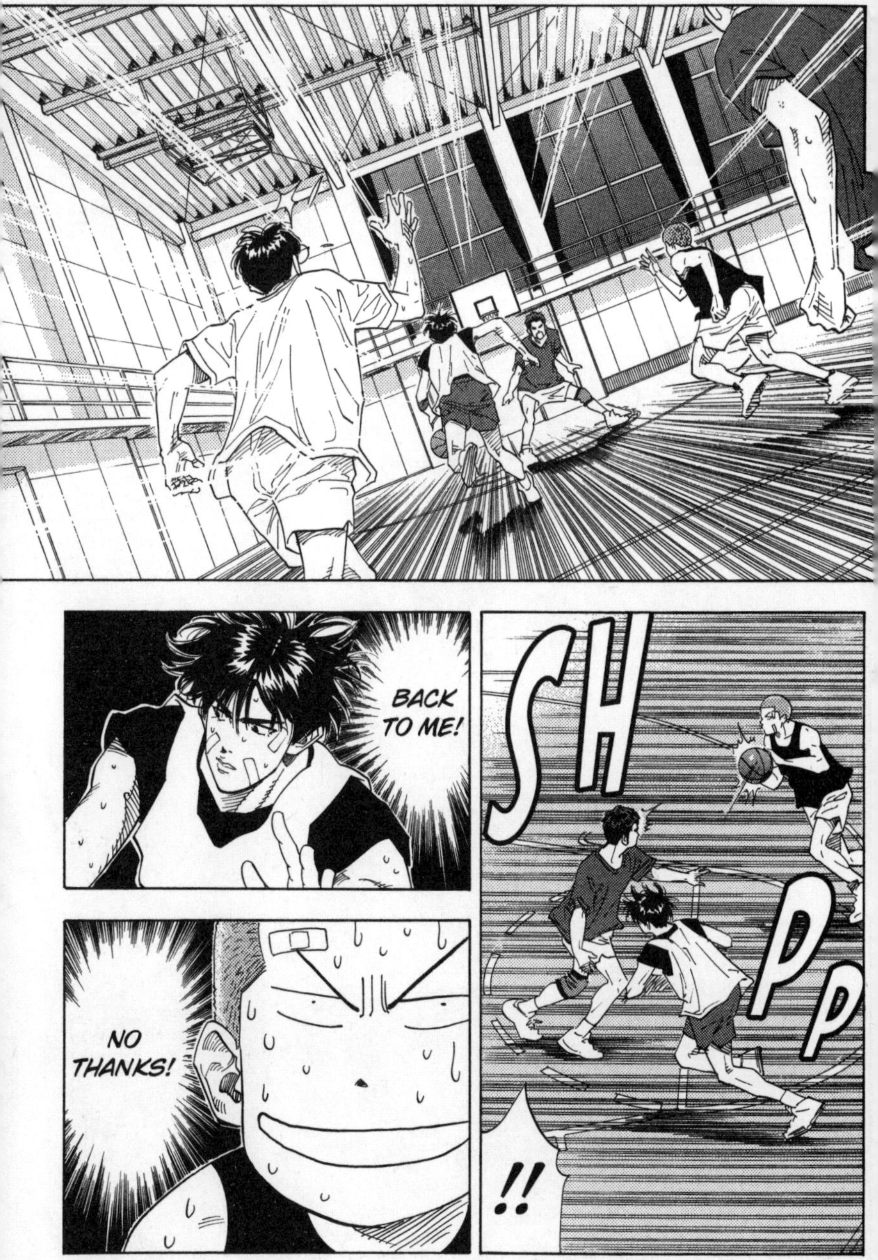
SH
PP
!!
BACK TO ME!
NO THANKS!

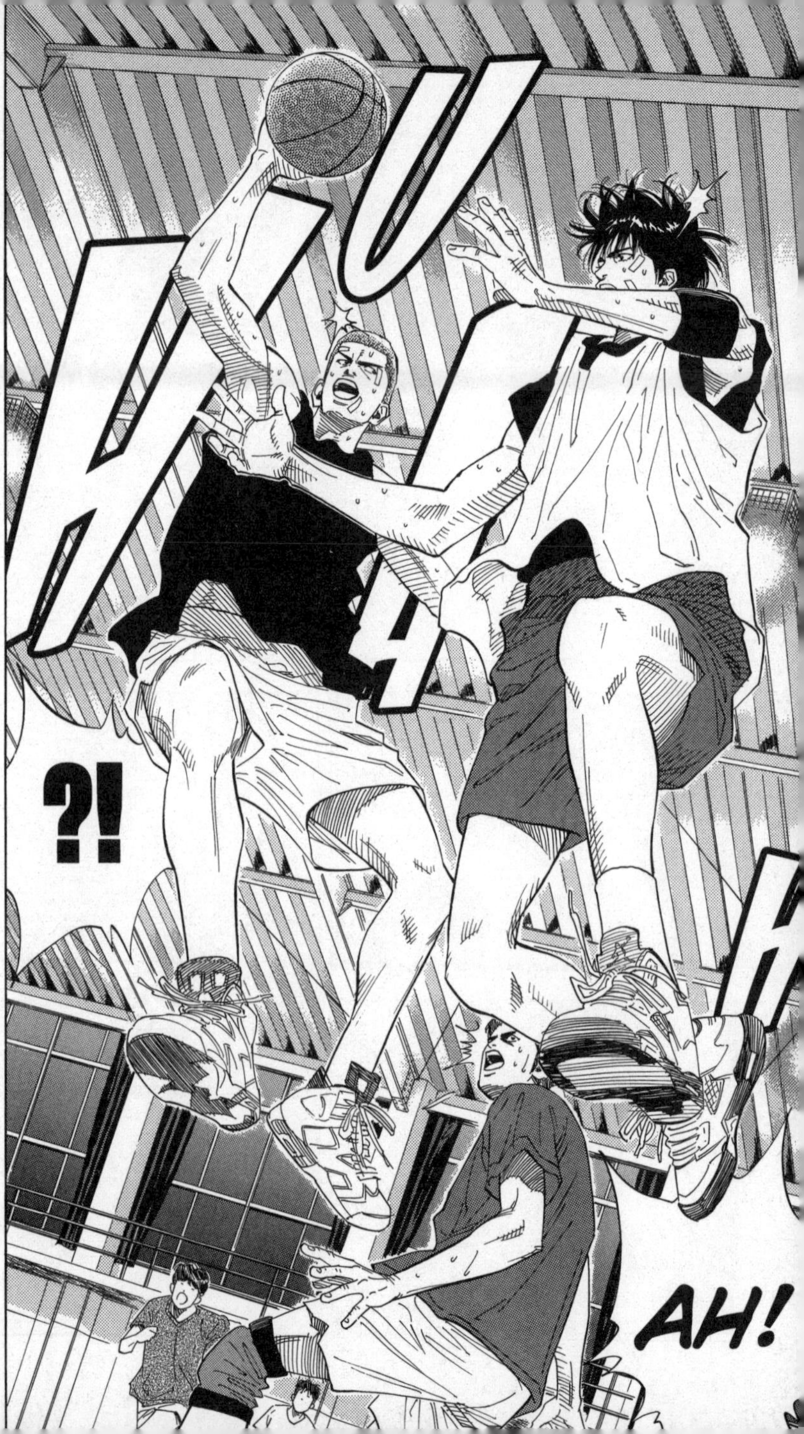
?!
AH!

READ THIS WAY

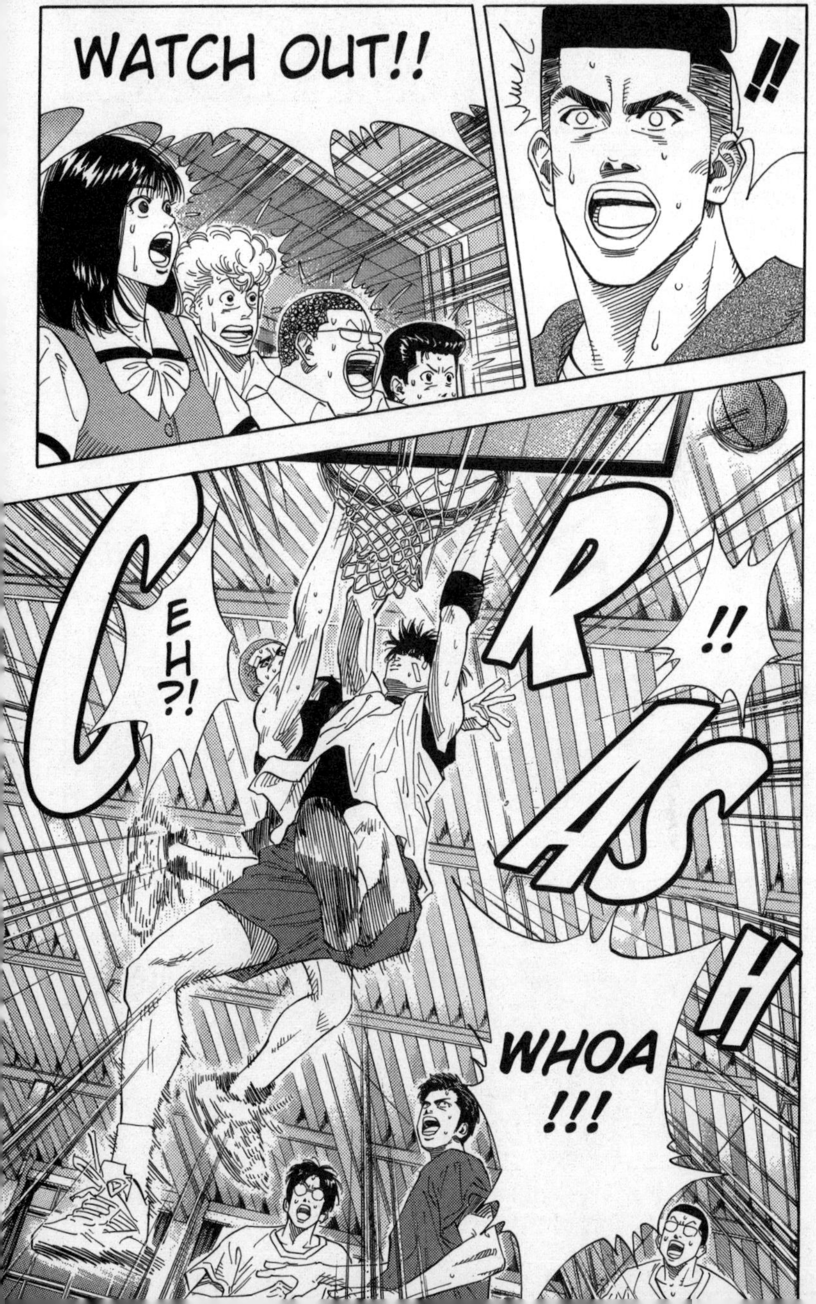
!!
WATCH OUT!!
CRASH
!!
EH?!
WHOA !!!

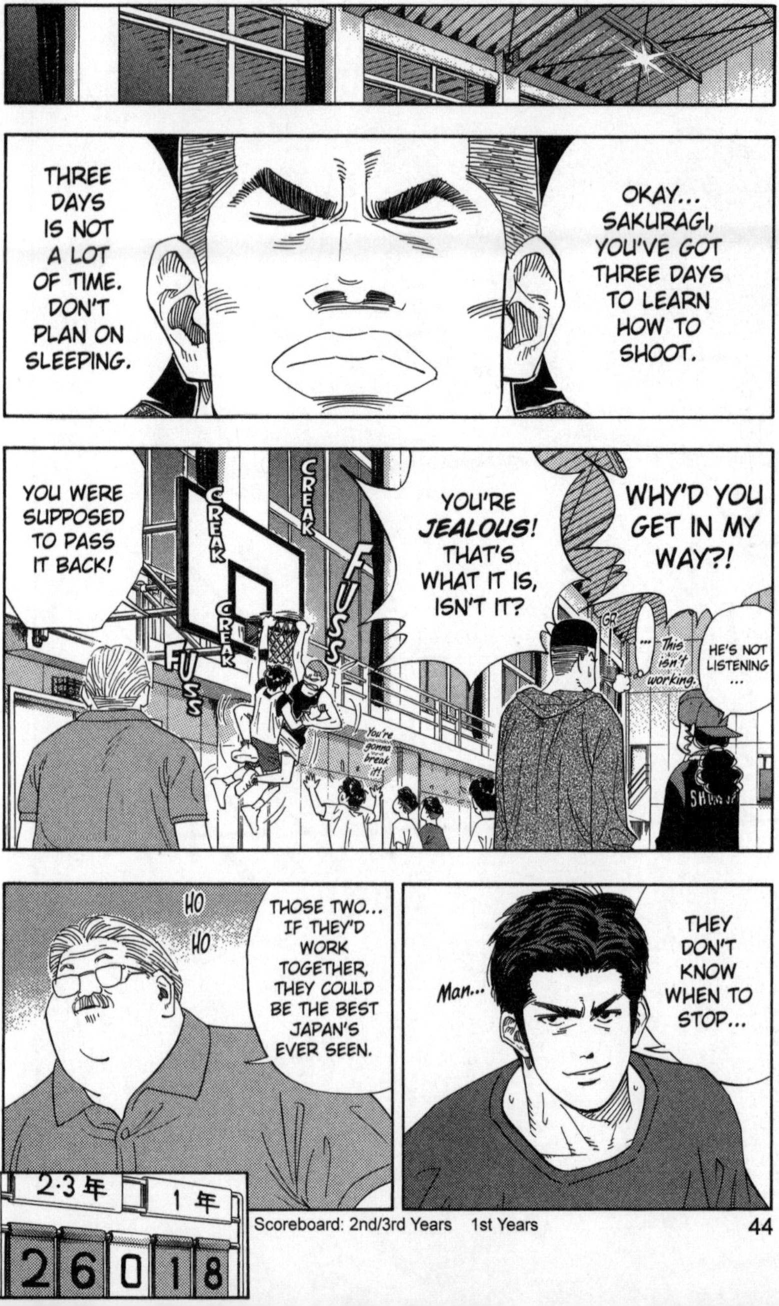
OKAY... SAKURAGI, YOU'VE GOT THREE DAYS TO LEARN HOW TO SHOOT.
THREE DAYS IS NOT A LOT OF TIME. DON'T PLAN ON SLEEPING.
WHY'D YOU GET IN MY WAY?!
YOU'RE *JEALOUS*! THAT'S WHAT IT IS, ISN'T IT?
HE'S NOT LISTENING...
... This isn't working.
GR
CREAK
FUSS
CREAK
CREAK
FUSS
You're gonna break it!
YOU WERE SUPPOSED TO PASS IT BACK!
THEY DON'T KNOW WHEN TO STOP...
Man...
HO
HO
THOSE TWO... IF THEY'D WORK TOGETHER, THEY COULD BE THE BEST JAPAN'S EVER SEEN.
2·3年
1年
26018
Scoreboard: 2nd/3rd Years 1st Years

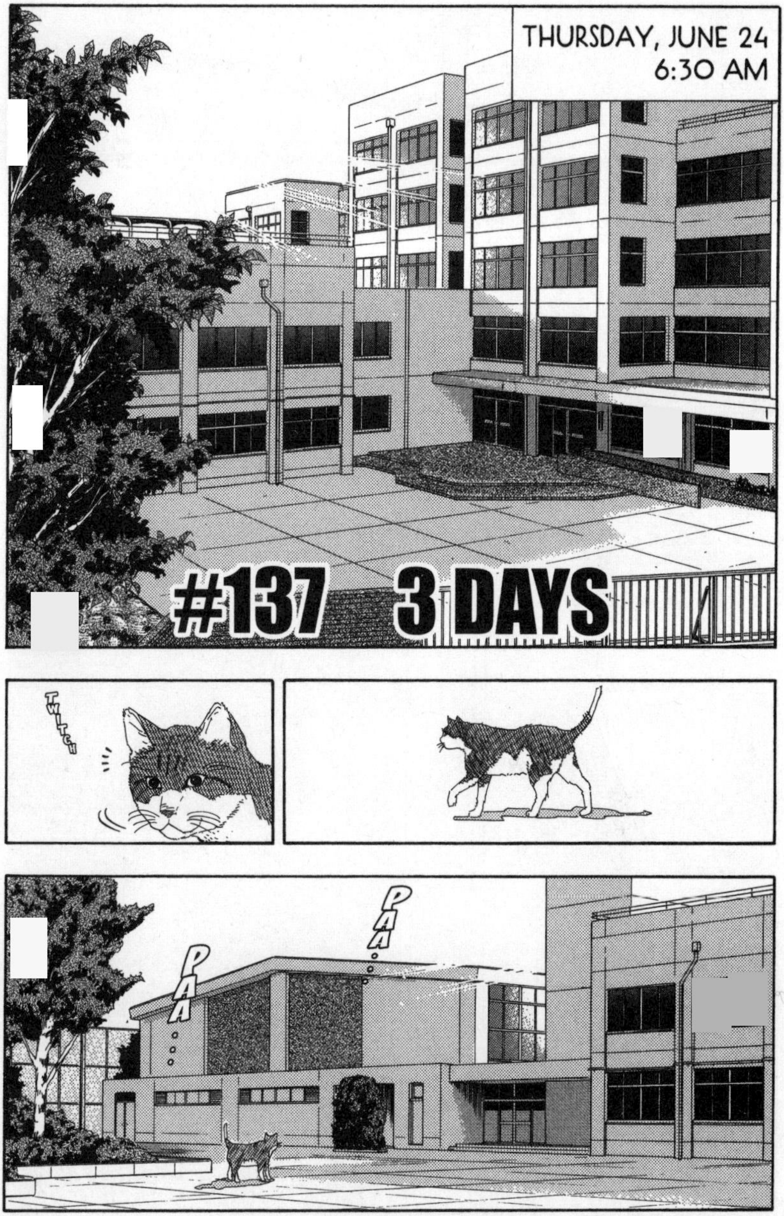
THURSDAY, JUNE 24
6:30 AM
#137 3 DAYS
TWITCH
PAA...
PAA...

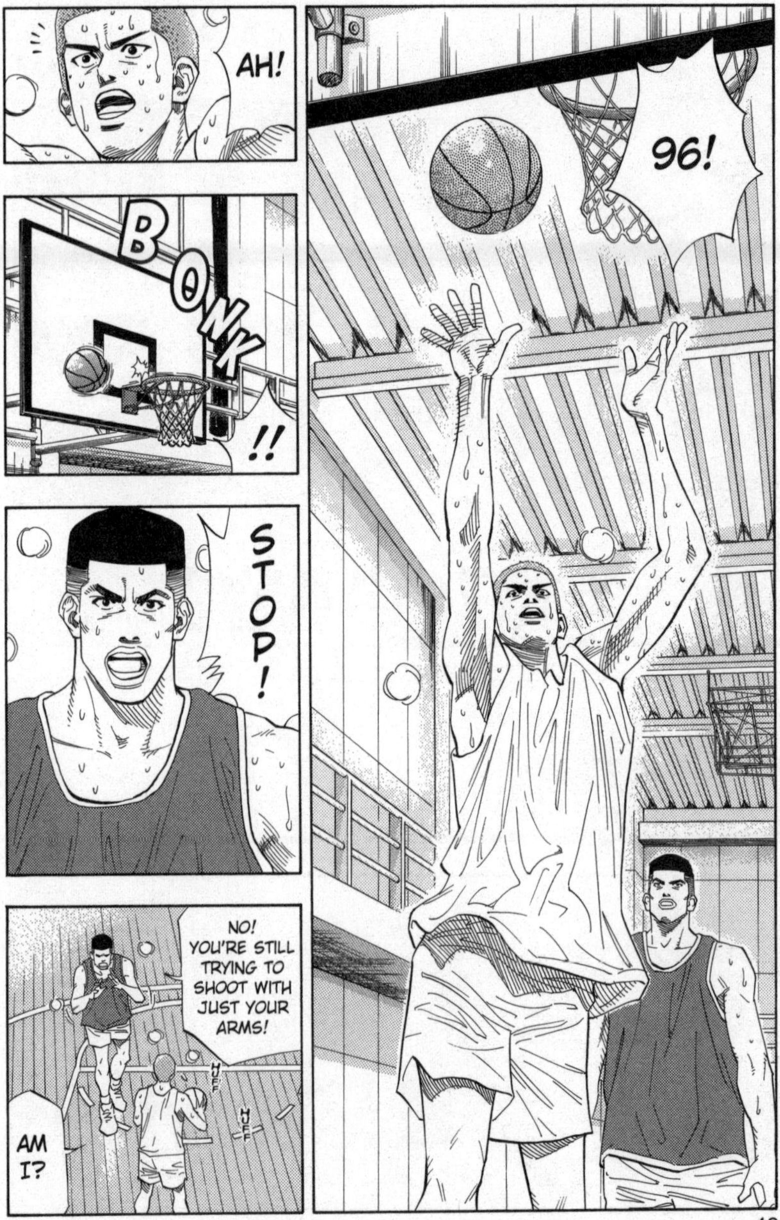
96!
AH!
BONK!!
STOP!
NO! YOU'RE STILL TRYING TO SHOOT WITH JUST YOUR ARMS!
HUFF
HUFF
AM I?

READ THIS WAY

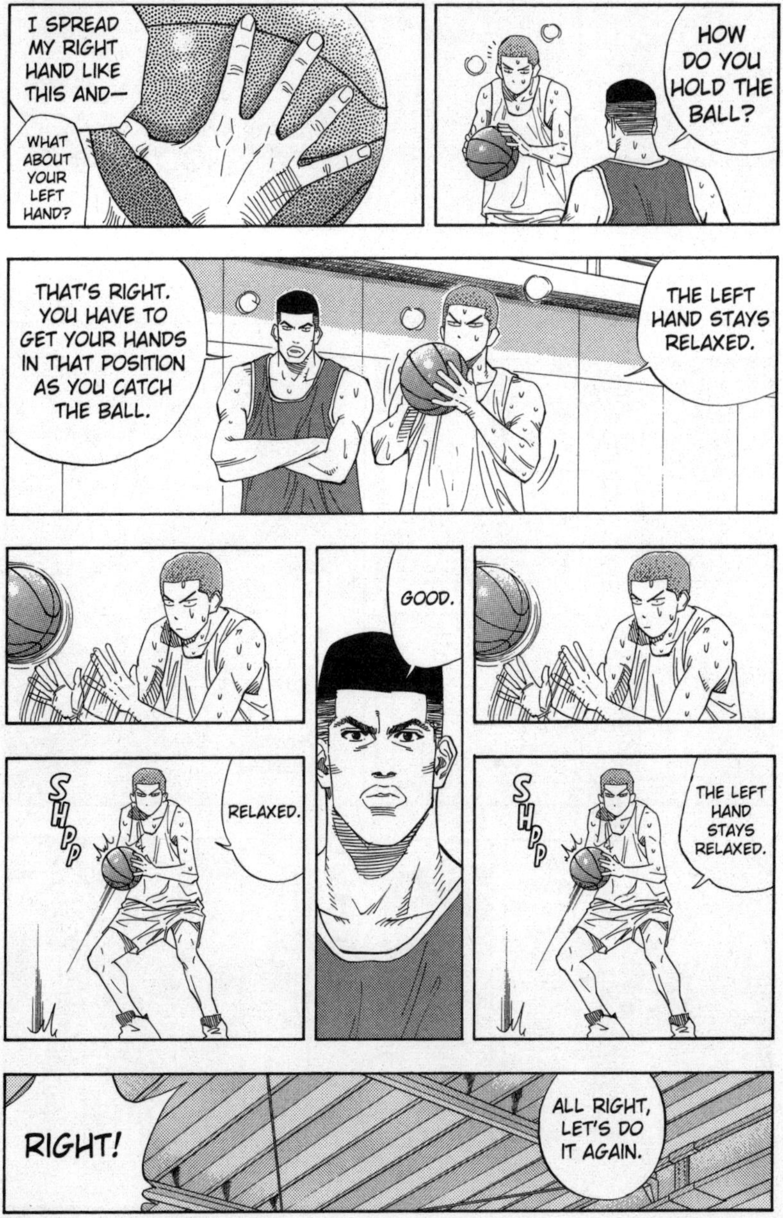
HOW DO YOU HOLD THE BALL?
I SPREAD MY RIGHT HAND LIKE THIS AND—
WHAT ABOUT YOUR LEFT HAND?
THE LEFT HAND STAYS RELAXED.
THAT'S RIGHT. YOU HAVE TO GET YOUR HANDS IN THAT POSITION AS YOU CATCH THE BALL.
SHPP
THE LEFT HAND STAYS RELAXED.
GOOD.
SHPP
RELAXED.
ALL RIGHT, LET'S DO IT AGAIN.
RIGHT!

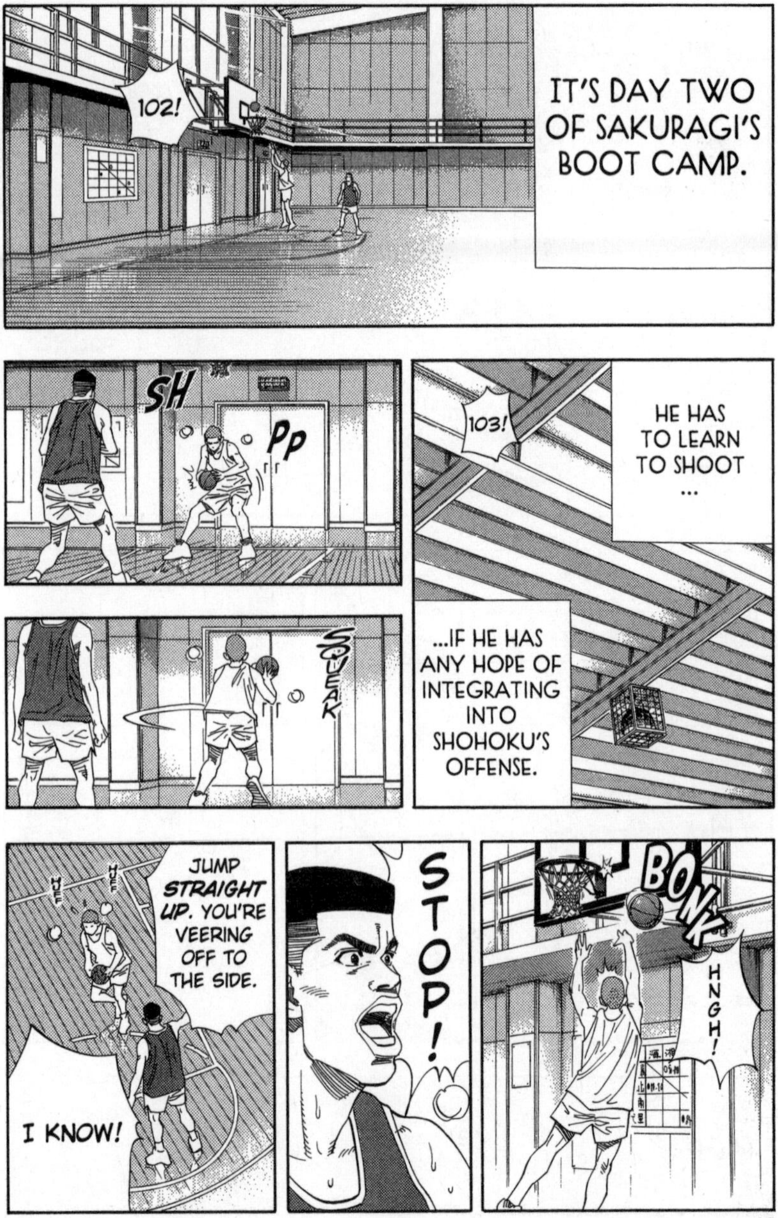
IT'S DAY TWO OF SAKURAGI'S BOOT CAMP.
102!
103!
HE HAS TO LEARN TO SHOOT ...
...IF HE HAS ANY HOPE OF INTEGRATING INTO SHOHOKU'S OFFENSE.
SH
PP
SQUEAK
BONK
HNGH!
STOP!
HUFF
HUFF
JUMP STRAIGHT UP. YOU'RE VEERING OFF TO THE SIDE.
I KNOW!

READ THIS WAY

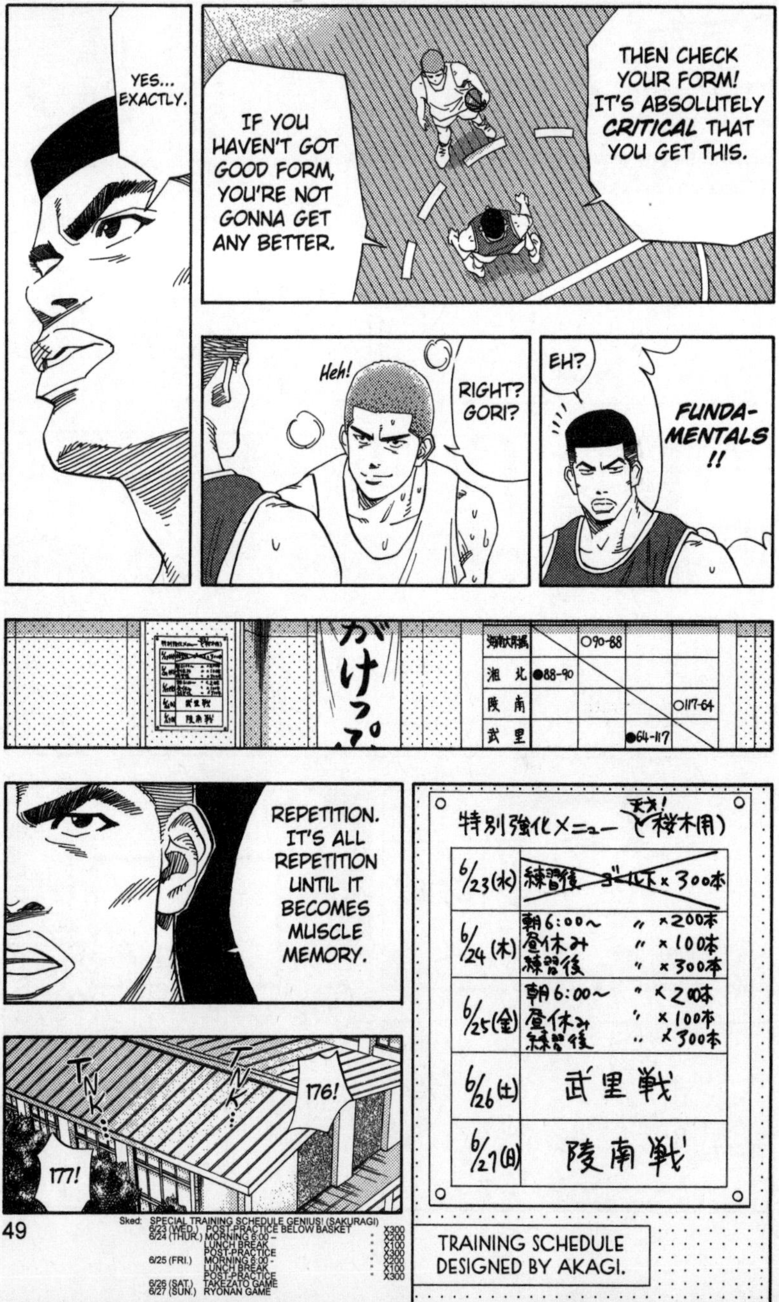
THEN CHECK YOUR FORM! IT'S ABSOLUTELY CRITICAL THAT YOU GET THIS.
IF YOU HAVEN'T GOT GOOD FORM, YOU'RE NOT GONNA GET ANY BETTER.
FUNDA-MENTALS !!
EH?
RIGHT? GORI?
Heh!
YES... EXACTLY.
がけっぷ
海南大附属
○90-88
湘北
●88-90
陵南
○117-64
武里
●64-117
特別強化メニュー（天才！桜木用）
6/23(水) 練習後 ゴール下 ×300本
6/24(木) 朝6:00～ 〃 ×200本
昼休み 〃 ×100本
練習後 〃 ×300本
6/25(金) 朝6:00～ 〃 ×200本
昼休み 〃 ×100本
練習後 〃 ×300本
6/26(土) 武里戦
6/27(日) 陵南戦
TRAINING SCHEDULE DESIGNED BY AKAGI.
REPETITION. IT'S ALL REPETITION UNTIL IT BECOMES MUSCLE MEMORY.
TNK
176!
TNK...
177!

Sked: SPECIAL TRAINING SCHEDULE GENIUS! (SAKURAGI)
6/23 (WED.) POST-PRACTICE BELOW BASKET X300
6/24 (THUR.) MORNING 6:00 – X200
LUNCH BREAK X100
POST-PRACTICE X300
6/25 (FRI.) MORNING 6:00 – X200
LUNCH BREAK X100
POST-PRACTICE X300
6/26 (SAT.) TAKEZATO GAME
6/27 (SUN.) RYONAN GAME

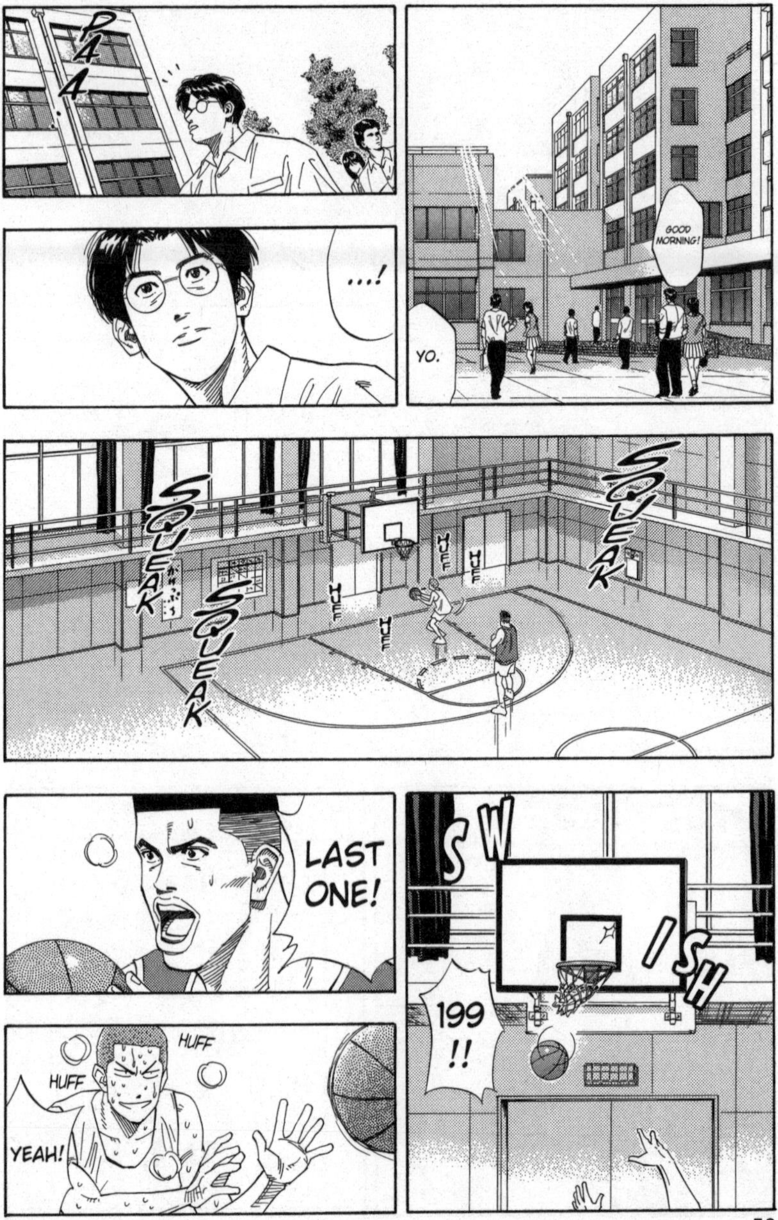
GOOD MORNING!
YO.
...!
SQUEAK
HUFF
HUFF
HUFF
HUFF
SQUEAK
SQUEAK
SWISH
199 !!
LAST ONE!
HUFF
HUFF
YEAH!

READ THIS WAY

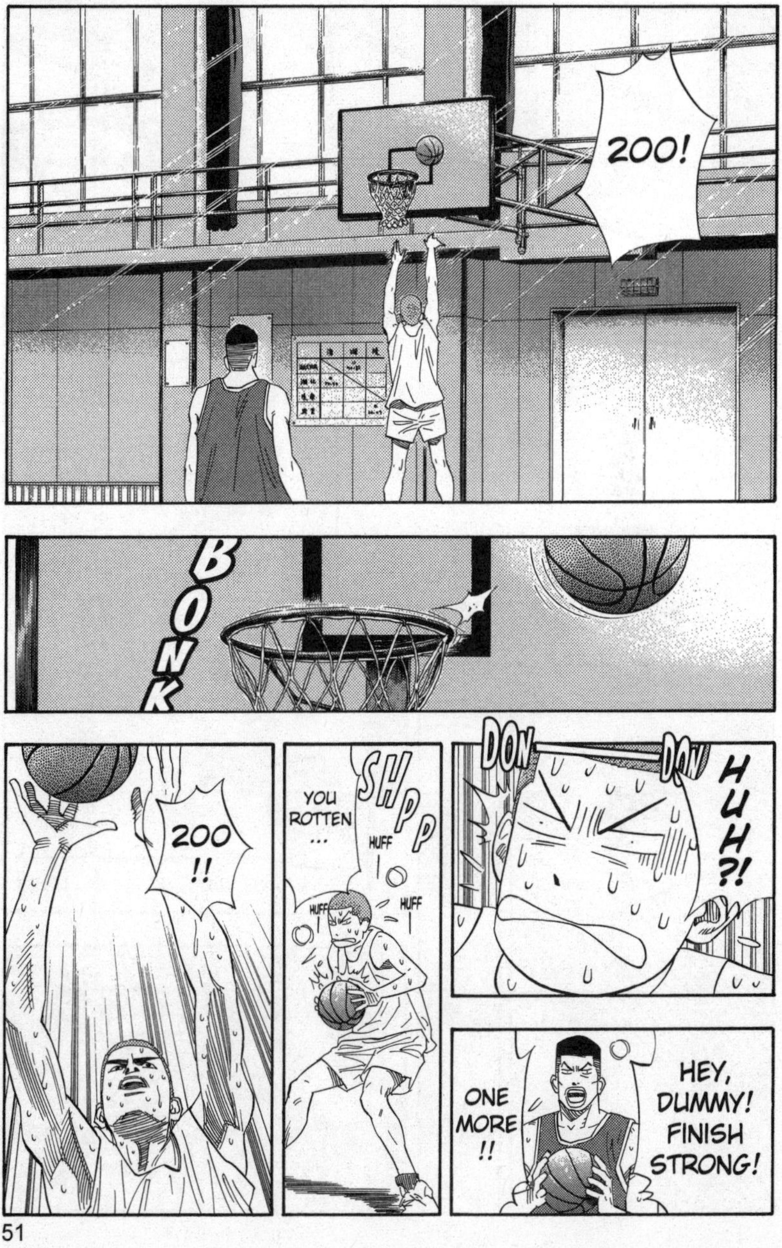
200!
BONK
DON DON
HUH?!
HEY, DUMMY! FINISH STRONG!
ONE MORE !!
SHPP
YOU ROTTEN ...
HUFF
HUFF
HUFF
200 !!

SWISH

16!

T N K . . . .

T N K . . . .

ZZZ ZZZ

RECHARGING HIS BATTERIES.

I SEE YOU SLEEPING IN MY CLASS! Punk!

52

READ THIS WAY

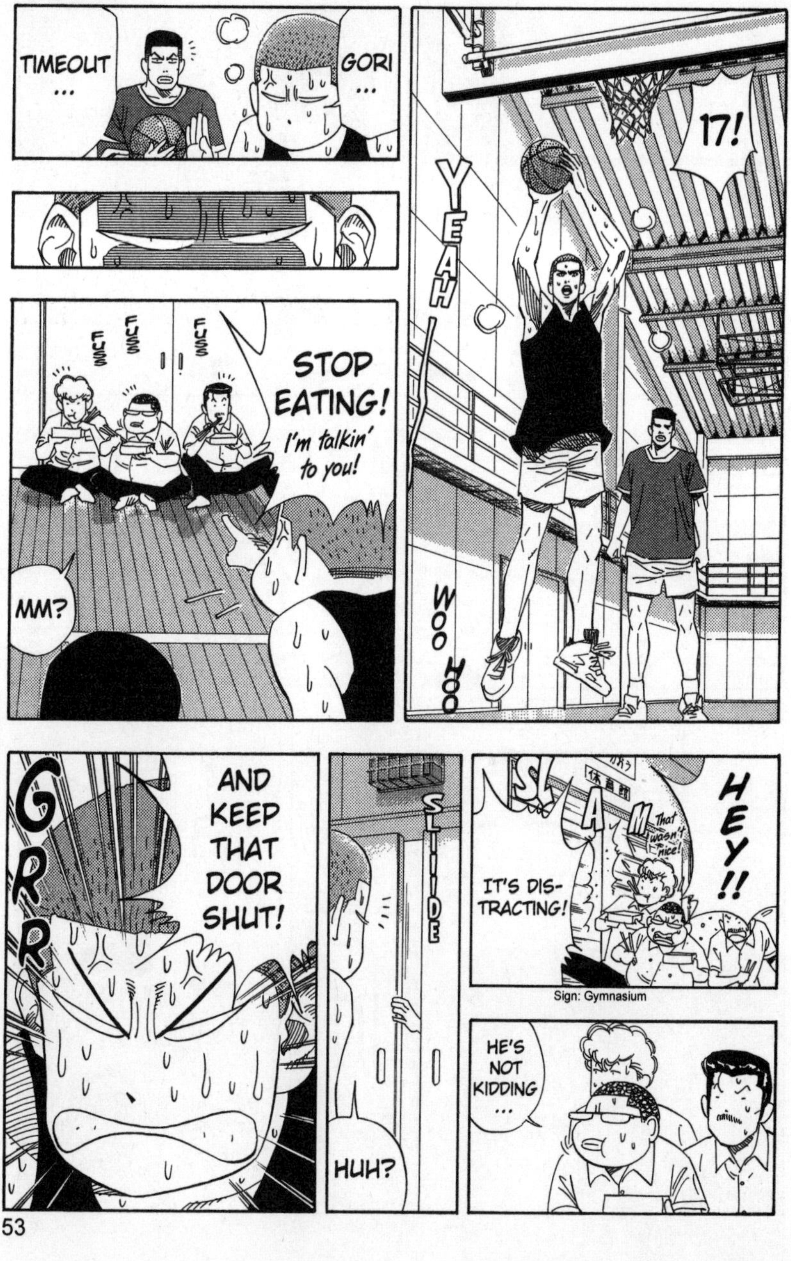
17!
YEAH
WOO HOO
GORI ...
TIMEOUT ...
STOP EATING!
I'm talkin' to you!
FUSS FUSS FUSS
MM?
HEY!!
That wasn't nice!
SLAM
IT'S DIS-TRACTING!
HE'S NOT KIDDING ...
SLIIIDE
HUH?
AND KEEP THAT DOOR SHUT!
GRR

Sign: Gymnasium

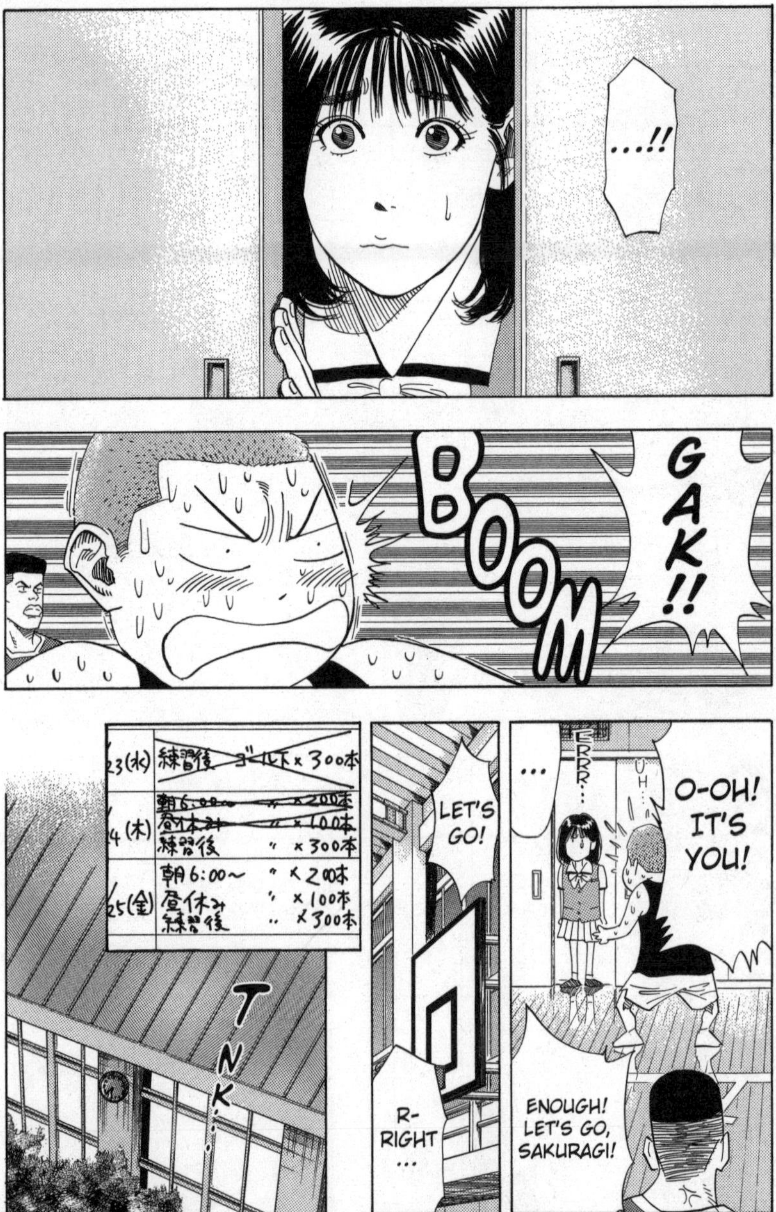
...!!
GAK!!
BOOM
O-OH! IT'S YOU!
UH...
ERRR...
...
ENOUGH! LET'S GO, SAKURAGI!
LET'S GO!
R-RIGHT...
23(水) 練習後 ゴール下 ×300本
24(木) 朝6:00~ 〃 ×200本
昼休み 〃 ×100本
練習後 〃 ×300本
25(金) 朝6:00~ 〃 ×200本
昼休み 〃 ×100本
練習後 〃 ×300本
TNK...

Sked:	6/23 (WED.)	POST-PRACTICE BELOW BASKET		X300
	6/24 (THUR.)	MORNING 6:00 –	"	X200
		LUNCH BREAK	"	X100
		POST-PRACTICE	"	X300
	6/25 (FRI.)	MORNING 6:00 -	"	X200
		LUNCH BREAK	"	X100
		POST-PRACTICE	"	X300

READ THIS WAY

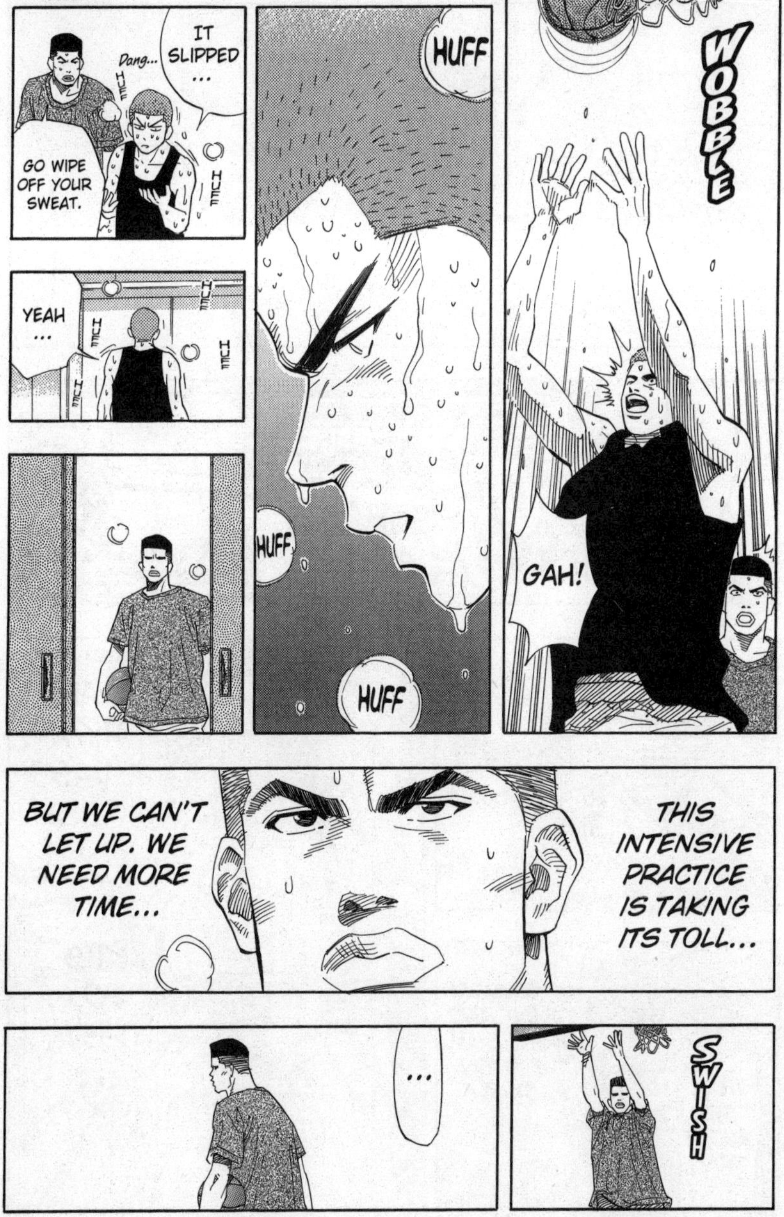
WOBBLE
GAH!
HUFF
HUFF
HUFF
IT SLIPPED...
Dang...
HUFF
HUFF
GO WIPE OFF YOUR SWEAT.
YEAH...
HUFF
HUFF
HUFF
HUFF
THIS INTENSIVE PRACTICE IS TAKING ITS TOLL...
BUT WE CAN'T LET UP. WE NEED MORE TIME...
SWISH
...

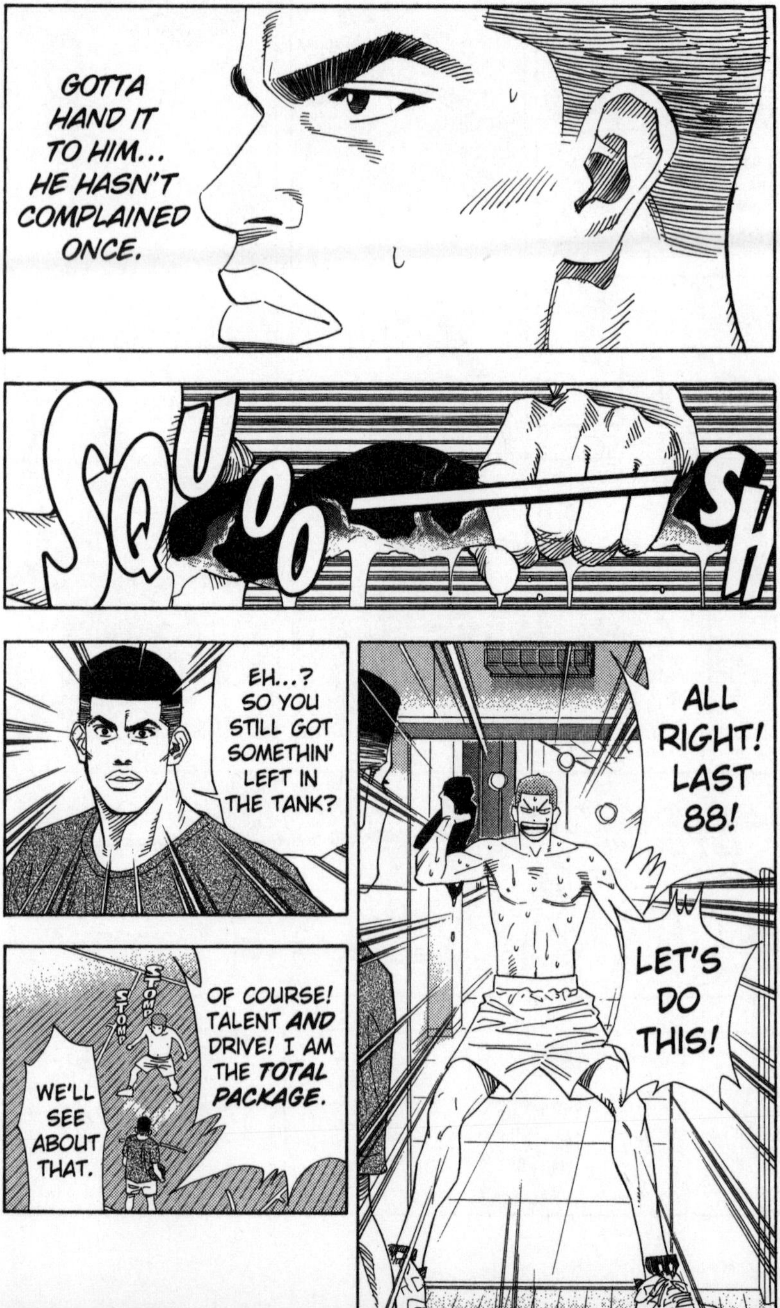
GOTTA HAND IT TO HIM... HE HASN'T COMPLAINED ONCE.
SQUOOSH
ALL RIGHT! LAST 88!
LET'S DO THIS!
EH...? SO YOU STILL GOT SOMETHIN' LEFT IN THE TANK?
OF COURSE! TALENT AND DRIVE! I AM THE TOTAL PACKAGE.
STOMP
STOMP
WE'LL SEE ABOUT THAT.

READ THIS WAY

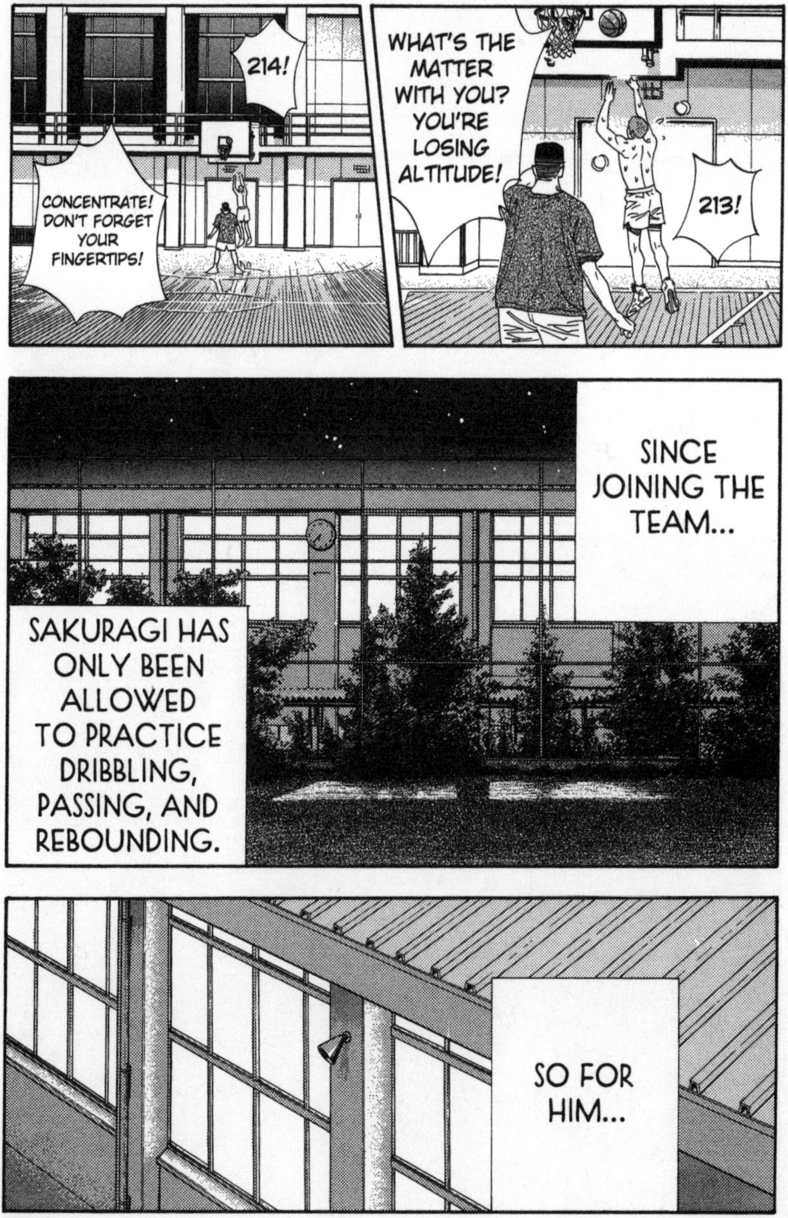
WHAT'S THE MATTER WITH YOU? YOU'RE LOSING ALTITUDE!
213!
214!
CONCENTRATE! DON'T FORGET YOUR FINGERTIPS!
SINCE JOINING THE TEAM...
SAKURAGI HAS ONLY BEEN ALLOWED TO PRACTICE DRIBBLING, PASSING, AND REBOUNDING.
SO FOR HIM...

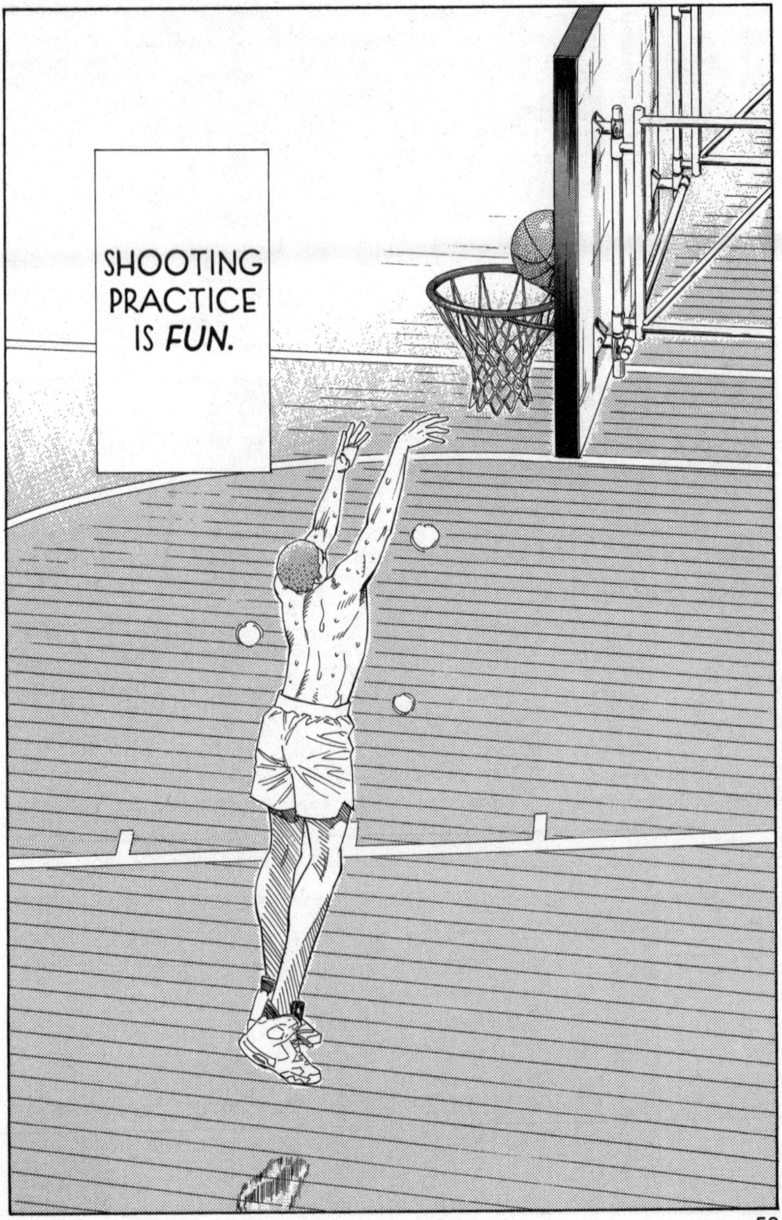
SHOOTING PRACTICE IS *FUN.*

READ THIS WAY

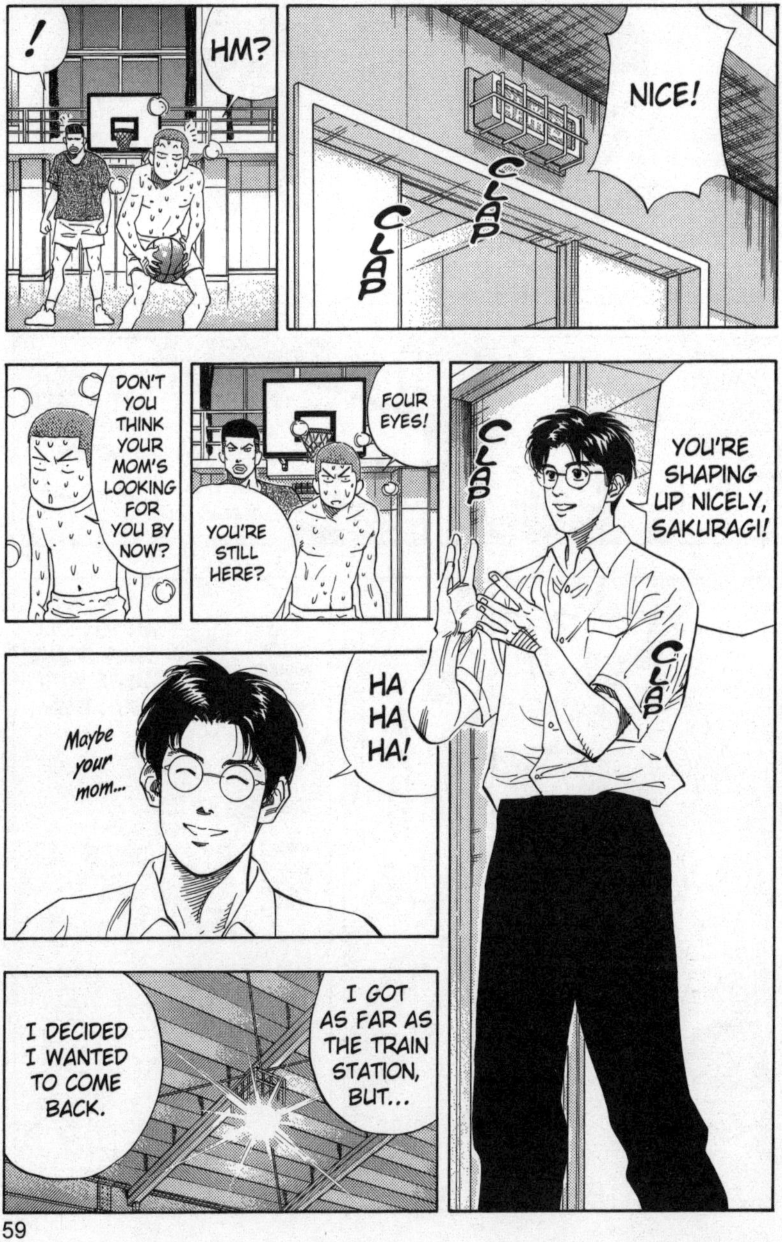
NICE!
CLAP
CLAP
HM?
!
CLAP
YOU'RE SHAPING UP NICELY, SAKURAGI!
CLAP
FOUR EYES!
YOU'RE STILL HERE?
DON'T YOU THINK YOUR MOM'S LOOKING FOR YOU BY NOW?
HA HA HA!
Maybe your mom...
I GOT AS FAR AS THE TRAIN STATION, BUT...
I DECIDED I WANTED TO COME BACK.

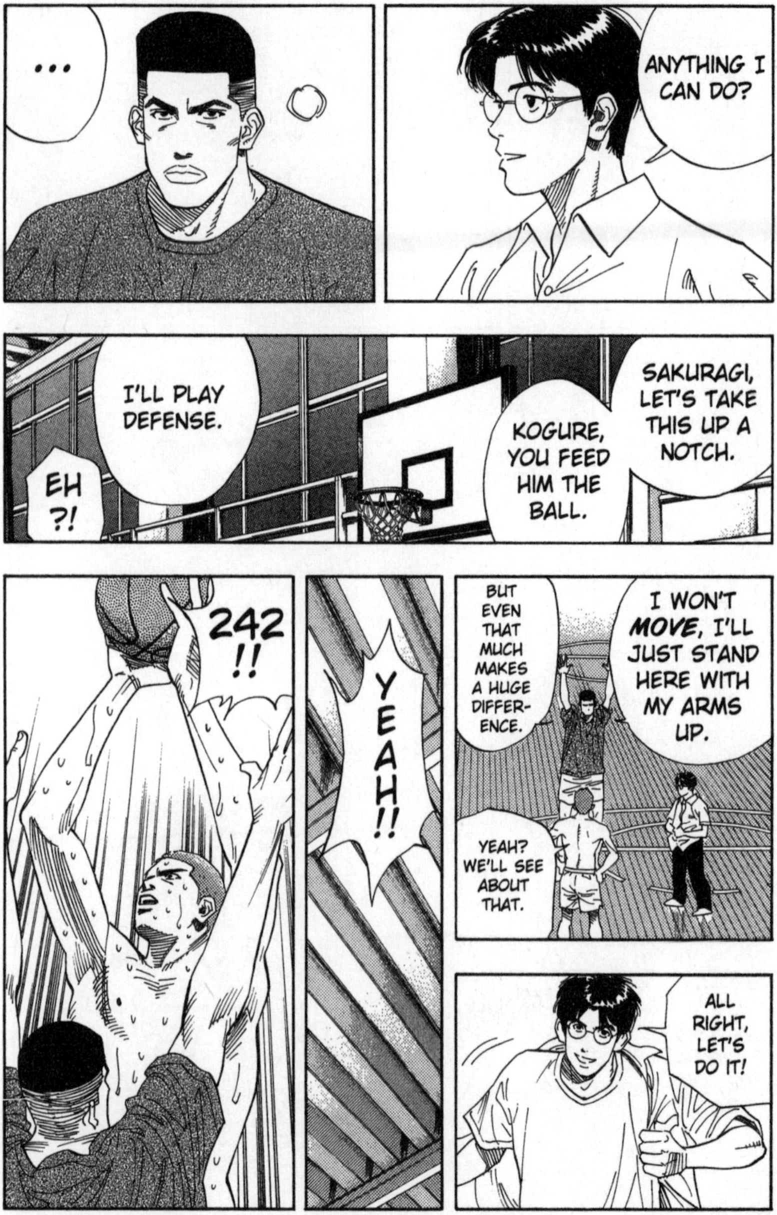
ANYTHING I CAN DO?
...
SAKURAGI, LET'S TAKE THIS UP A NOTCH.
KOGURE, YOU FEED HIM THE BALL.
I'LL PLAY DEFENSE.
EH ?!
I WON'T *MOVE*, I'LL JUST STAND HERE WITH MY ARMS UP.
BUT EVEN THAT MUCH MAKES A HUGE DIFFER-ENCE.
YEAH? WE'LL SEE ABOUT THAT.
ALL RIGHT, LET'S DO IT!
YEAH!!
242 !!

READ THIS WAY

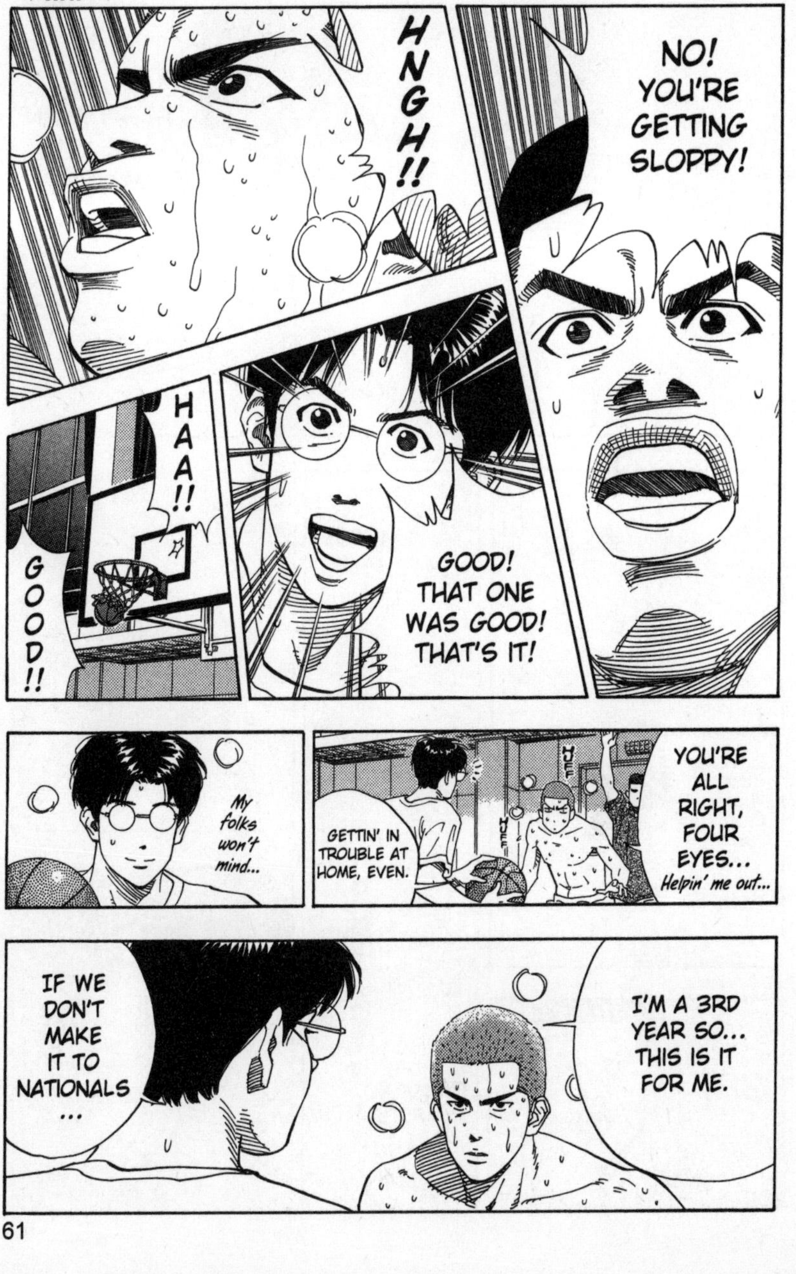

NO! YOU'RE GETTING SLOPPY!
HNGH!!
GOOD! THAT ONE WAS GOOD! THAT'S IT!
HAAA!!
GOOD!!
YOU'RE ALL RIGHT, FOUR EYES...
Helpin' me out...
HUFF
HUFF
GETTIN' IN TROUBLE AT HOME, EVEN.
My folks won't mind...
I'M A 3RD YEAR SO... THIS IS IT FOR ME.
IF WE DON'T MAKE IT TO NATIONALS ...

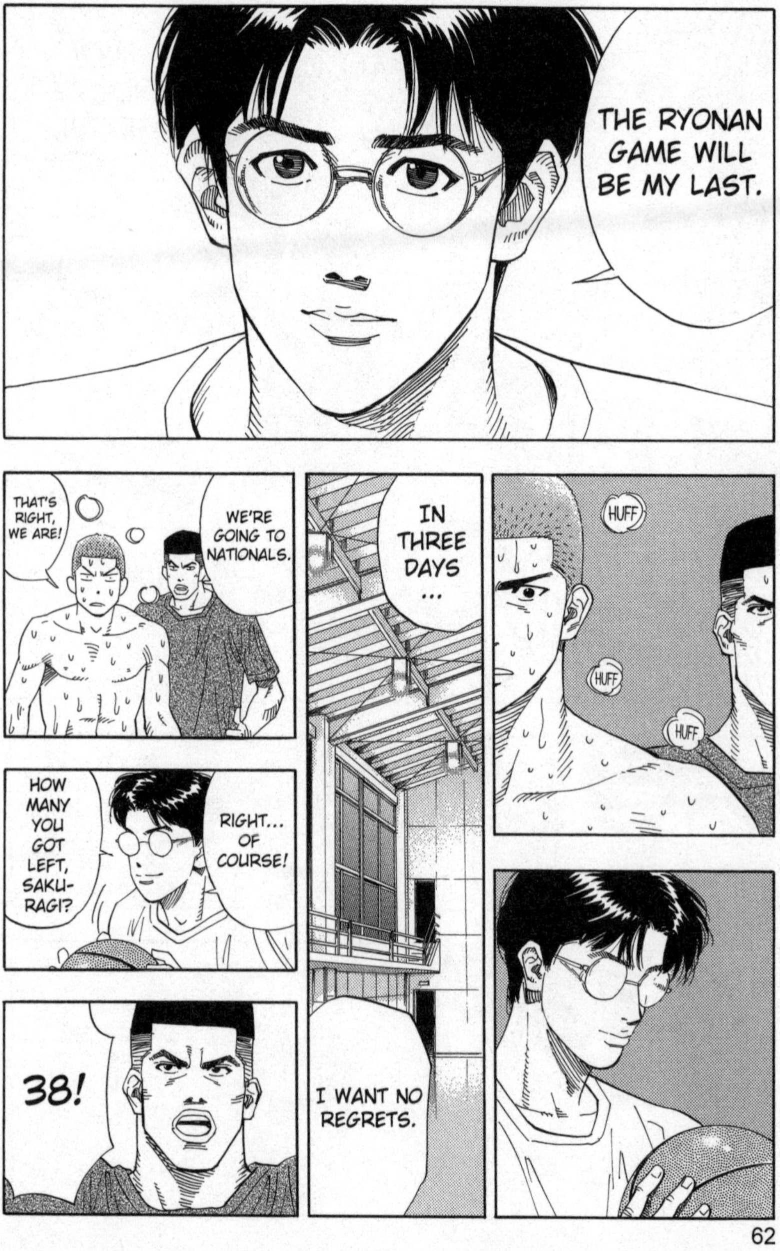
THE RYONAN GAME WILL BE MY LAST.
HUFF
HUFF
HUFF
IN THREE DAYS ...
I WANT NO REGRETS.
WE'RE GOING TO NATIONALS.
THAT'S RIGHT, WE ARE!
RIGHT... OF COURSE!
HOW MANY YOU GOT LEFT, SAKURAGI?
38!

ALL RIGHT! BRING IT ON!

YEAH!!

JUNE 26TH
SATURDAY

特別強化メニュー（桜木用）

6/23 (水)	練習後	ゴール下 x 30本
6/24 (木)	朝6:00～ 昼休み 練習後	x 200本 x 100本 x 300本
6/25 (金)	朝6:00～ 昼休み 練習後	x 200本 x 100本 x 300本
6/26 (土)	武里戦	
6/27 (日)	陵南戦	

かけっぷち

Sked: 6/26 (SAT.) TAKEZATO GAME
6/27 (SUN.) RYONAN GAME

Paper: On the Brink
By Ayako

SWISH
HEE... MUMBLE MUMBLE

SLAM DUNK

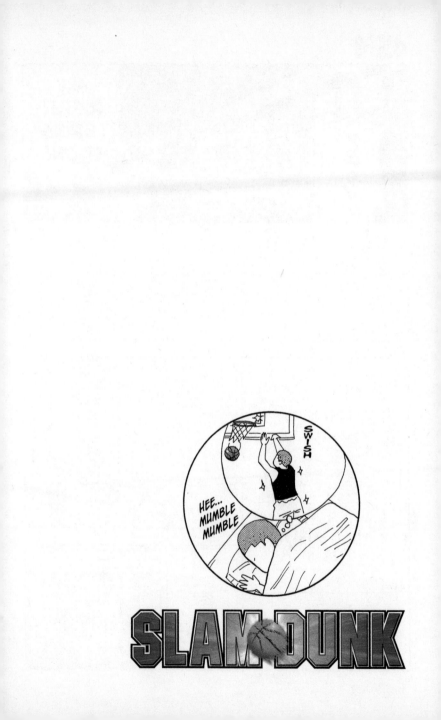

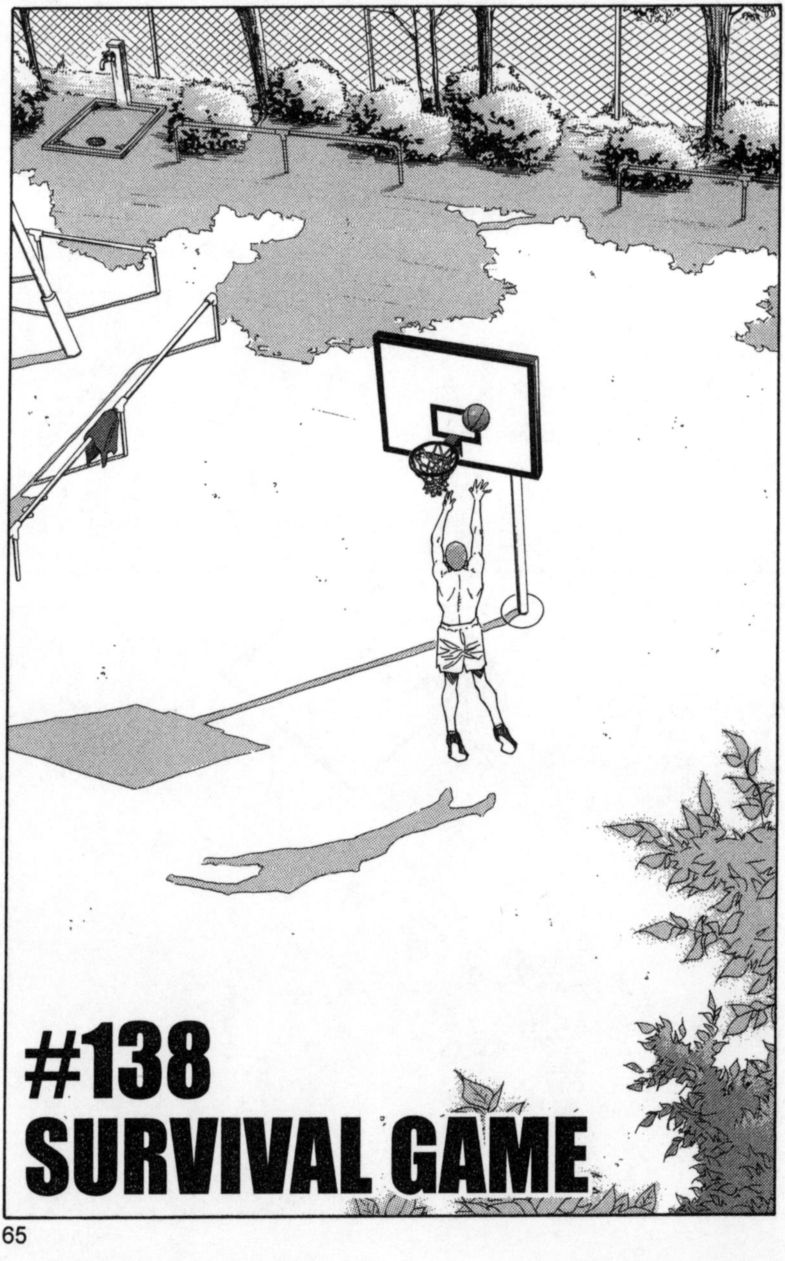
#138
SURVIVAL GAME

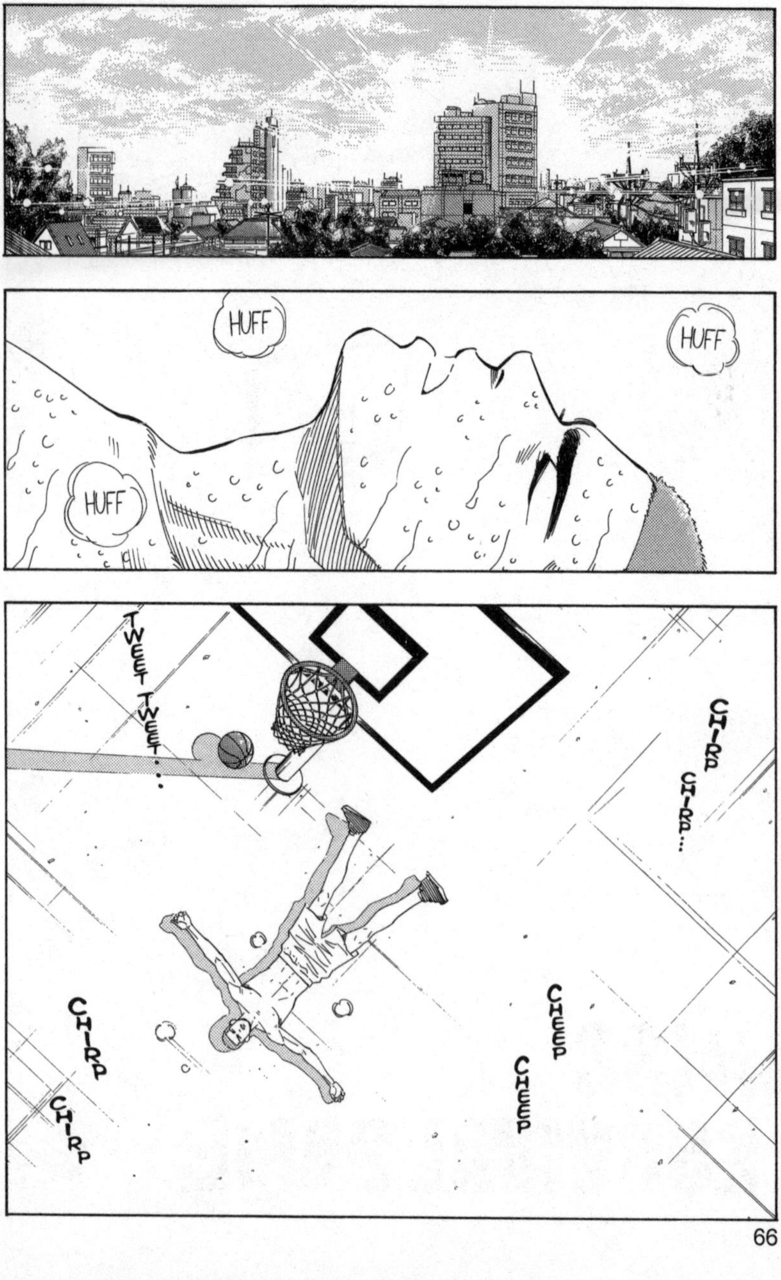
HUFF
HUFF
HUFF
CHIRP CHIRP...
TWEET TWEET...
CHEEP CHEEP
CHIRP CHIRP

READ THIS WAY

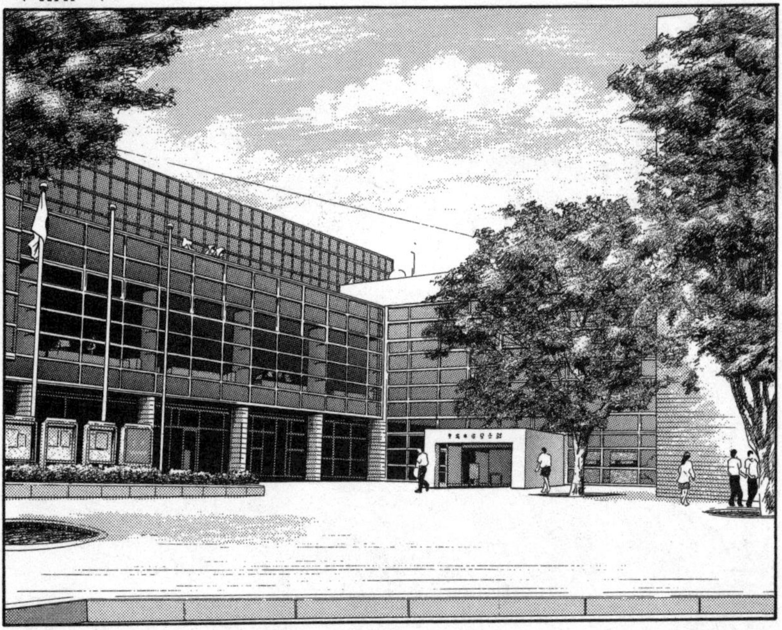

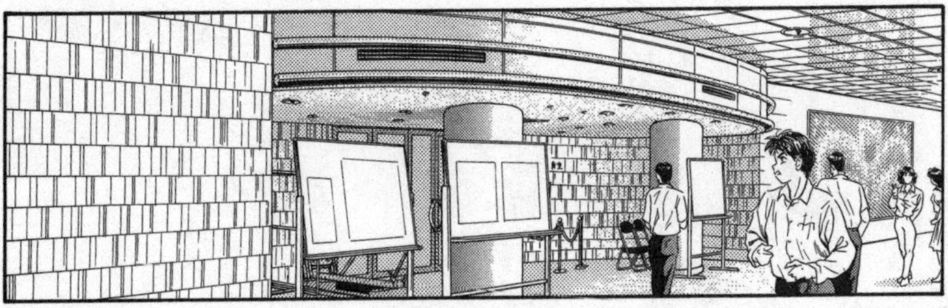

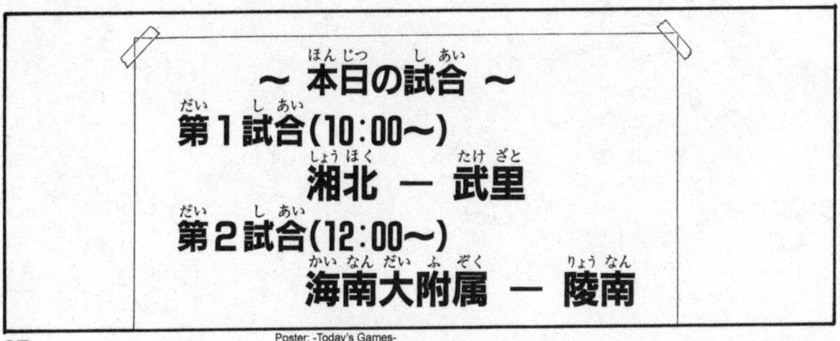
～ 本日の試合 ～
第1試合(10:00～)
湘北 ― 武里
第2試合(12:00～)
海南大附属 ― 陵南

Poster: -Today's Games-
1st Game (10:00 -)
Shohoku – Takezato
2nd Game (12:00 -)
Kainan University Affiliate – Ryonan

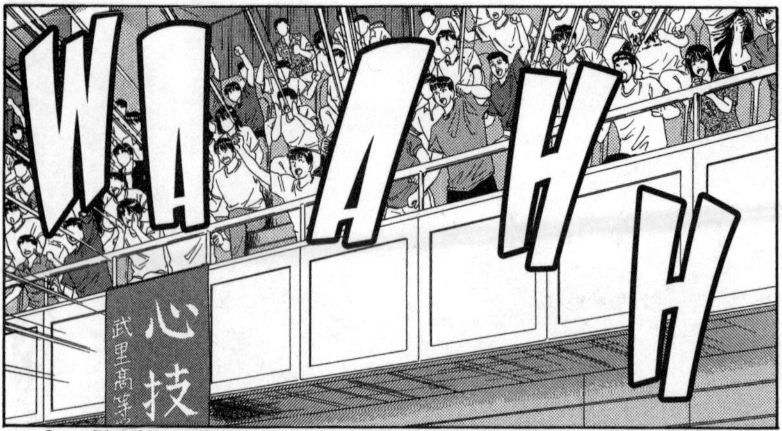
WAAHH

Banner: *Shingitai* [shin – mind/heart, gi – technique/skill, tai – body]
Takezato High School

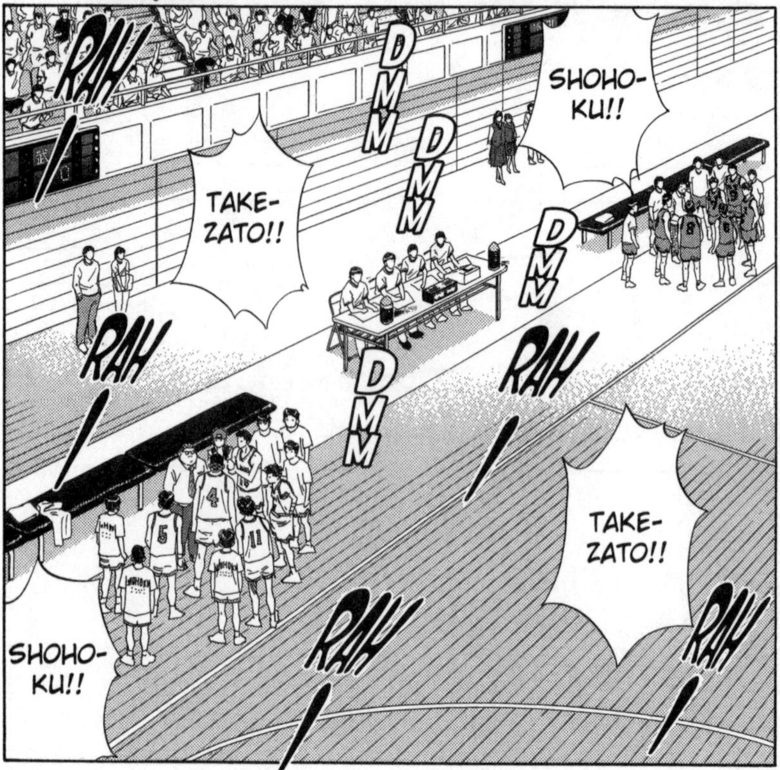
SHOHO-KU!!
DMM
DMM
DMM
TAKE-ZATO!!
RAH!
RAH!
RAH!
DMM
TAKE-ZATO!!
RAH!
RAH!
SHOHO-KU!!

READ THIS WAY

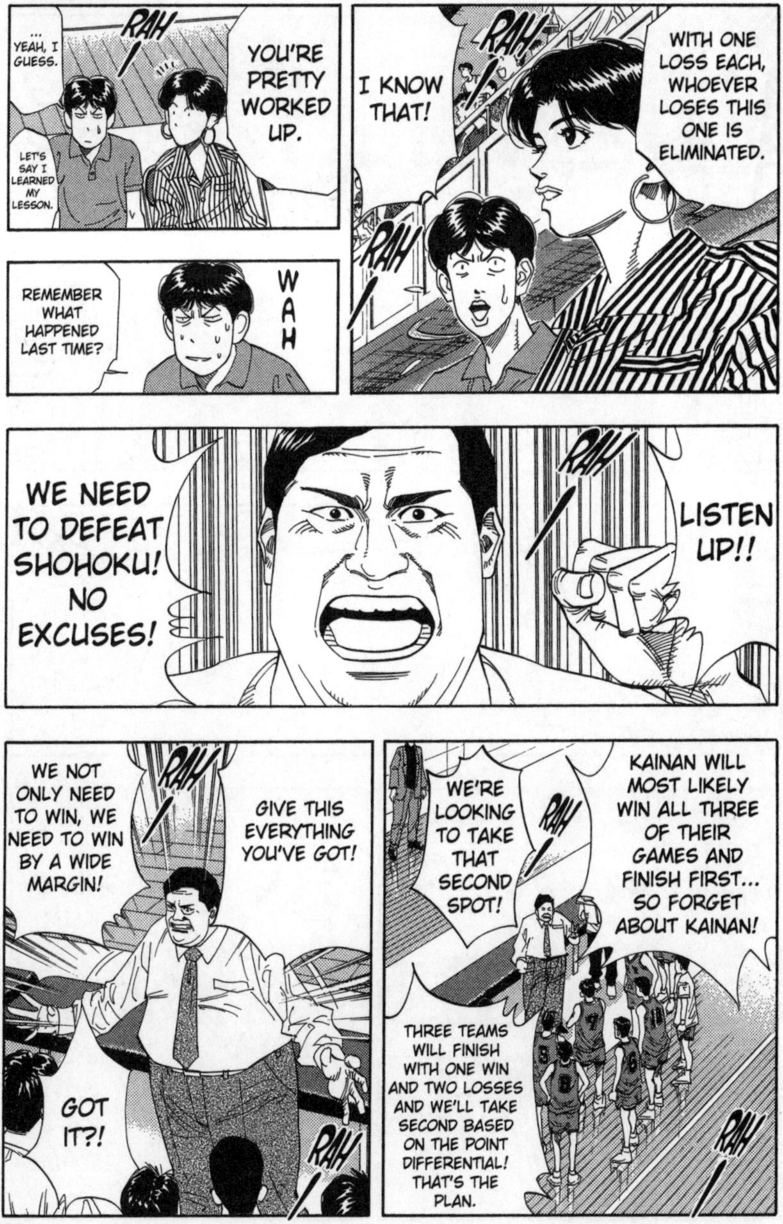
WITH ONE LOSS EACH, WHOEVER LOSES THIS ONE IS ELIMINATED.
RAH!
I KNOW THAT!
RAH!
YOU'RE PRETTY WORKED UP.
RAH!
... YEAH, I GUESS.
LET'S SAY I LEARNED MY LESSON.
WAH
REMEMBER WHAT HAPPENED LAST TIME?
RAH!
LISTEN UP!!
WE NEED TO DEFEAT SHOHOKU! NO EXCUSES!
KAINAN WILL MOST LIKELY WIN ALL THREE OF THEIR GAMES AND FINISH FIRST... SO FORGET ABOUT KAINAN!
RAH!
WE'RE LOOKING TO TAKE THAT SECOND SPOT!
THREE TEAMS WILL FINISH WITH ONE WIN AND TWO LOSSES AND WE'LL TAKE SECOND BASED ON THE POINT DIFFERENTIAL! THAT'S THE PLAN.
RAH!
GIVE THIS EVERYTHING YOU'VE GOT!
RAH!
WE NOT ONLY NEED TO WIN, WE NEED TO WIN BY A WIDE MARGIN!
GOT IT?!
RAH!

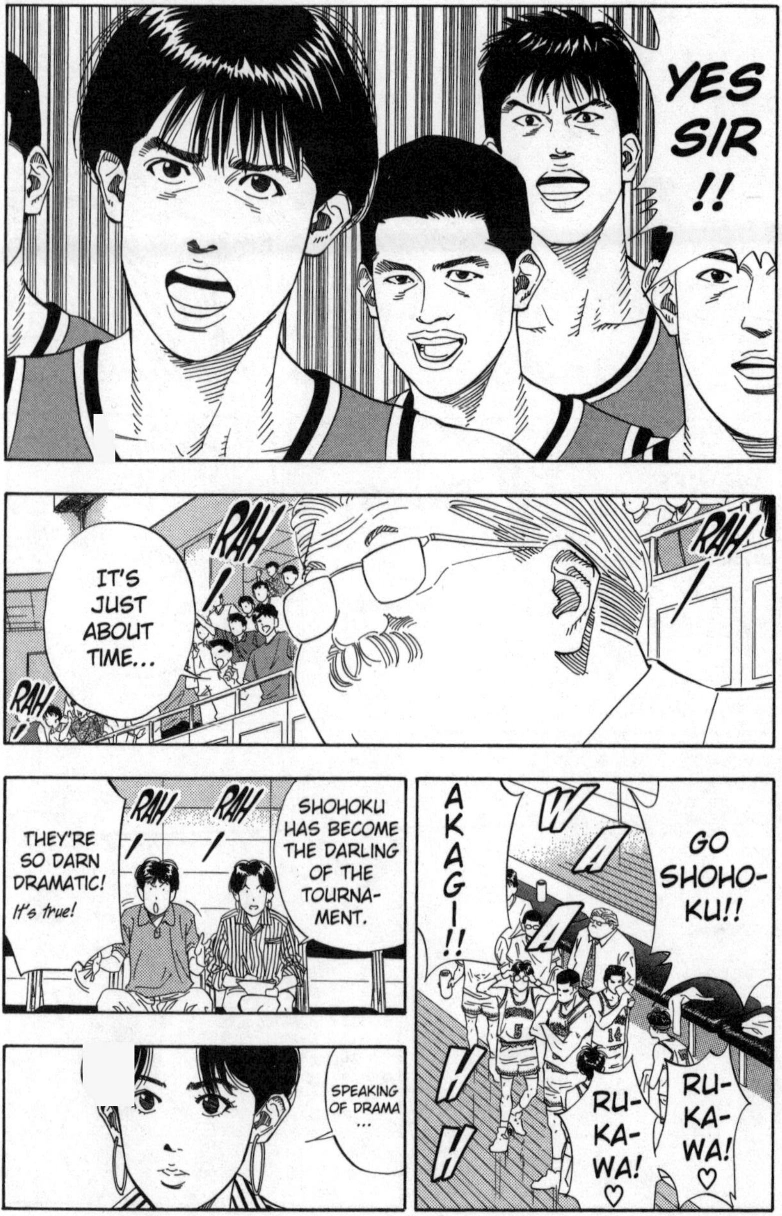
YES SIR!!
RAH!
IT'S JUST ABOUT TIME...
RAH!
RAH!
AKAGI!!
WAAHH
GO SHOHOKU!!
RU-KA-WA! ♡
RU-KA-WA! ♡
SHOHOKU HAS BECOME THE DARLING OF THE TOURNAMENT.
RAH!
RAH!
THEY'RE SO DARN DRAMATIC!
It's true!
SPEAKING OF DRAMA...

READ THIS WAY

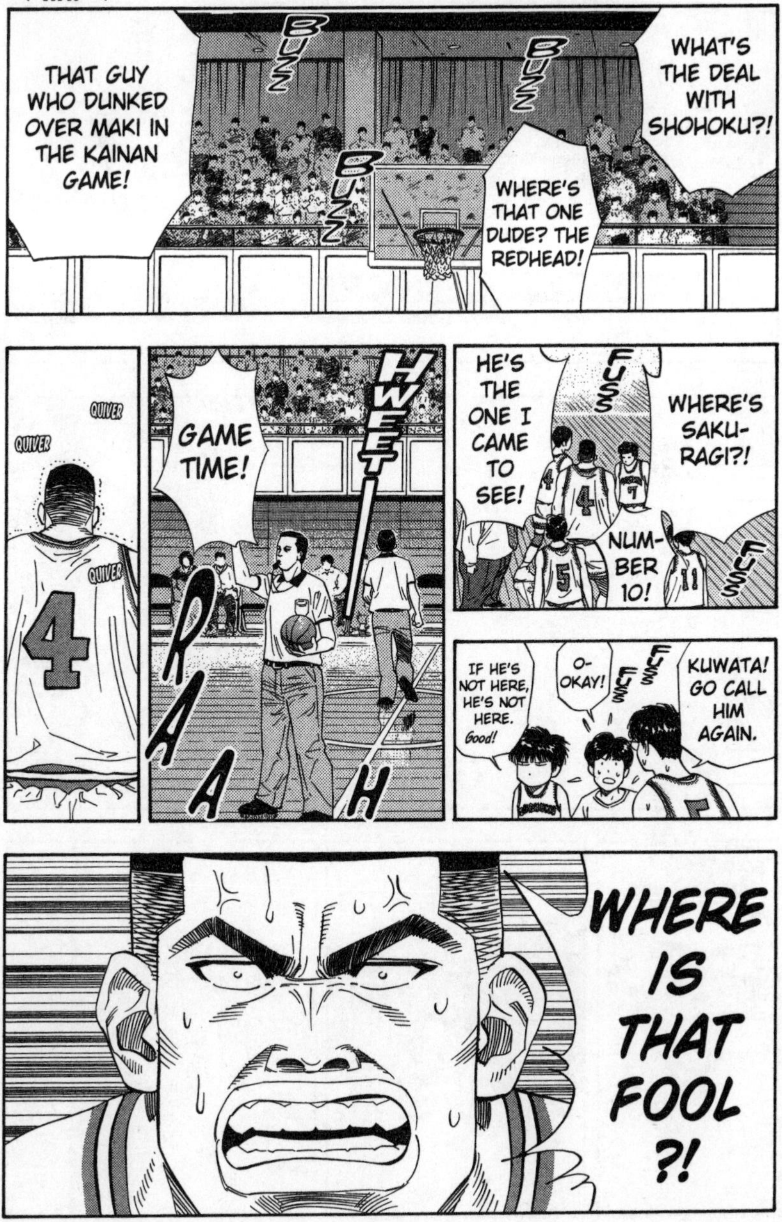
WHAT'S THE DEAL WITH SHOHOKU?!
BUZZ
WHERE'S THAT ONE DUDE? THE REDHEAD!
BUZZ
BUZZ
THAT GUY WHO DUNKED OVER MAKI IN THE KAINAN GAME!
WHERE'S SAKU-RAGI?!
FUSS
HE'S THE ONE I CAME TO SEE!
NUM-BER 10!
FUSS
KUWATA! GO CALL HIM AGAIN.
FUSS
FUSS
O-OKAY!
IF HE'S NOT HERE, HE'S NOT HERE. Good!
HWEET
GAME TIME!
RAAAH
QUIVER
QUIVER
QUIVER
WHERE IS THAT FOOL ?!

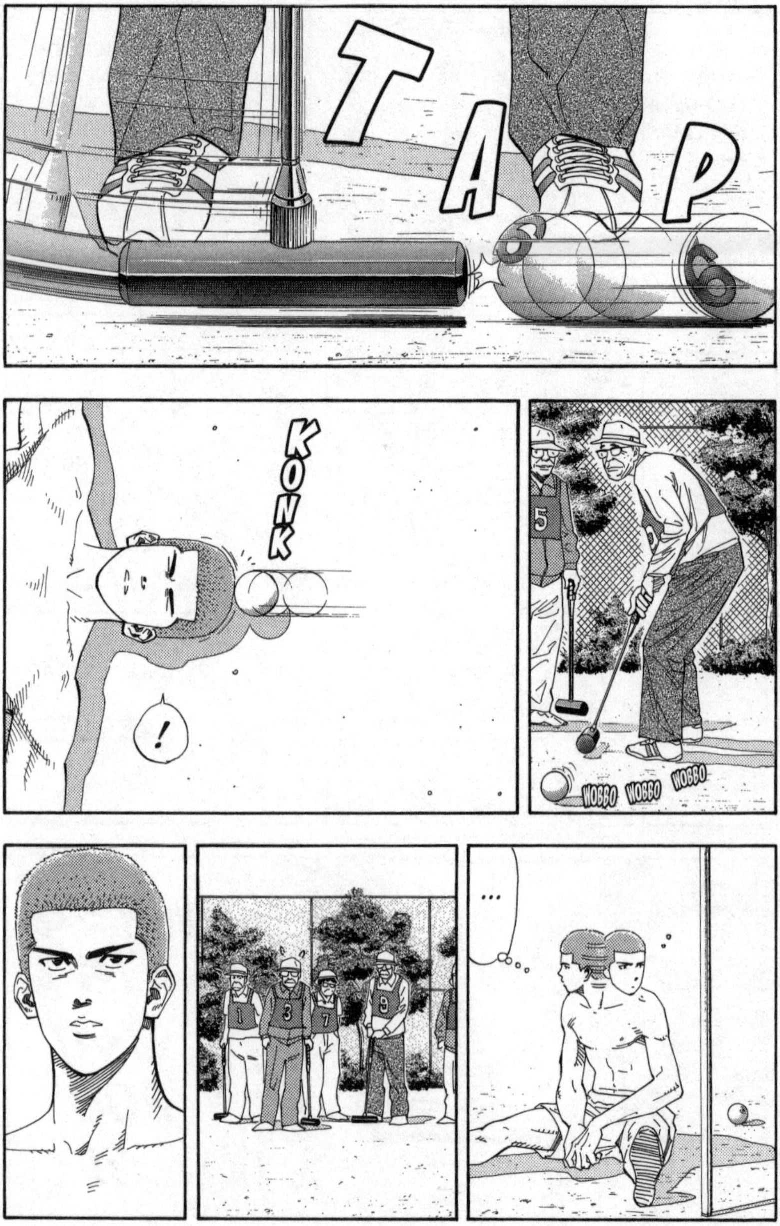
TAP
KONK
!
WOBBO WOBBO WOBBO
...

READ THIS WAY

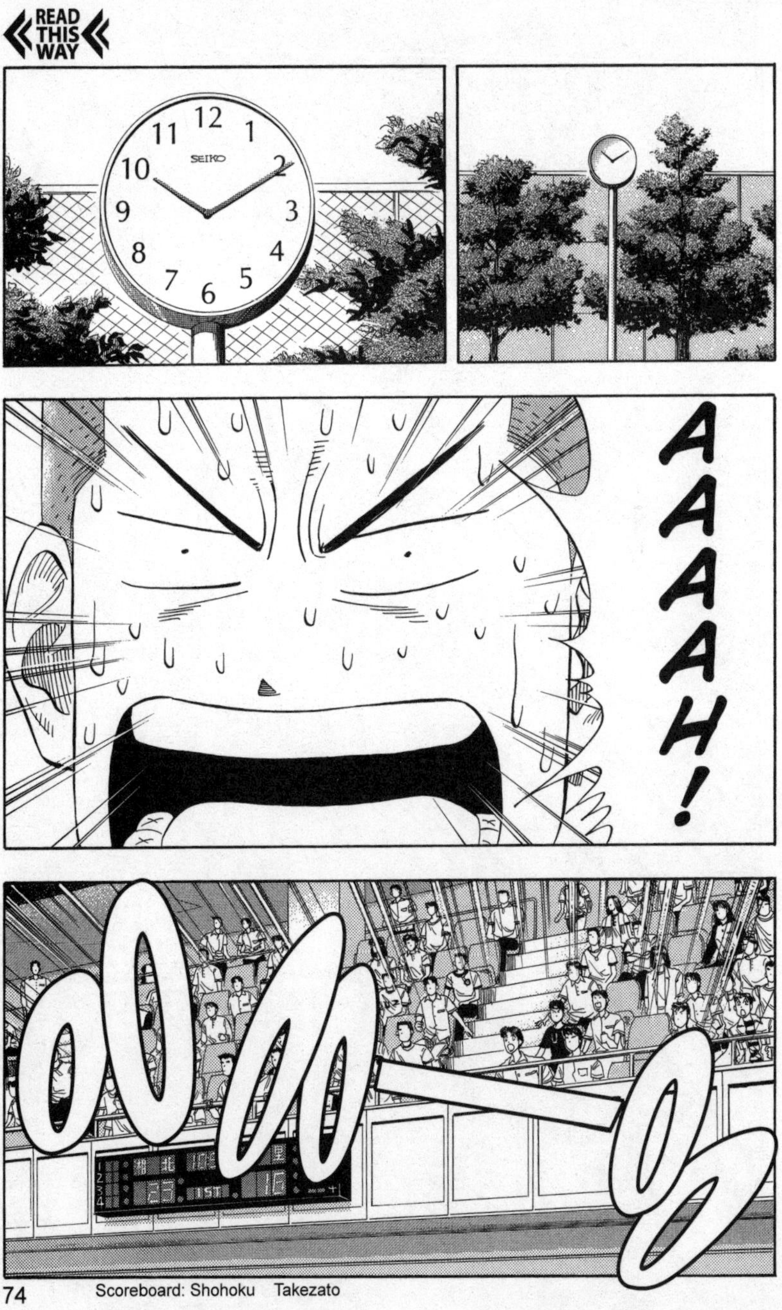
SEIKO
AAAAAH!
OOOO—OO

Scoreboard: Shohoku Takezato

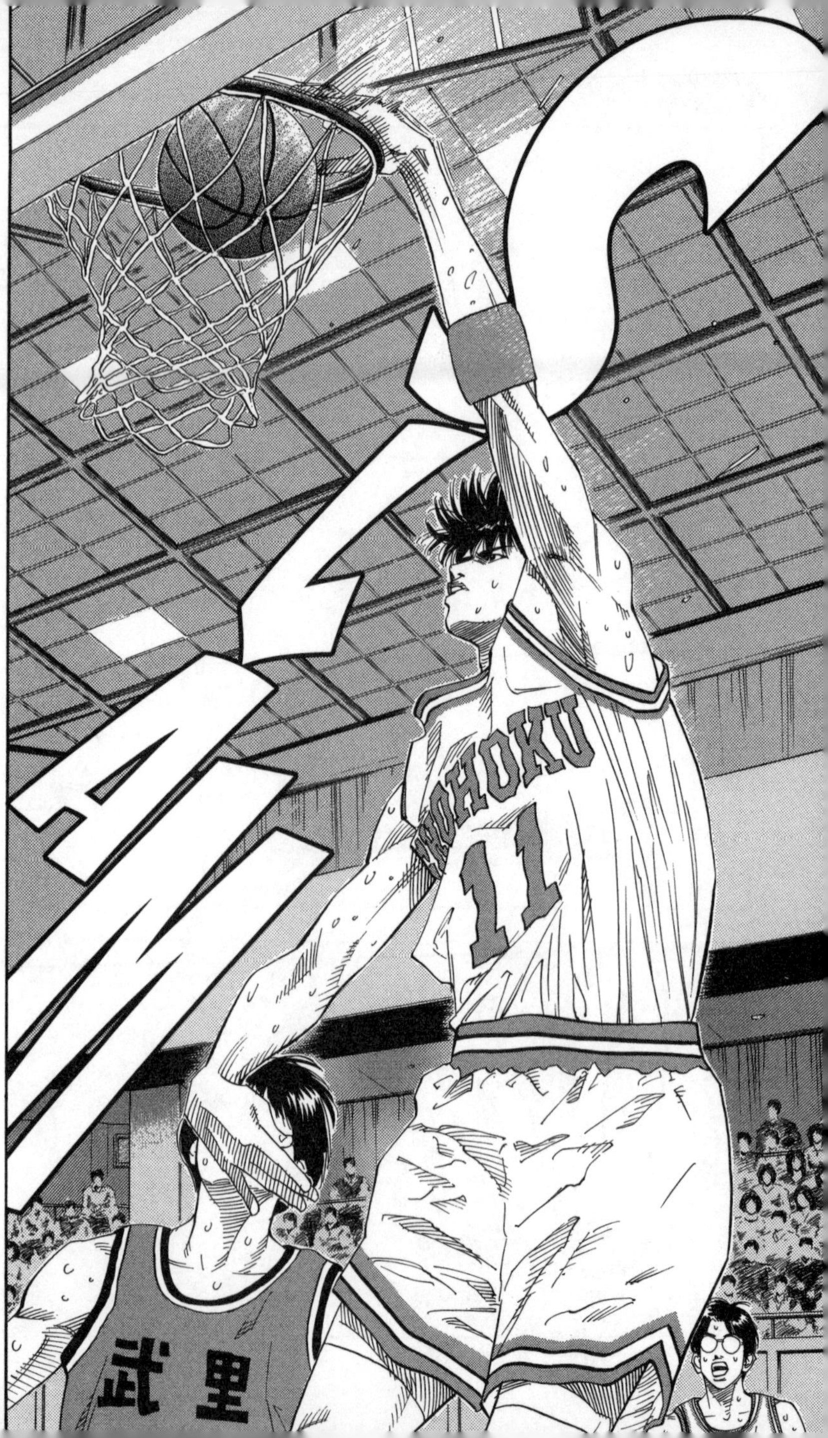
SLAM
11
武里

READ THIS WAY

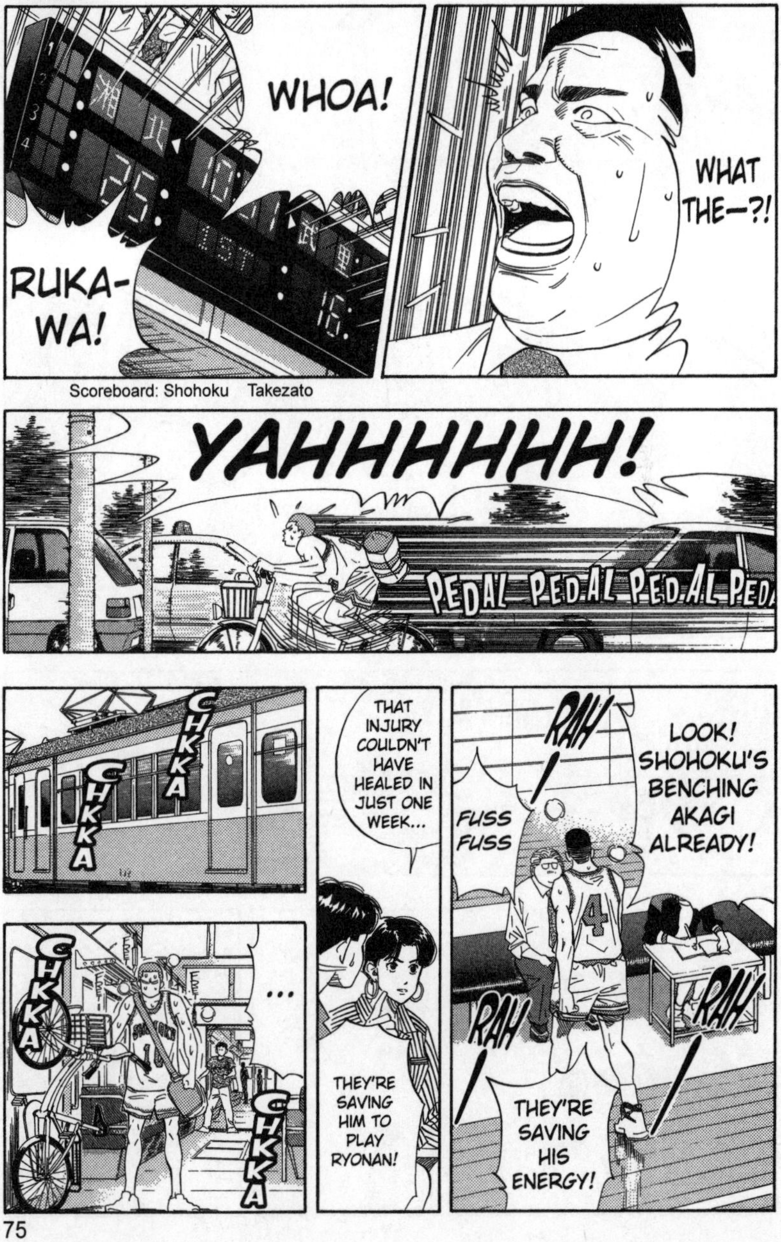
WHAT THE—?!
WHOA!
RUKA-WA!
Scoreboard: Shohoku Takezato
YAHHHHHH!
PEDAL PEDAL PEDAL PEDA
LOOK! SHOHOKU'S BENCHING AKAGI ALREADY!
RAH
FUSS FUSS
RAH
RAH
THEY'RE SAVING HIS ENERGY!
THAT INJURY COULDN'T HAVE HEALED IN JUST ONE WEEK...
THEY'RE SAVING HIM TO PLAY RYONAN!
CHKKA
CHKKA
...
CHKKA
CHKKA

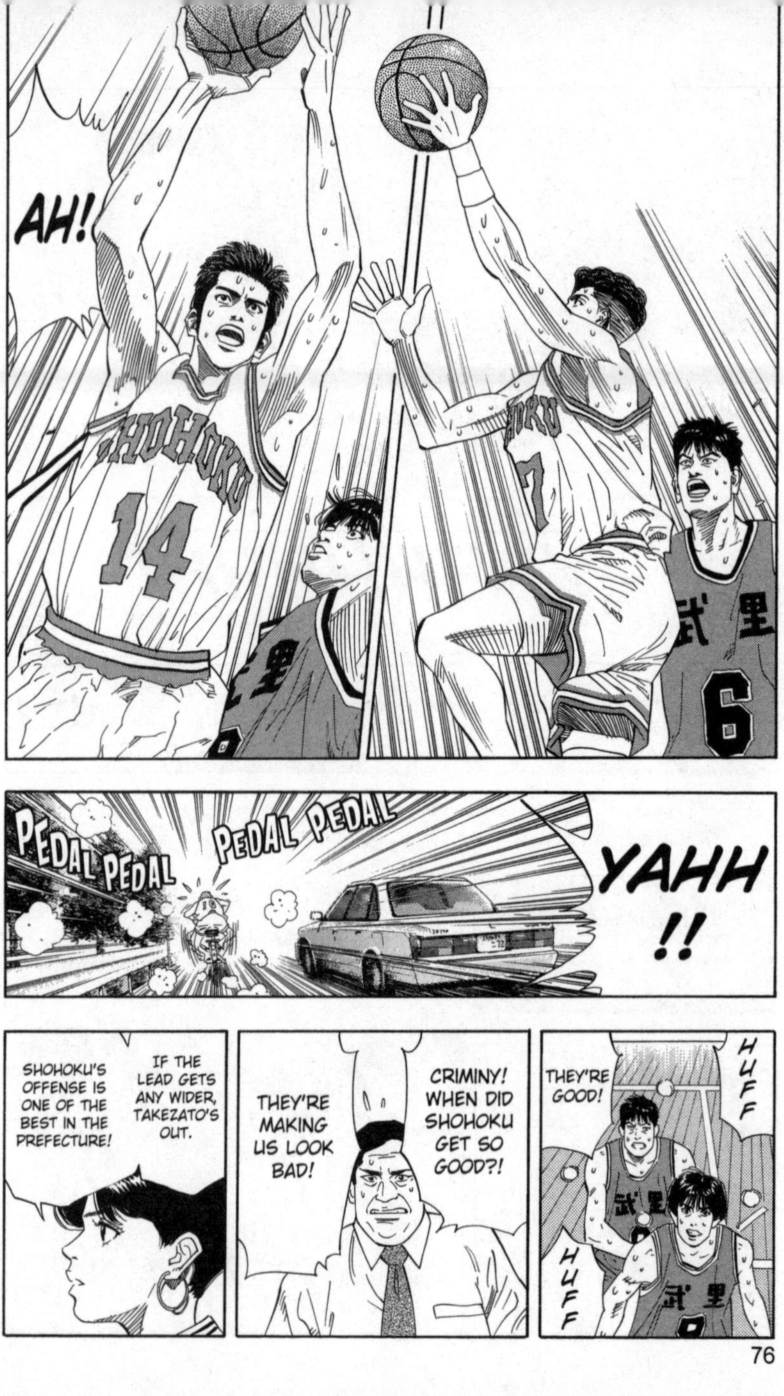
AH!
YAHH !!
PEDAL PEDAL
PEDAL PEDAL
HUFF
THEY'RE GOOD!
HUFF
CRIMINY! WHEN DID SHOHOKU GET SO GOOD?!
THEY'RE MAKING US LOOK BAD!
IF THE LEAD GETS ANY WIDER, TAKEZATO'S OUT.
SHOHOKU'S OFFENSE IS ONE OF THE BEST IN THE PREFECTURE!

READ THIS WAY

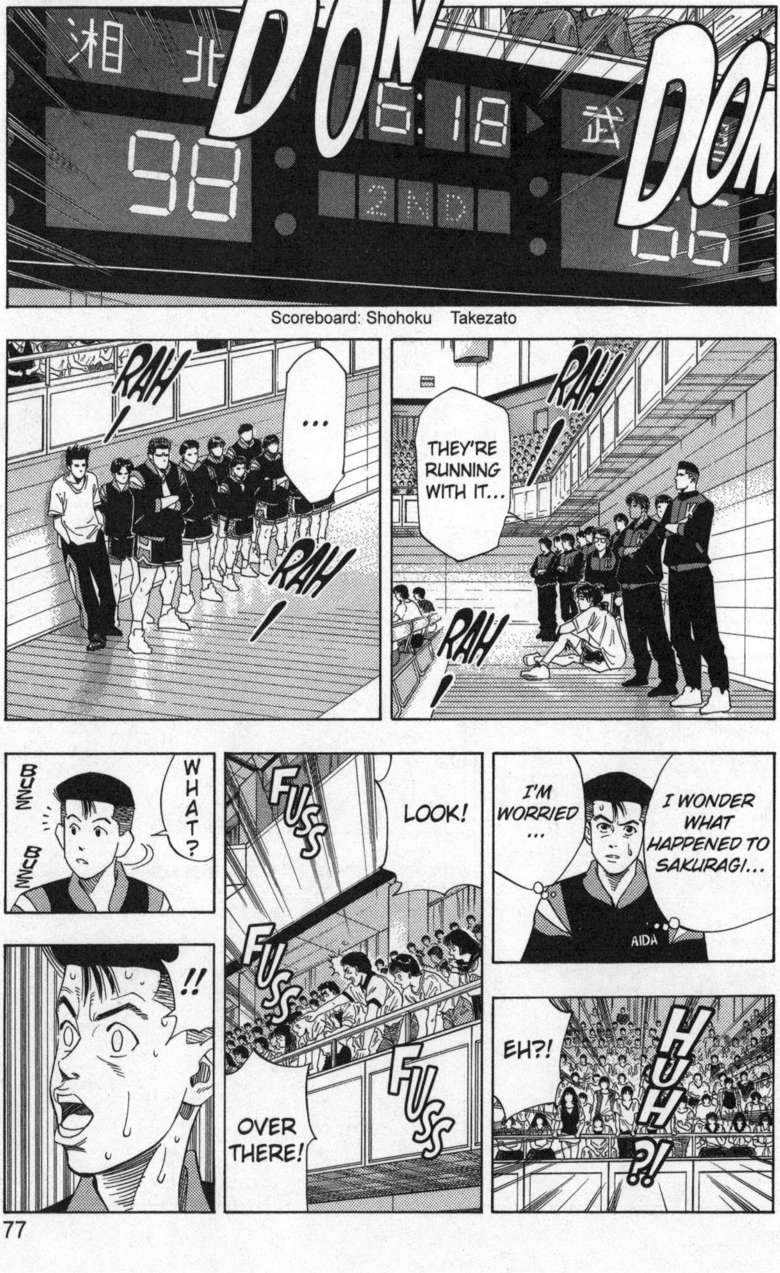
DON
DON
湘北
6:18
2ND
98
RAH!
THEY'RE RUNNING WITH IT...
RAH!
RAH!
...
RAH!
I WONDER WHAT HAPPENED TO SAKURAGI...
I'M WORRIED...
AIDA
HUH?!
EH?!
LOOK!
FUSS
FUSS
OVER THERE!
FUSS
BUZZ
BUZZ
WHAT?
!!

Scoreboard: Shohoku Takezato

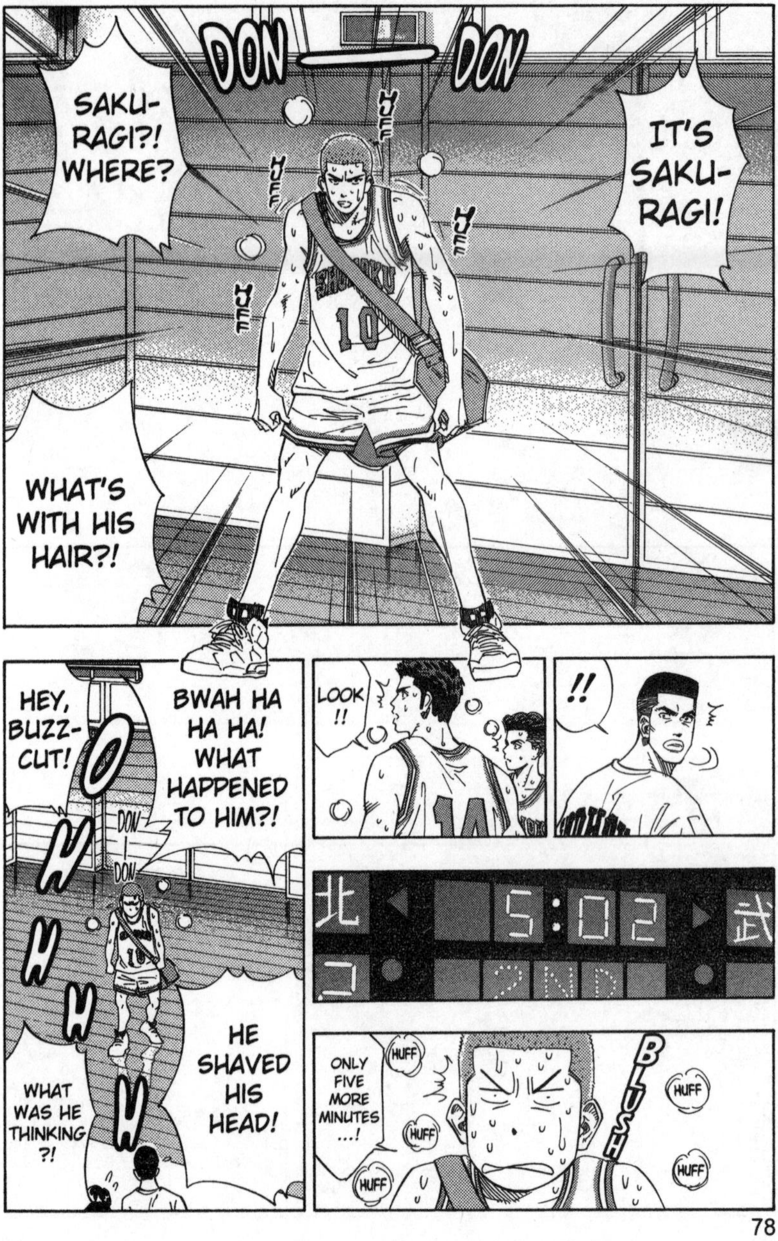

DON — DON
IT'S SAKU-RAGI!
SAKU-RAGI?! WHERE?
HUFF
HUFF
HUFF
HUFF
WHAT'S WITH HIS HAIR?!
!!
LOOK !!
北
5:02
武
2ND
HUFF
HUFF
HUFF
HUFF
HUFF
BLUSH
ONLY FIVE MORE MINUTES ...!
BWAH HA HA HA! WHAT HAPPENED TO HIM?!
HEY, BUZZ-CUT!
OHHHHHH
DON-DON
HE SHAVED HIS HEAD!
WHAT WAS HE THINKING ?!

READ THIS WAY

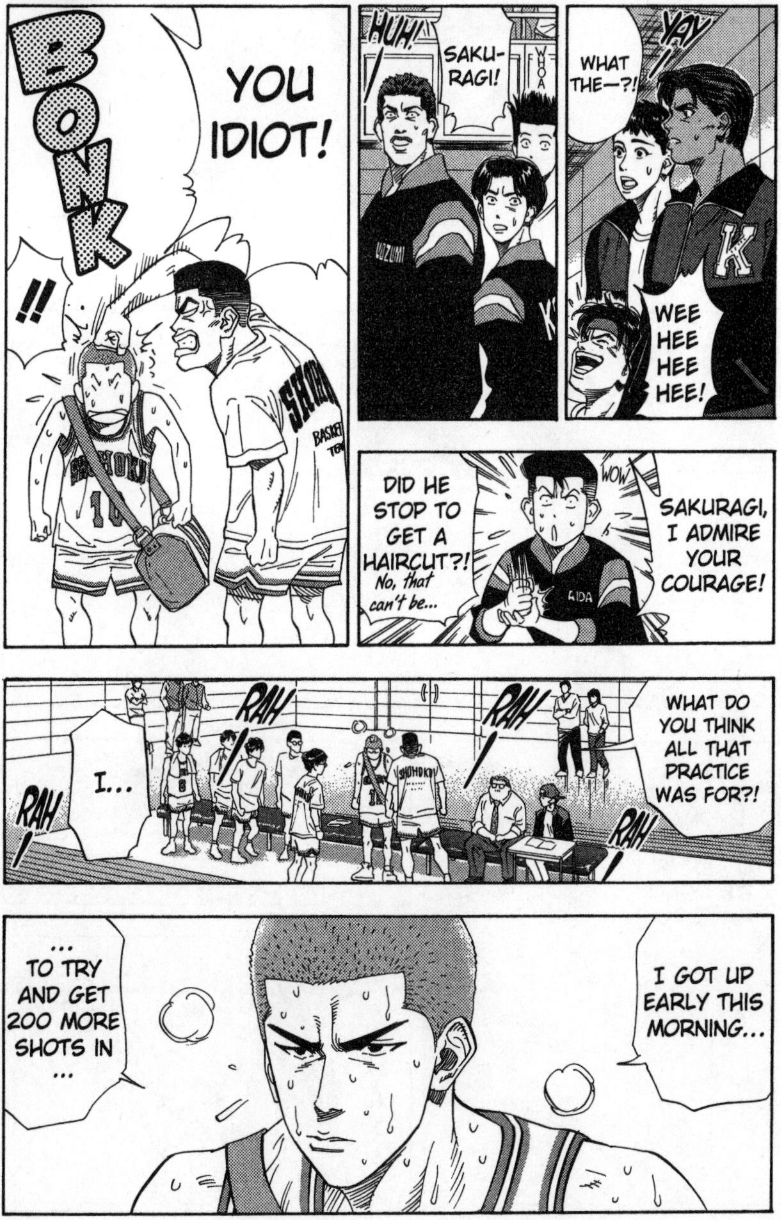
YAY!
WHAT THE—?!
WEE HEE HEE HEE!
HUH!
SAKU-RAGI!
WHOA
SAKURAGI, I ADMIRE YOUR COURAGE!
WOW
DID HE STOP TO GET A HAIRCUT?!
No, that can't be...
YOU IDIOT!
BONK
!!
WHAT DO YOU THINK ALL THAT PRACTICE WAS FOR?!
RAH!
RAH!
RAH!
RAH!
I...
I GOT UP EARLY THIS MORNING...
... TO TRY AND GET 200 MORE SHOTS IN ...

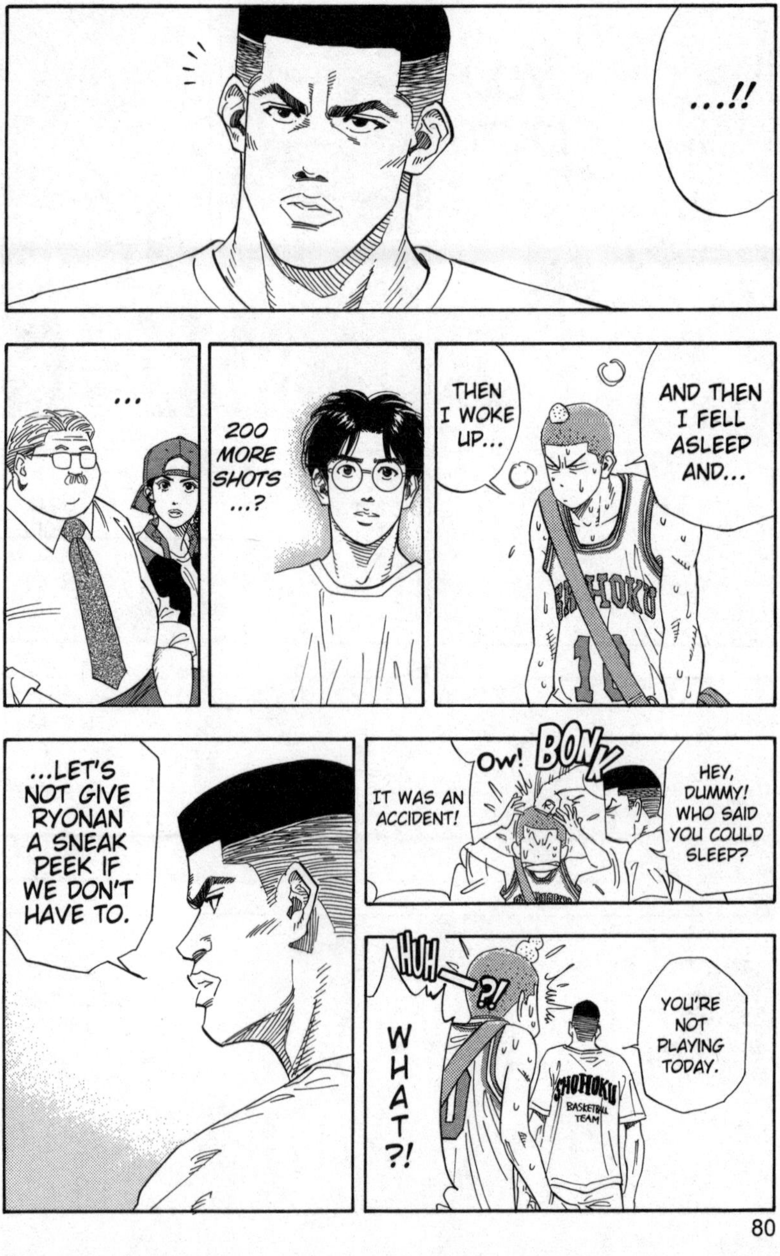
...!!
...
200 MORE SHOTS ...?
AND THEN I FELL ASLEEP AND...
THEN I WOKE UP...
SHOHOKU
...LET'S NOT GIVE RYONAN A SNEAK PEEK IF WE DON'T HAVE TO.
HEY, DUMMY! WHO SAID YOU COULD SLEEP?
BONK
Ow!
IT WAS AN ACCIDENT!
YOU'RE NOT PLAYING TODAY.
SHOHOKU BASKETBALL TEAM
HUH—?!
WHAT?!

READ THIS WAY

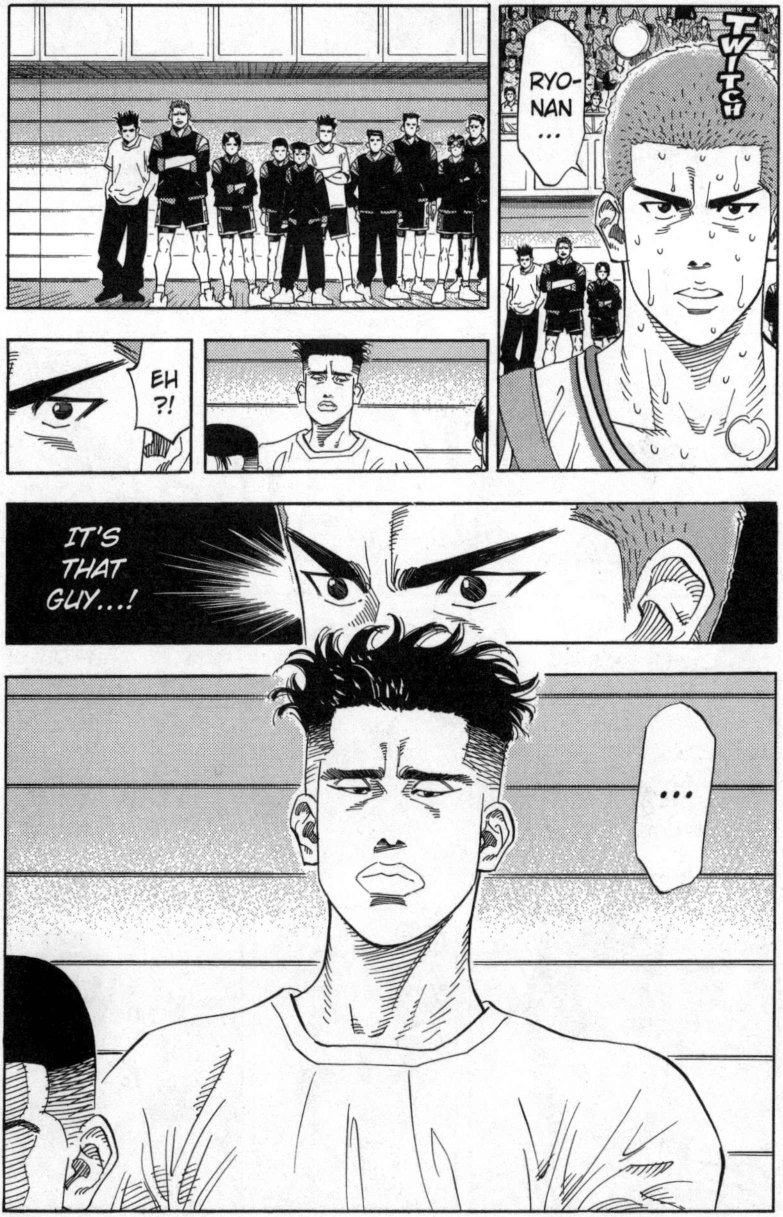
TWITCH
RYO-NAN ...
EH ?!
IT'S THAT GUY...!
...

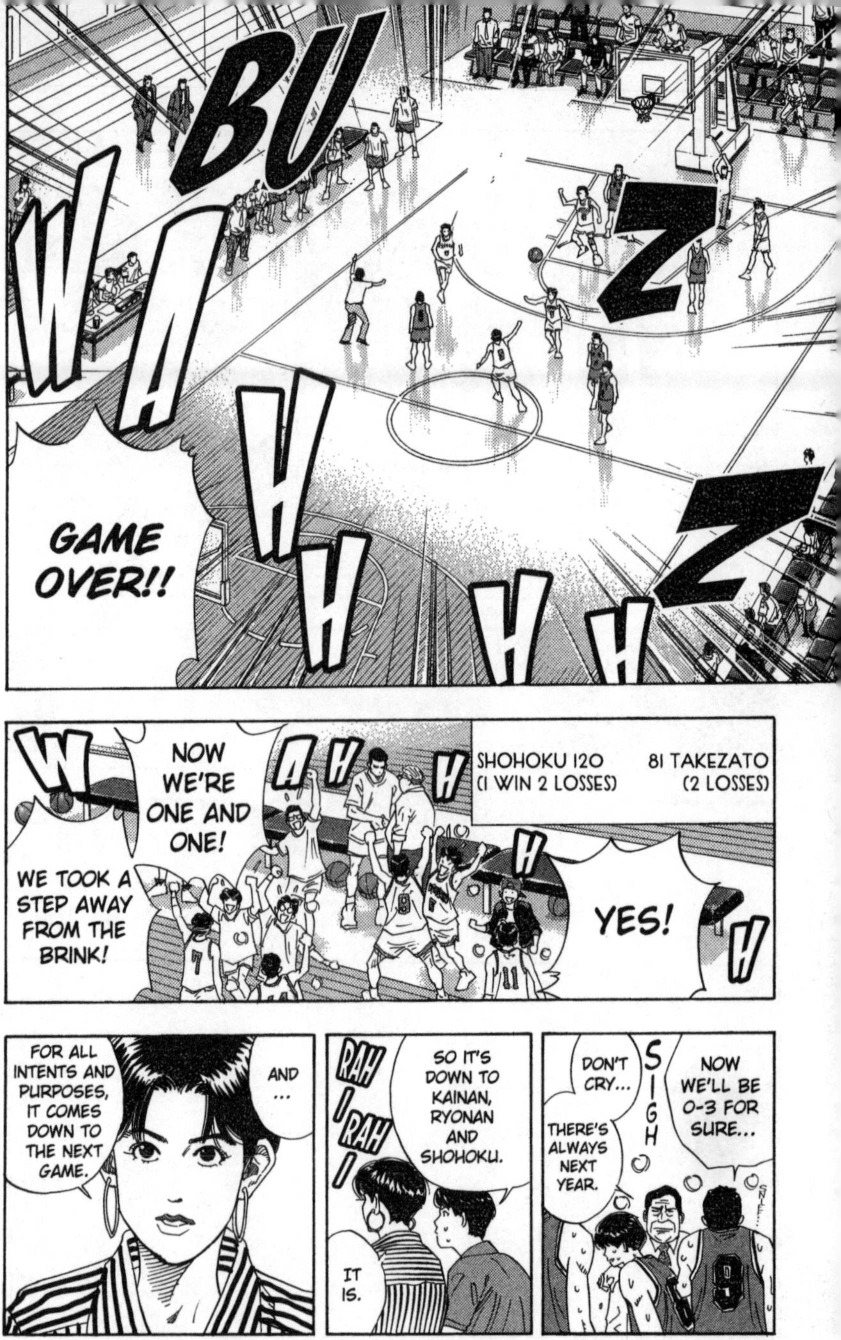
BUZZZ
WAHHHH
GAME OVER!!
SHOHOKU 120 (1 WIN 2 LOSSES)
81 TAKEZATO (2 LOSSES)
YES!
NOW WE'RE ONE AND ONE!
WE TOOK A STEP AWAY FROM THE BRINK!
WAHHHH
NOW WE'LL BE 0-3 FOR SURE...
SIGH
DON'T CRY...
THERE'S ALWAYS NEXT YEAR.
SNIFF...
SO IT'S DOWN TO KAINAN, RYONAN AND SHOHOKU.
RAH RAH
IT IS.
AND ...
FOR ALL INTENTS AND PURPOSES, IT COMES DOWN TO THE NEXT GAME.

READ THIS WAY

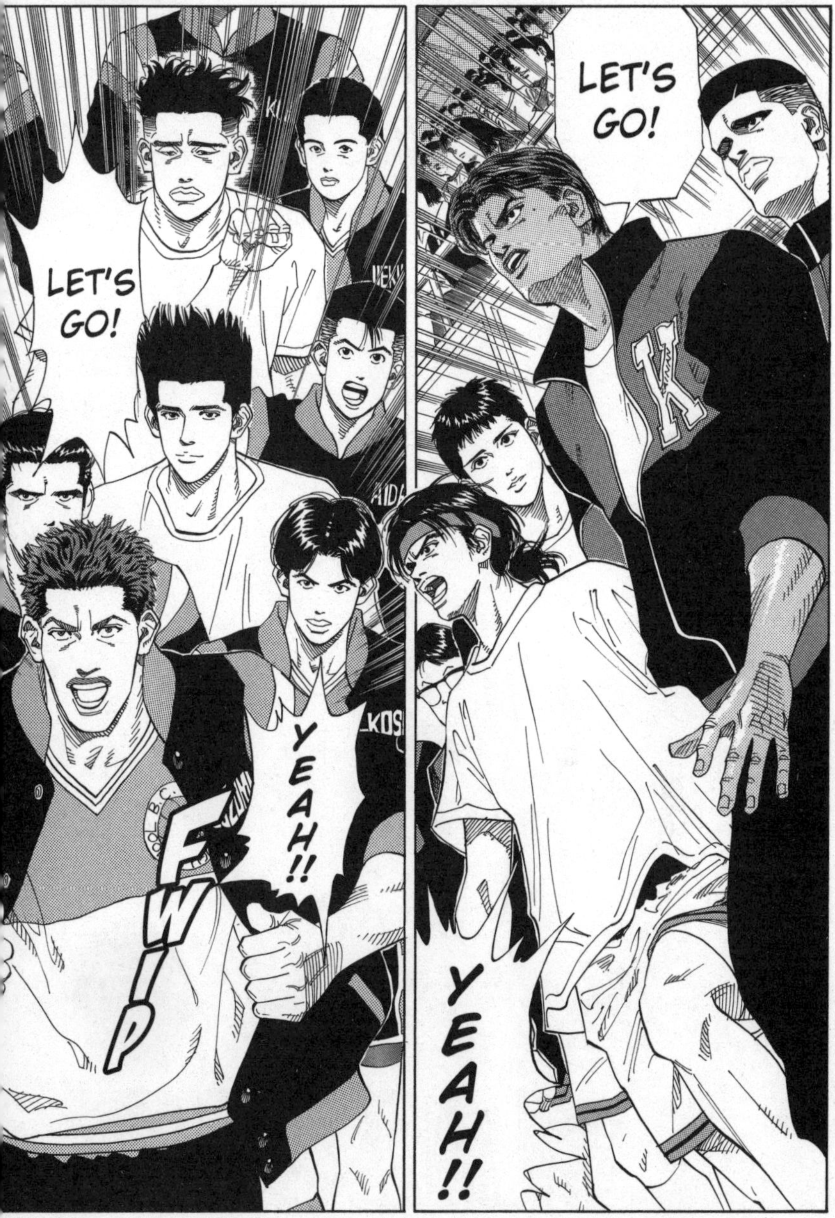

LET'S GO!
YEAH!!
LET'S GO!
YEAH!!
FWIP

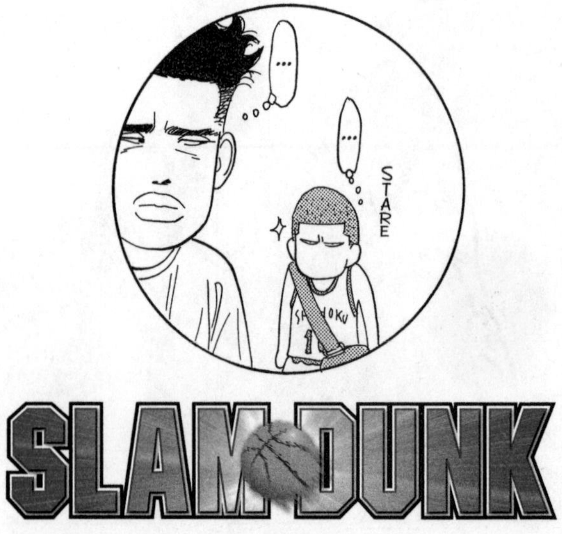
...
...
STARE

SLAM DUNK

#139 RYONAN'S CHALLENGE

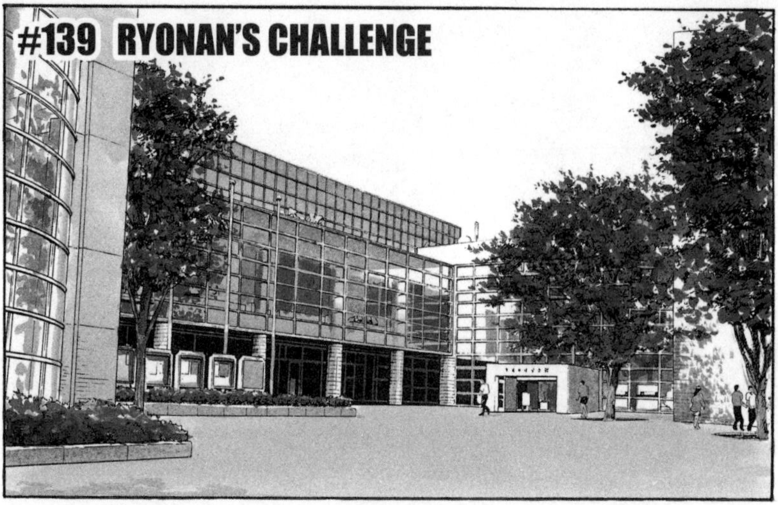

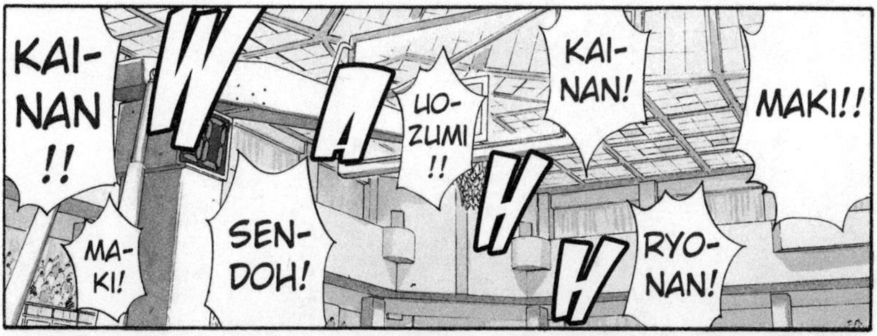
MAKI!!
KAI-NAN!
UO-ZUMI!!
RYO-NAN!
WAHH
SEN-DOH!
MA-KI!
KAI-NAN!!

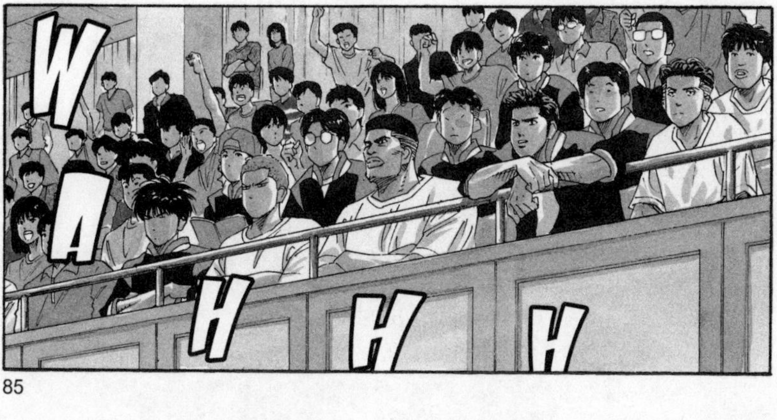
WAHHH

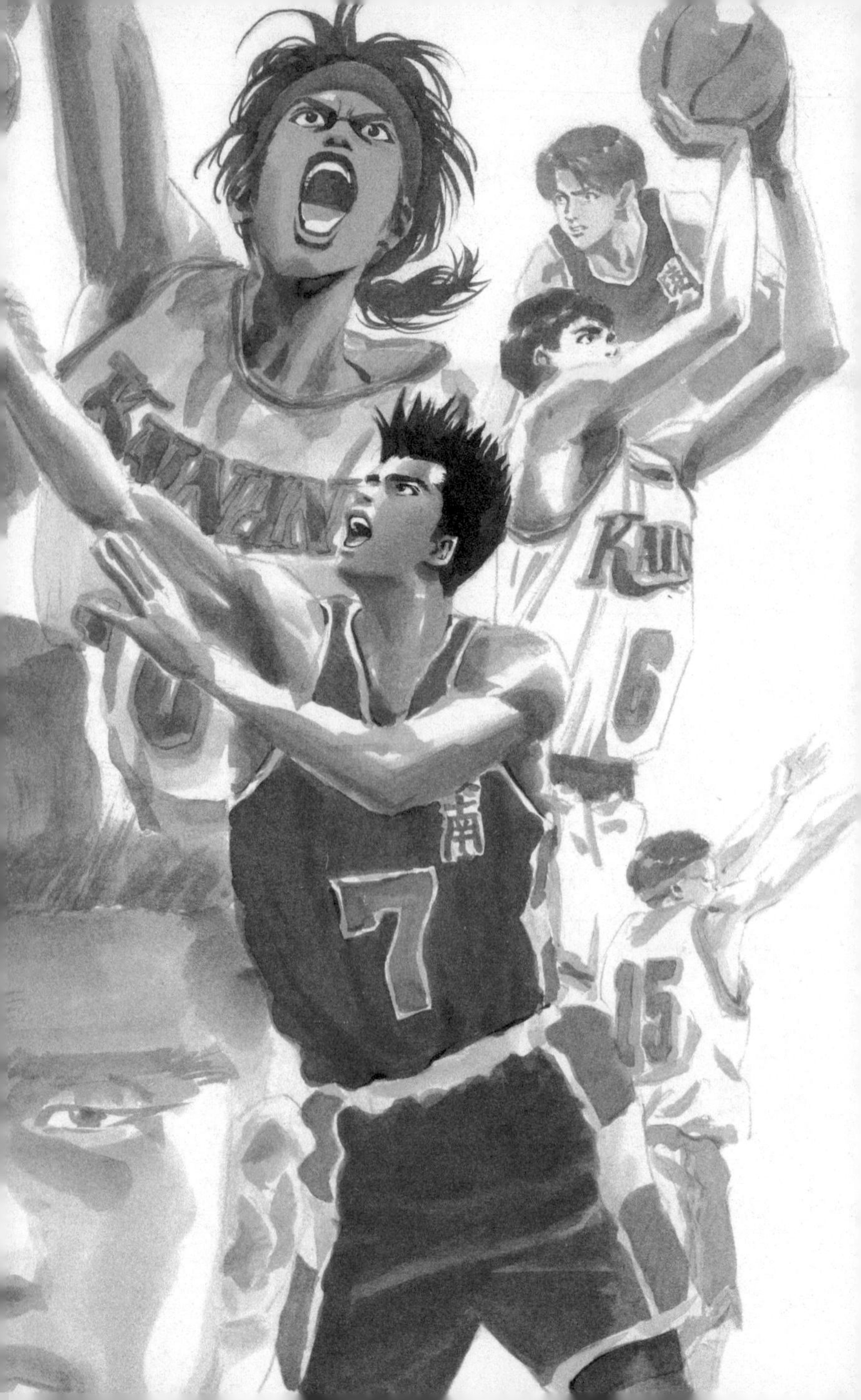

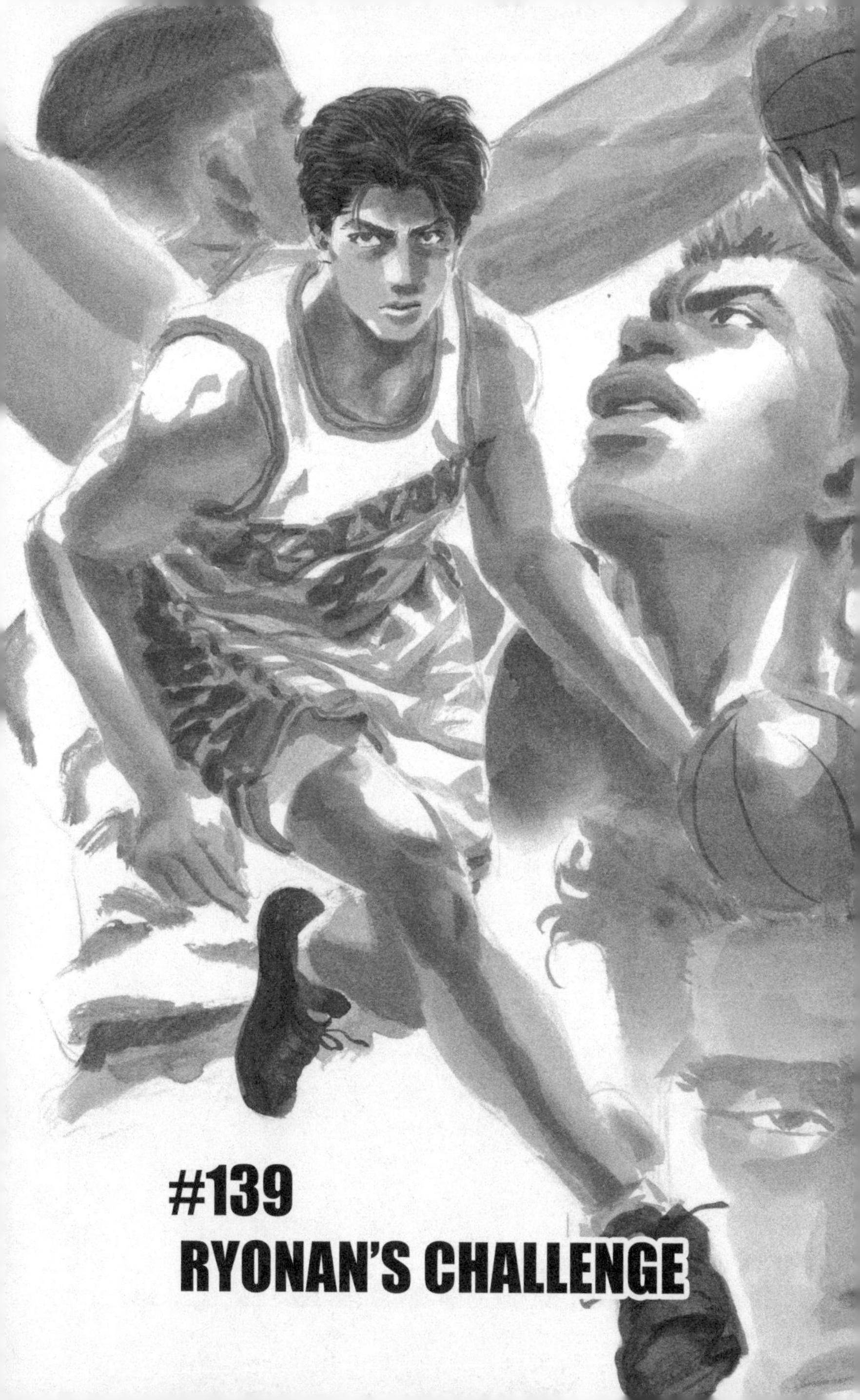

#139 RYONAN'S CHALLENGE

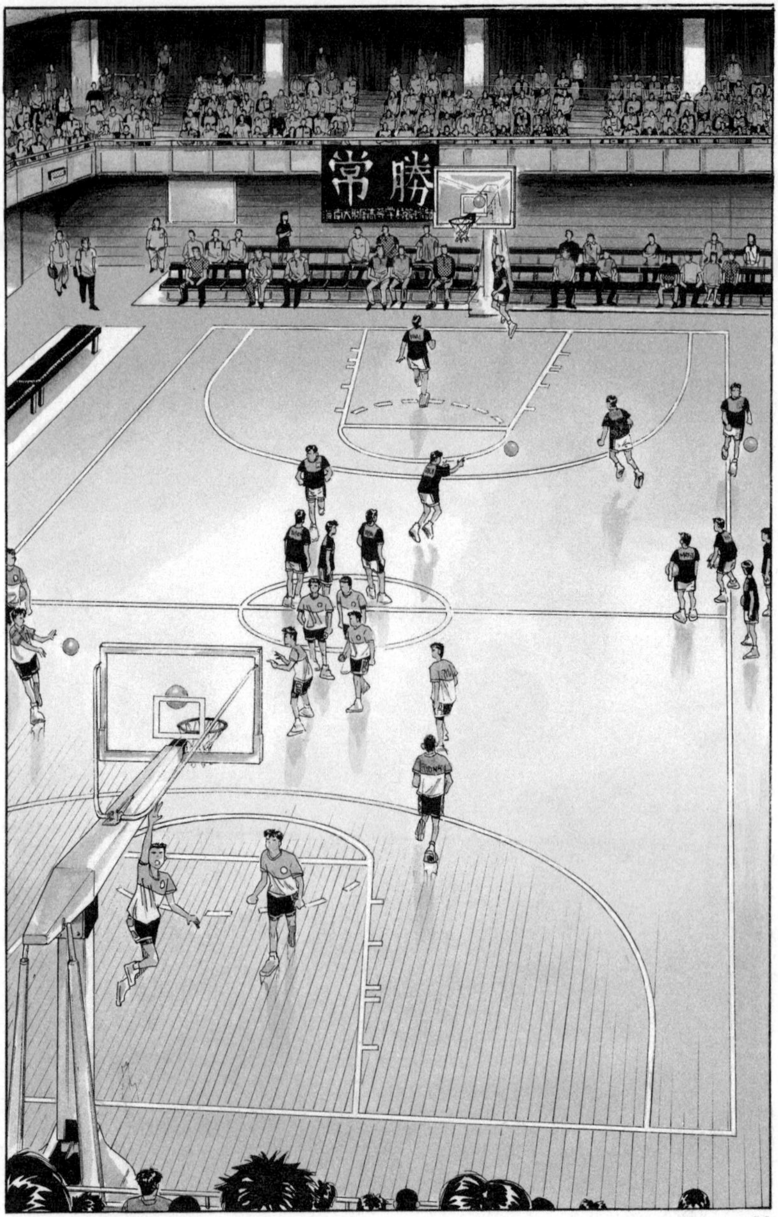
常勝

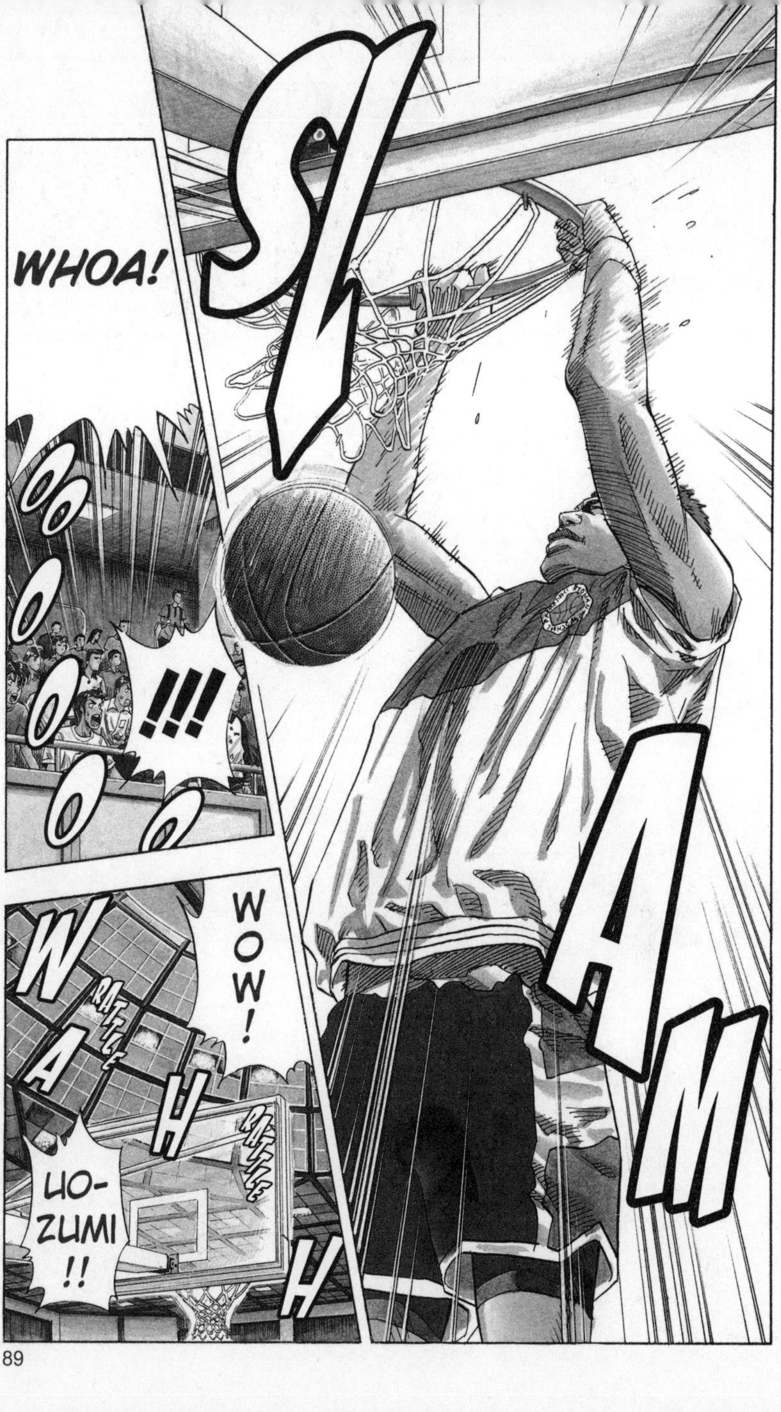

SLAM
WHOA!
OOOOOOOO
!!!
WOW!
WAHH
RATTLE
RATTLE
UO-ZUMI!!

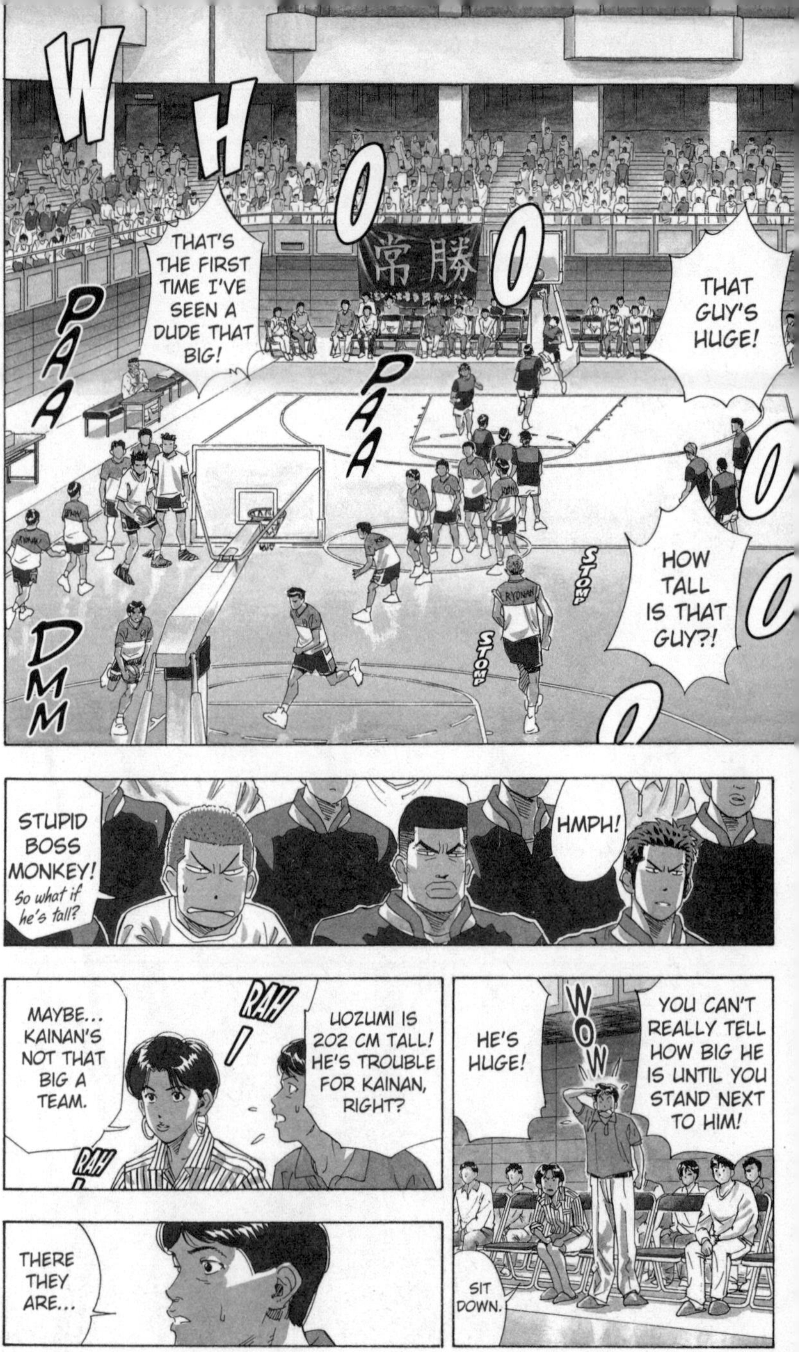
WHOOOOOO
THAT GUY'S HUGE!
HOW TALL IS THAT GUY?!
常勝
THAT'S THE FIRST TIME I'VE SEEN A DUDE THAT BIG!
PAA PAA
STOMP
STOMP
DMM
HMPH!
STUPID BOSS MONKEY! So what if he's tall?
WOW
YOU CAN'T REALLY TELL HOW BIG HE IS UNTIL YOU STAND NEXT TO HIM!
HE'S HUGE!
SIT DOWN.
RAH
UOZUMI IS 202 CM TALL! HE'S TROUBLE FOR KAINAN, RIGHT?
MAYBE... KAINAN'S NOT THAT BIG A TEAM.
RAH
THERE THEY ARE...

READ THIS WAY

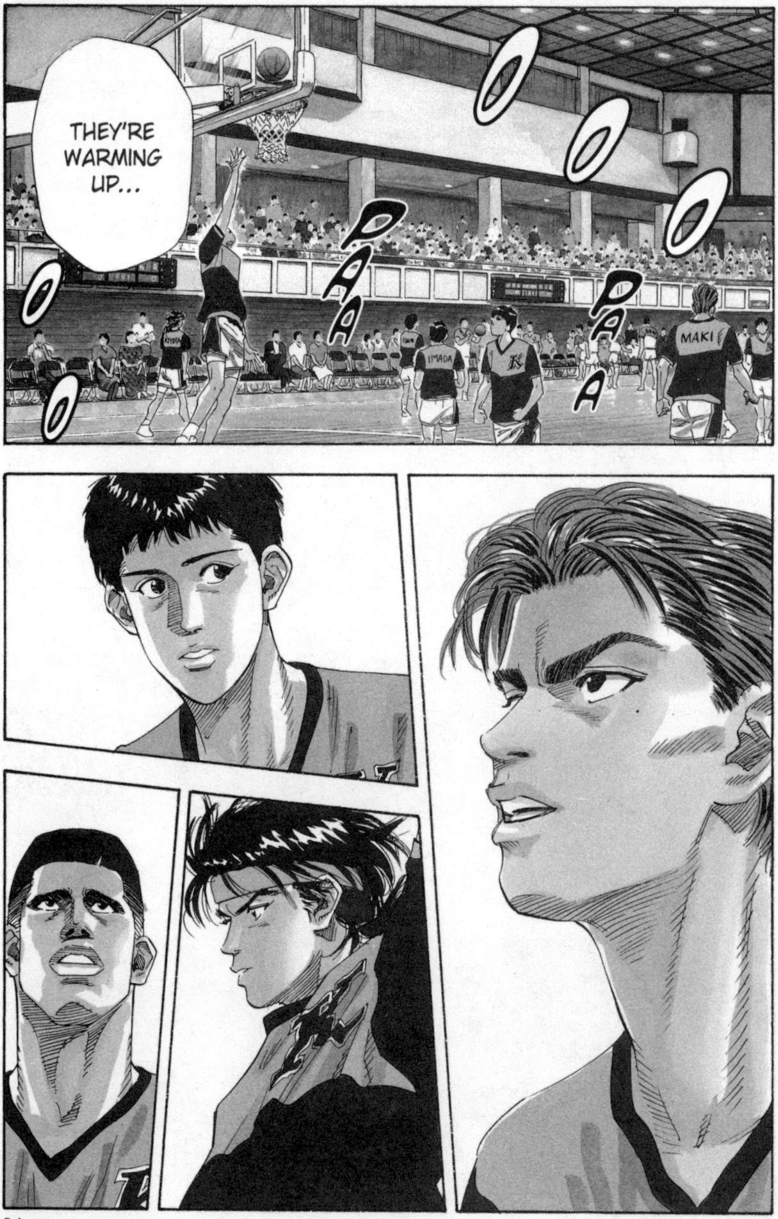
OOOO
PAA
PAA
THEY'RE WARMING UP...
OO

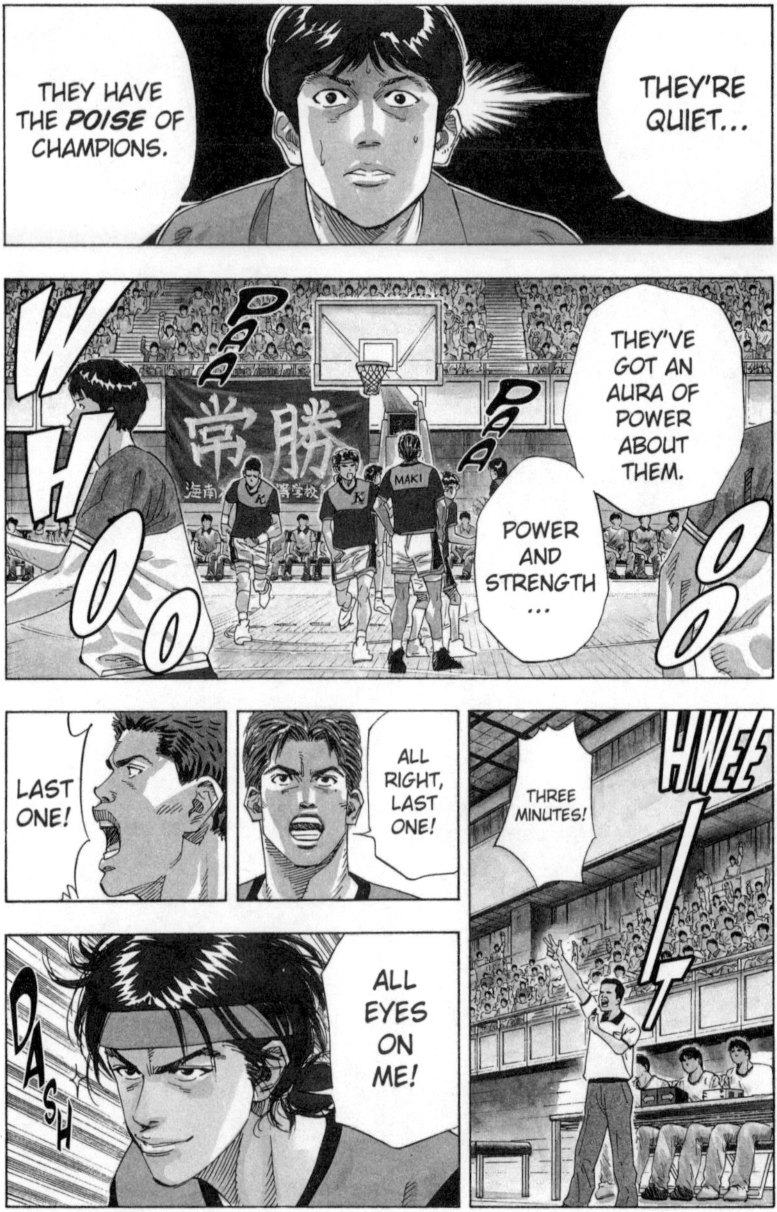
THEY'RE QUIET...
THEY HAVE THE *POISE* OF CHAMPIONS.
THEY'VE GOT AN AURA OF POWER ABOUT THEM.
OOO
PAA PAA
POWER AND STRENGTH...
常勝
MAKI
WHOOO
HWEET
THREE MINUTES!
ALL RIGHT, LAST ONE!
LAST ONE!
ALL EYES ON ME!
DASH

READ THIS WAY

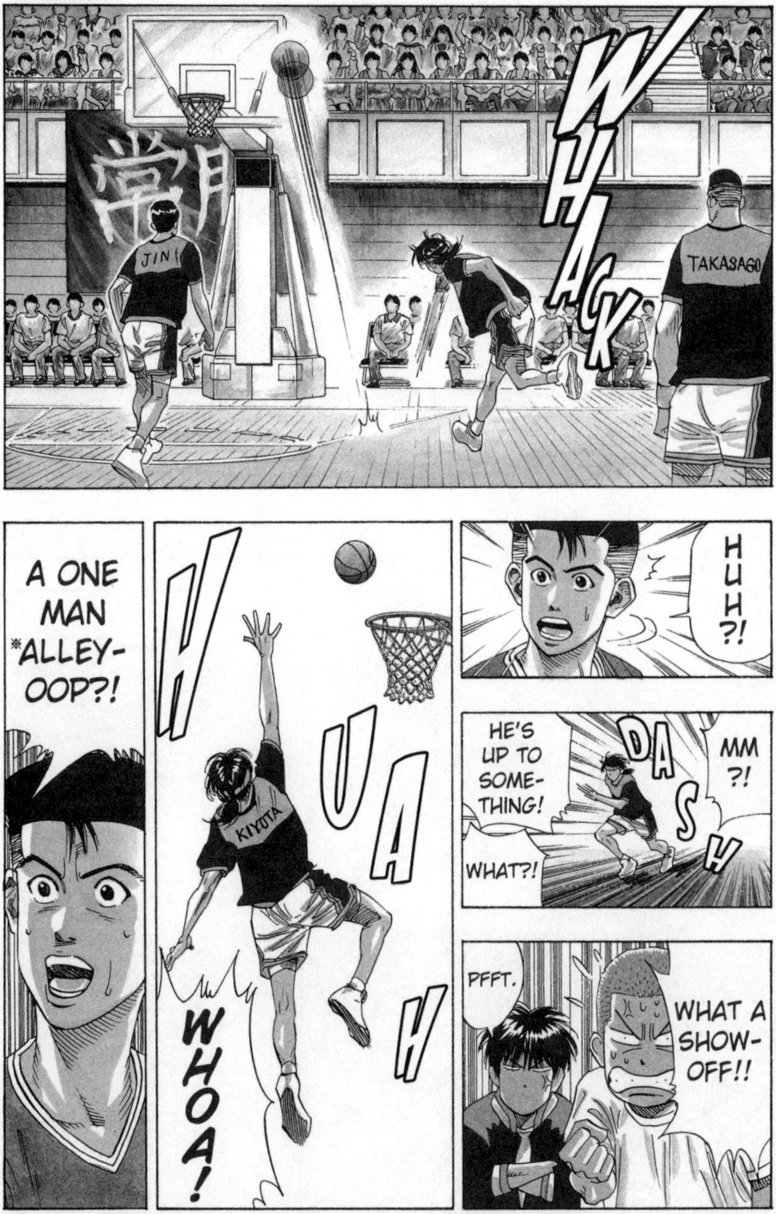
WHACK
HUH?!
MM?!
DASH
HE'S UP TO SOMETHING!
WHAT?!
WHAT A SHOW-OFF!!
PFFT.
HUAH
WHOA!
A ONE MAN ※ALLEY-OOP?!

※ALLEY-OOP = A SLAM DUNK MADE DIRECTLY FROM A MID-AIR CATCH USUALLY OFF A PASS.

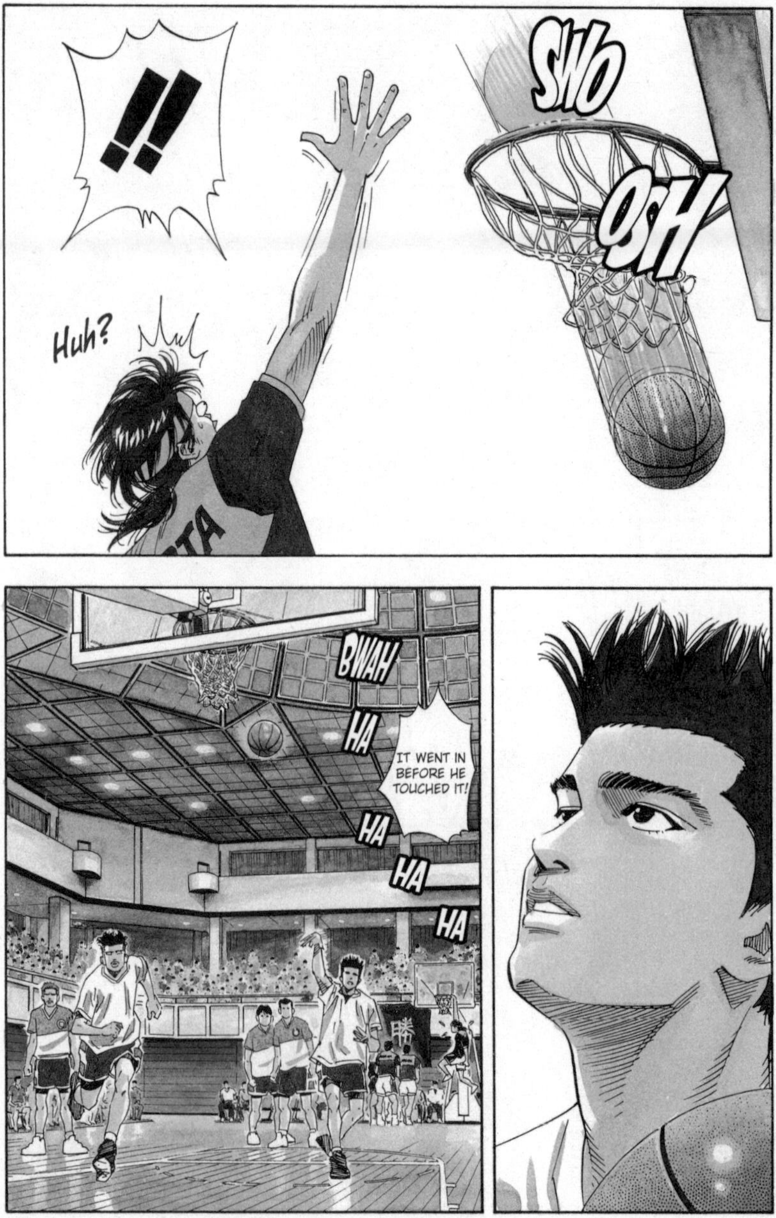
SWO OSH
!!
Huh?
BWAH HA
IT WENT IN BEFORE HE TOUCHED IT!
HA HA HA

READ THIS WAY

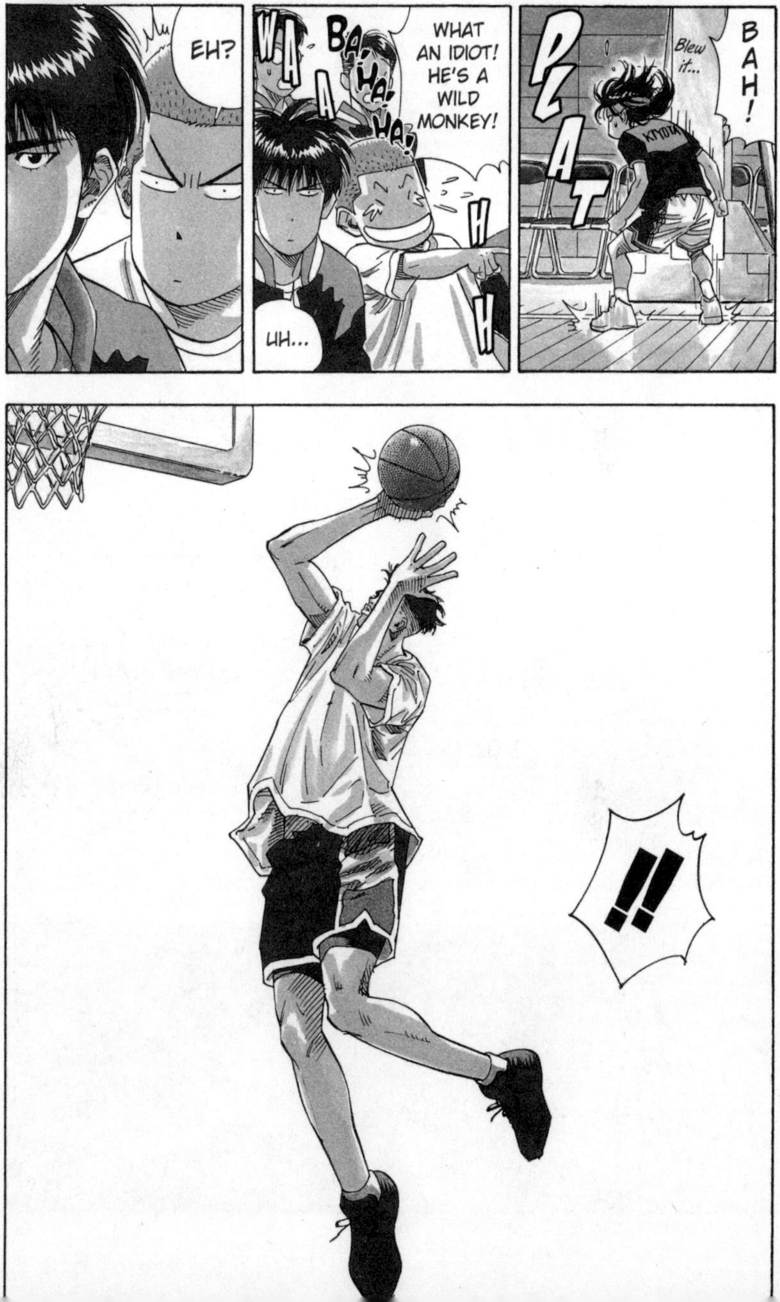
BAH!
Blew it...
PLAT
WHAT AN IDIOT! HE'S A WILD MONKEY!
BAHAHAHA!
WAAA
HH
UH...
EH?
!!

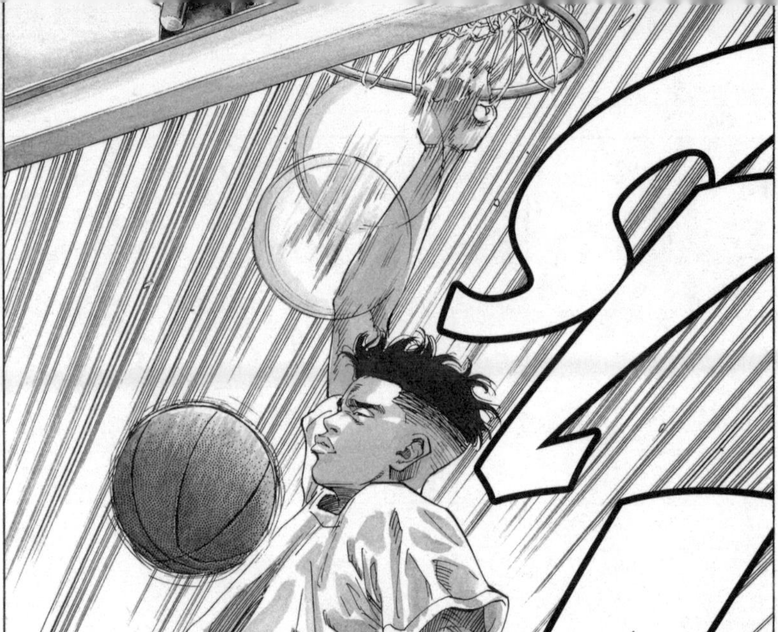
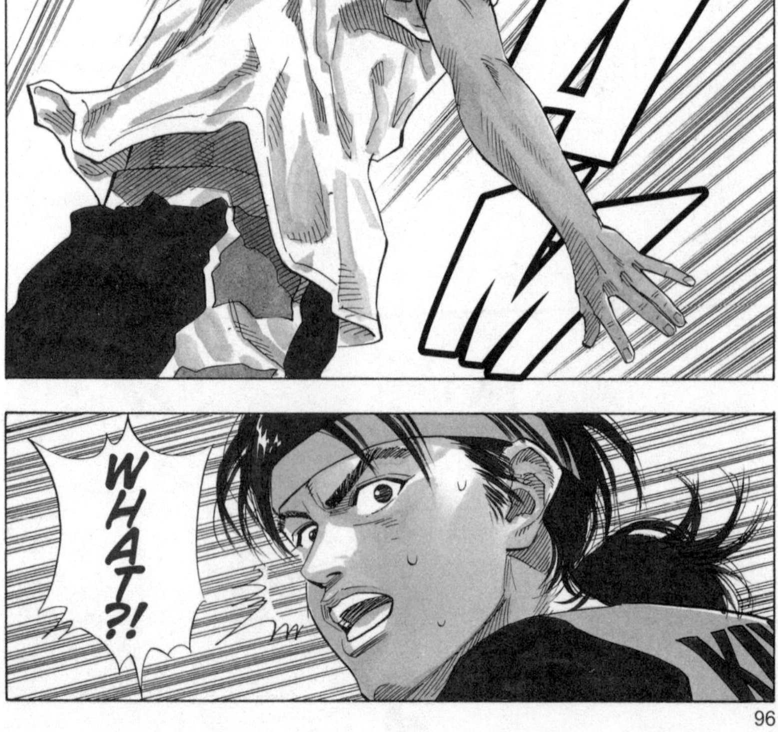
WHAT?!

READ THIS WAY

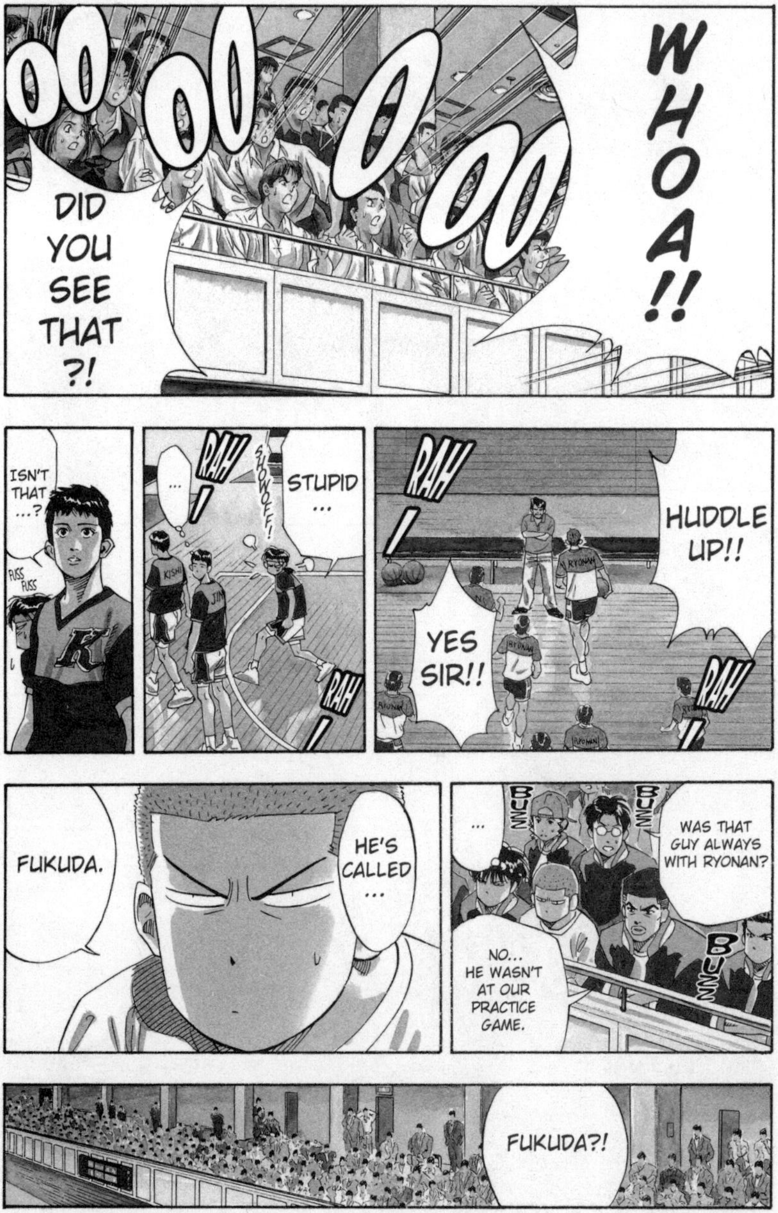
WHOA!!
OOOOOOO
DID YOU SEE THAT?!
HUDDLE UP!!
RAH
YES SIR!!
RAH
RAH
STUPID...
SHOWOFF!
RAH
...
RAH
ISN'T THAT...?
FUSS FUSS
BUZZ
WAS THAT GUY ALWAYS WITH RYONAN?
BUZZ
...
BUZZ
NO... HE WASN'T AT OUR PRACTICE GAME.
HE'S CALLED...
FUKUDA.
FUKUDA?!

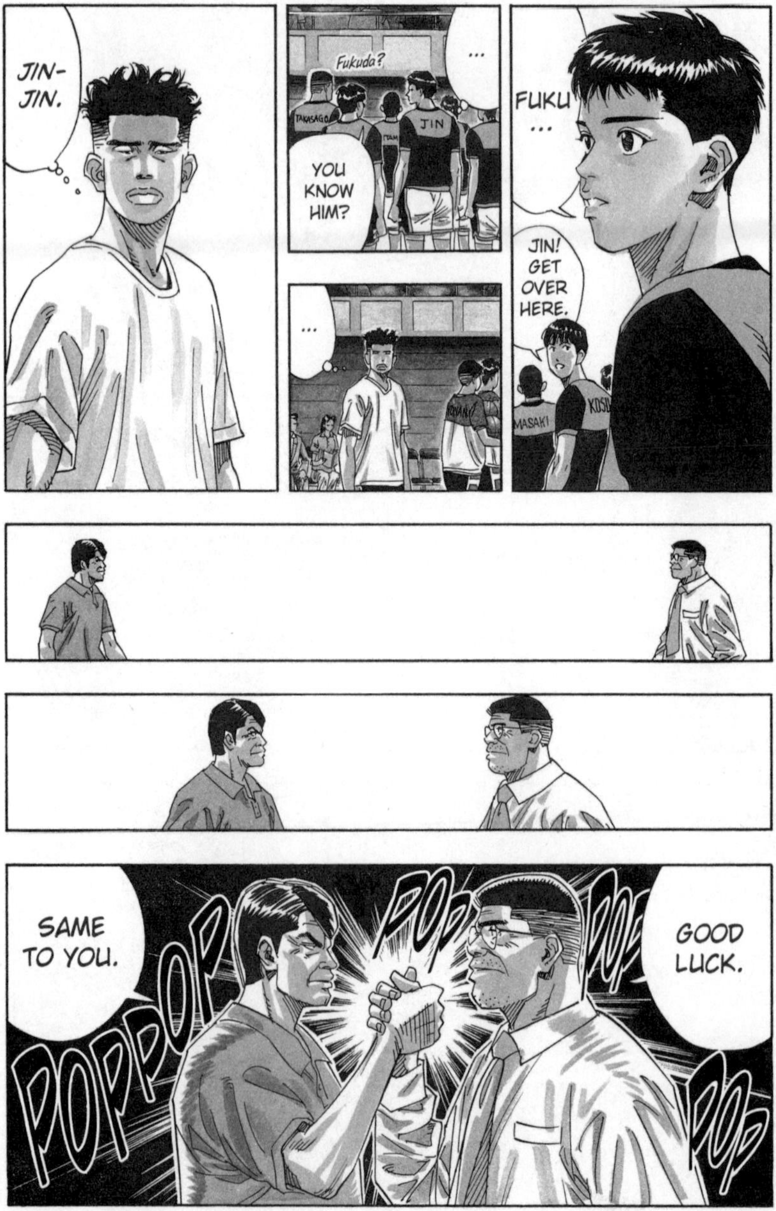
FUKU ...
JIN! GET OVER HERE.
...
Fukuda?
YOU KNOW HIM?
...
JIN-JIN.
GOOD LUCK.
POP
POP
SAME TO YOU.
POPPOP
POPPOP
POP

READ THIS WAY

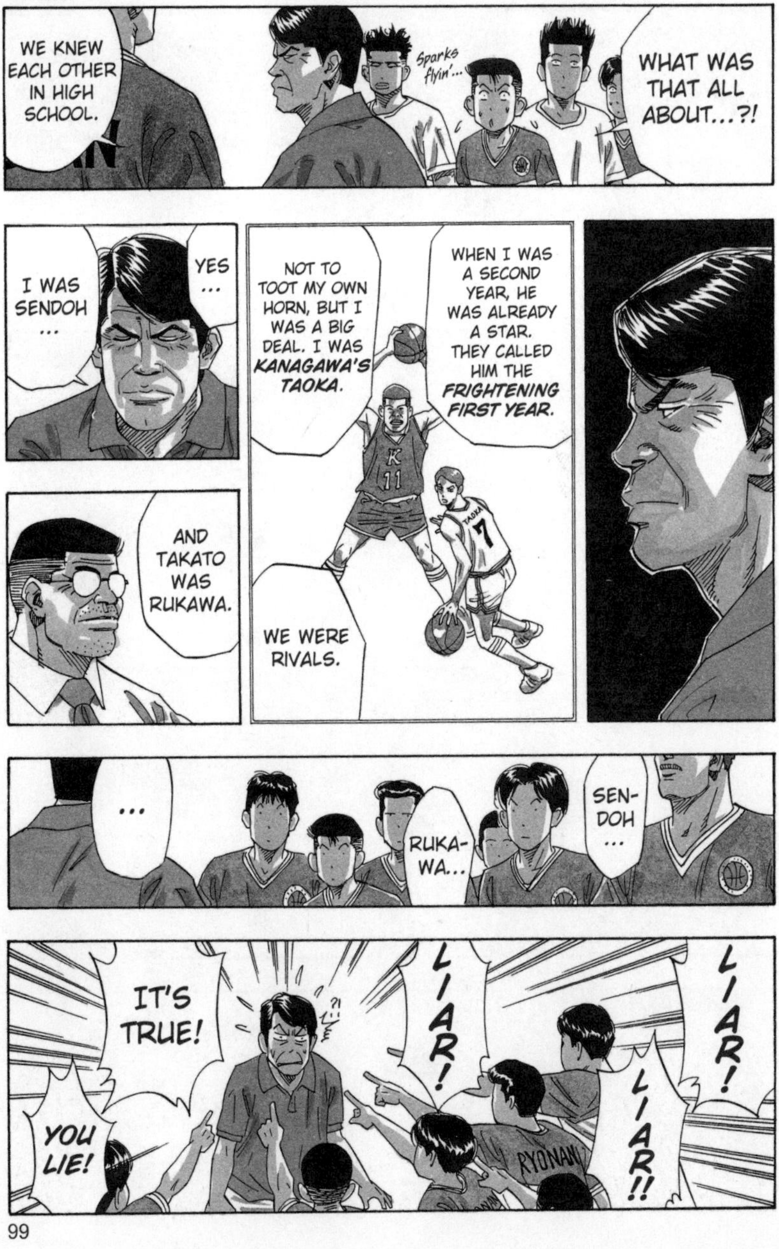

WHAT WAS THAT ALL ABOUT...?!
Sparks flyin'...
WE KNEW EACH OTHER IN HIGH SCHOOL.
WHEN I WAS A SECOND YEAR, HE WAS ALREADY A STAR. THEY CALLED HIM THE FRIGHTENING FIRST YEAR.
NOT TO TOOT MY OWN HORN, BUT I WAS A BIG DEAL. I WAS KANAGAWA'S TAOKA.
WE WERE RIVALS.
YES...
I WAS SENDOH...
AND TAKATO WAS RUKAWA.
SEN-DOH...
RUKA-WA...
...
LIAR!
LIAR!!
LIAR!
IT'S TRUE!
YOU LIE!

DOESN'T MATTER!

Scoreboard: Kainan U.   Ryonan

LISTEN UP...

CLOSE YOUR EYES.

VISUALIZE ONE OF OUR PRACTICES ...

G R U N T

...

...

...

READ THIS WAY

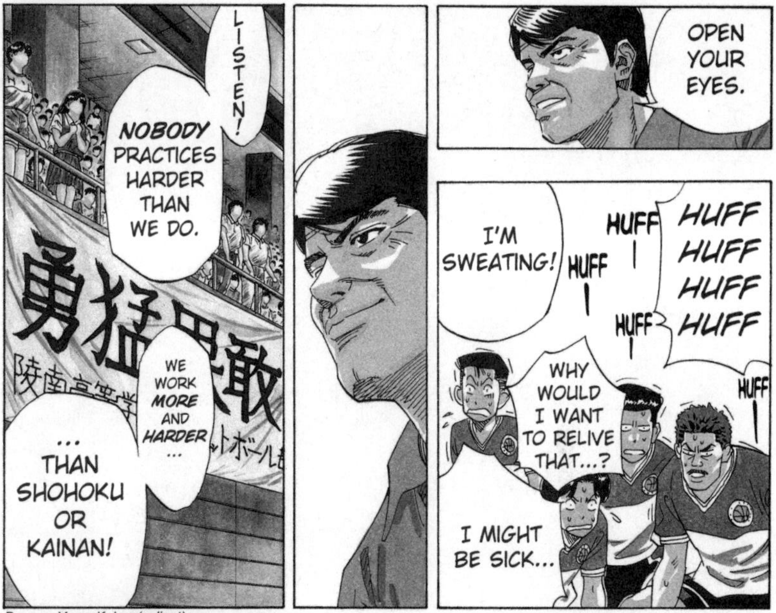
OPEN YOUR EYES.
HUFF HUFF HUFF HUFF
HUFF
HUFF
HUFF
HUFF
HUFF
I'M SWEATING!
WHY WOULD I WANT TO RELIVE THAT...?
I MIGHT BE SICK...
LISTEN!
NOBODY PRACTICES HARDER THAN WE DO.
WE WORK MORE AND HARDER...
... THAN SHOHOKU OR KAINAN!

Banner: *Yumo Kakan* (valiant)
Ryonan High School Basketball Team

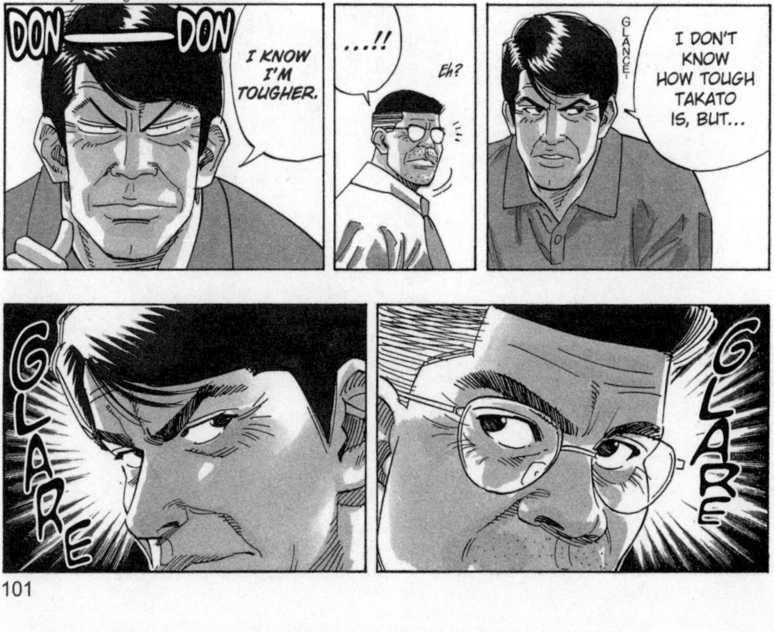
GLANCE
I DON'T KNOW HOW TOUGH TAKATO IS, BUT...
...!!
Eh?
DON—DON
I KNOW I'M TOUGHER.
GLARE
GLARE

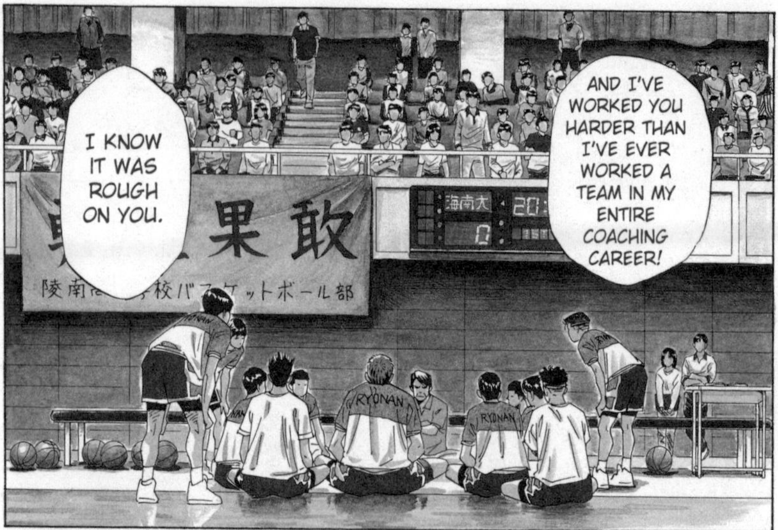
AND I'VE WORKED YOU HARDER THAN I'VE EVER WORKED A TEAM IN MY ENTIRE COACHING CAREER!
I KNOW IT WAS ROUGH ON YOU.

Banner: *Yumo Kakan* (valiant)
Ryonan High School Basketball Team

Scoreboard: Kainan U. Ryonan

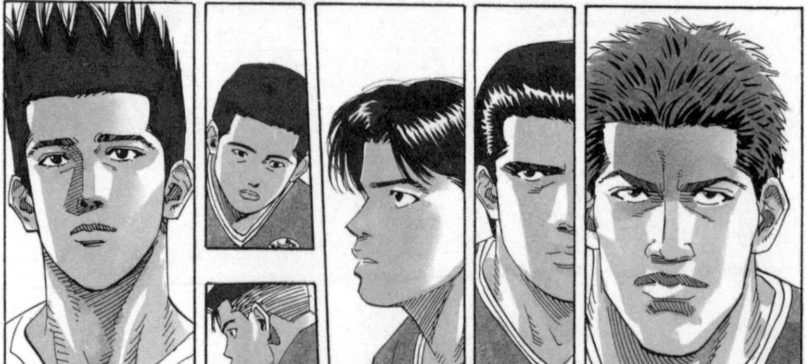

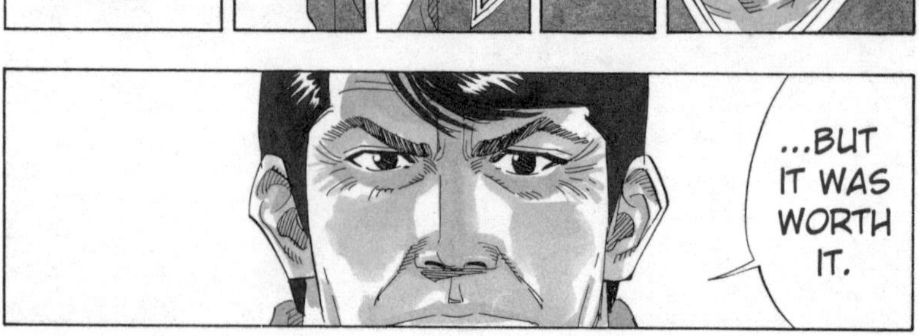
...BUT IT WAS WORTH IT.

READ THIS WAY

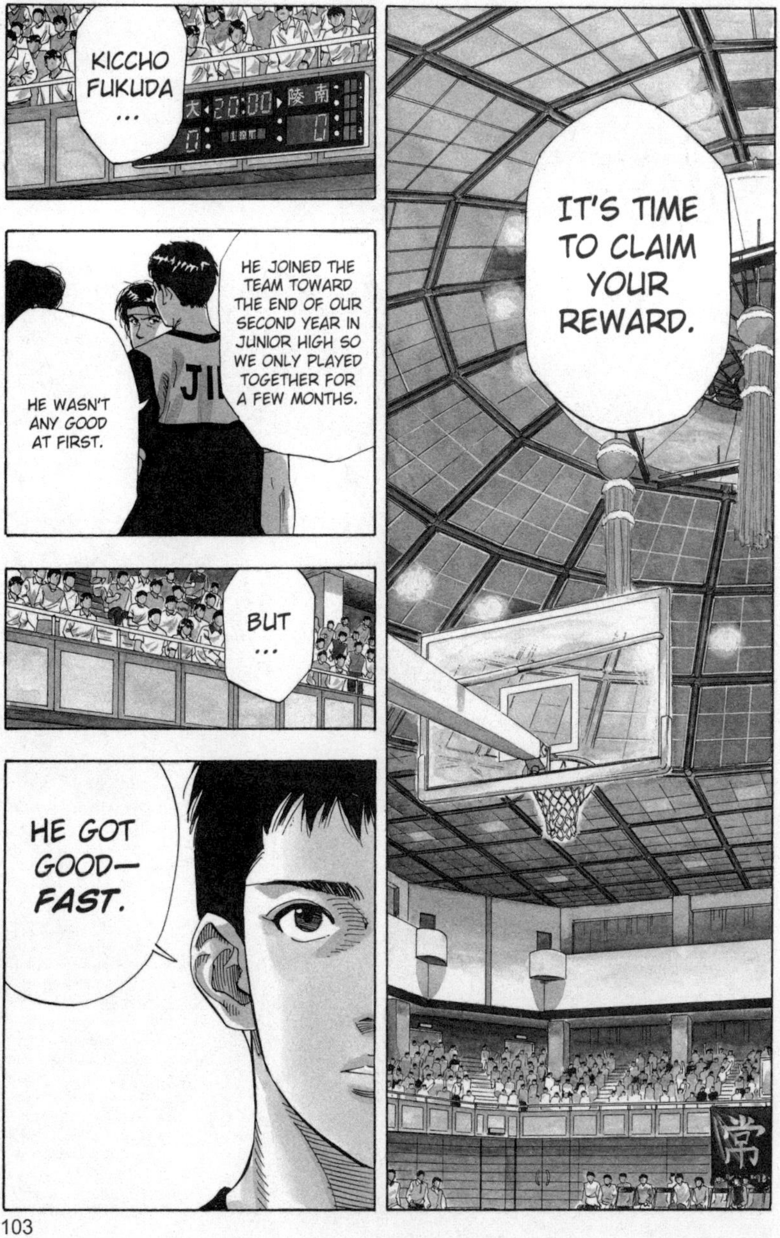
IT'S TIME TO CLAIM YOUR REWARD.
KICCHO FUKUDA ...
HE JOINED THE TEAM TOWARD THE END OF OUR SECOND YEAR IN JUNIOR HIGH SO WE ONLY PLAYED TOGETHER FOR A FEW MONTHS.
HE WASN'T ANY GOOD AT FIRST.
BUT ...
HE GOT GOOD— FAST.

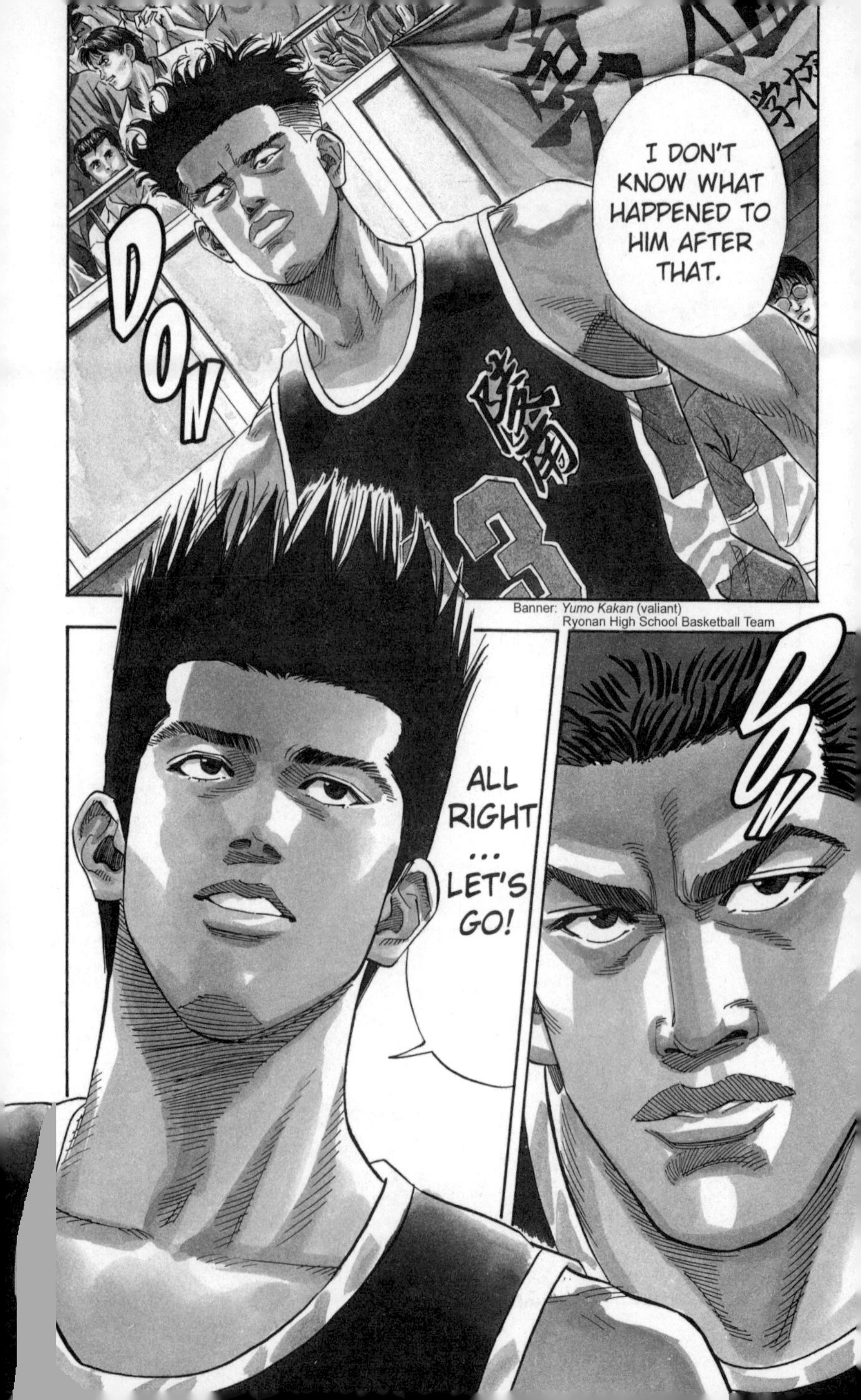
I DON'T KNOW WHAT HAPPENED TO HIM AFTER THAT.
DON
Banner: *Yumo Kakan* (valiant)
Ryonan High School Basketball Team
DON
ALL RIGHT ... LET'S GO!

#140 AN UNORTHODOX STRATEGY

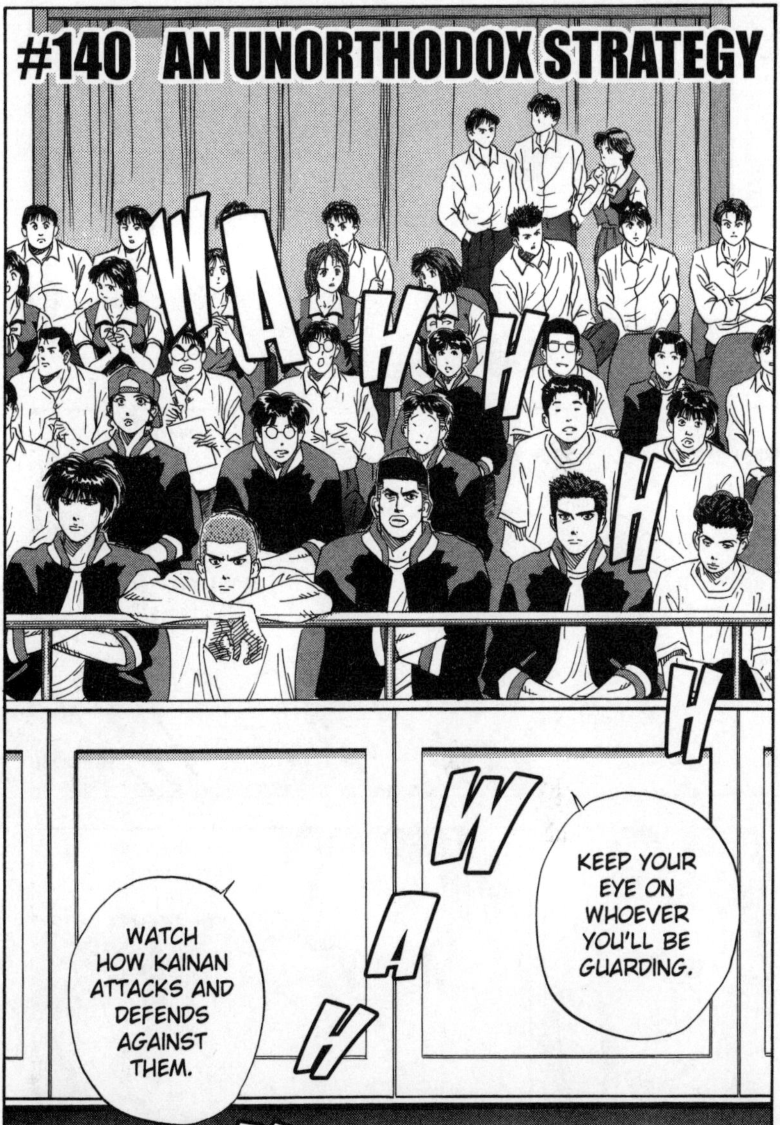
WAHHHHH
KEEP YOUR EYE ON WHOEVER YOU'LL BE GUARDING.
WAHHH
WATCH HOW KAINAN ATTACKS AND DEFENDS AGAINST THEM.

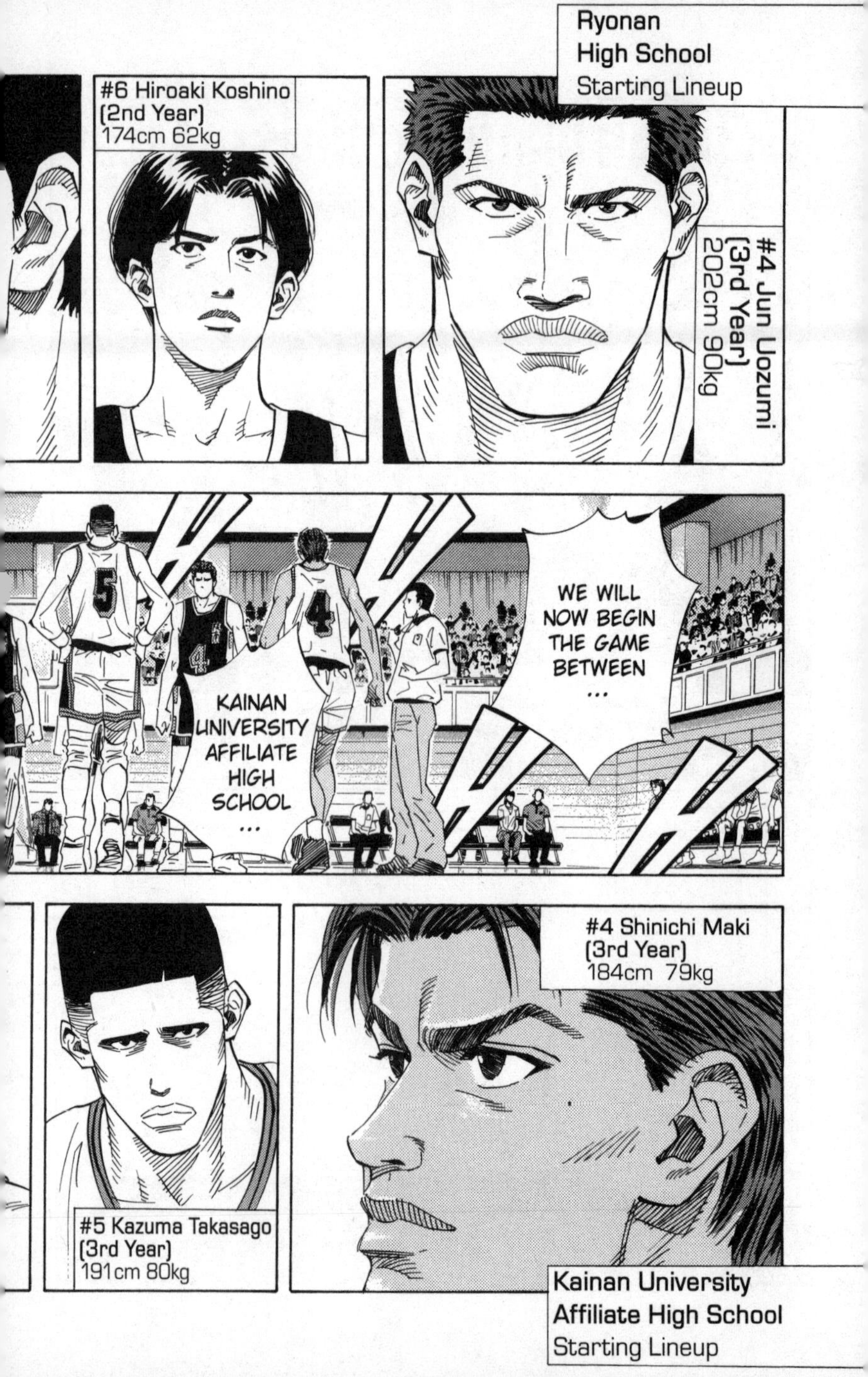
Ryonan
High School
Starting Lineup
#4 Jun Uozumi
(3rd Year)
202cm 90kg
#6 Hiroaki Koshino
(2nd Year)
174cm 62kg
WE WILL NOW BEGIN THE GAME BETWEEN ...
KAINAN UNIVERSITY AFFILIATE HIGH SCHOOL ...
#4 Shinichi Maki
(3rd Year)
184cm 79kg
Kainan University
Affiliate High School
Starting Lineup
#5 Kazuma Takasago
(3rd Year)
191cm 80kg

READ THIS WAY

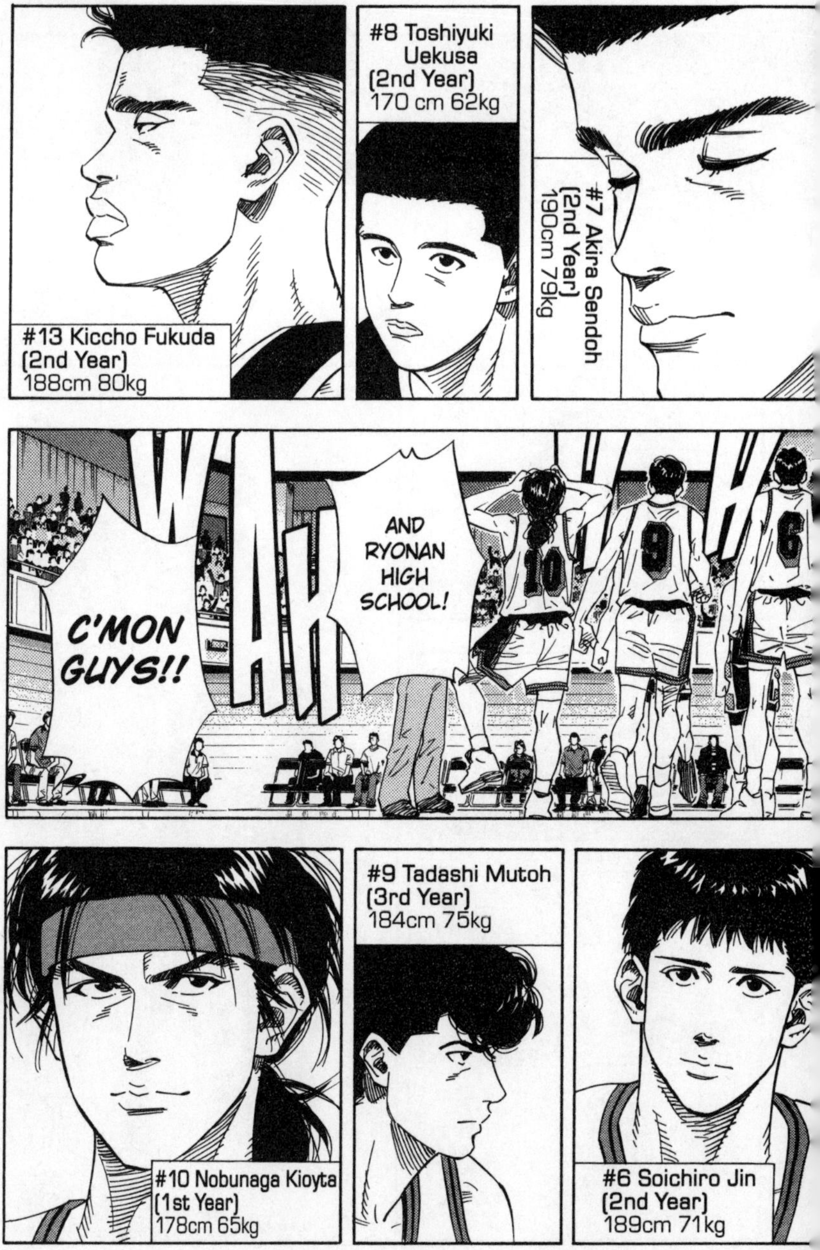
#7 Akira Sendoh
(2nd Year)
190cm 79kg
#8 Toshiyuki Uekusa
(2nd Year)
170 cm 62kg
#13 Kiccho Fukuda
(2nd Year)
188cm 80kg
AND RYONAN HIGH SCHOOL!
C'MON GUYS!!
#6 Soichiro Jin
(2nd Year)
189cm 71kg
#9 Tadashi Mutoh
(3rd Year)
184cm 75kg
#10 Nobunaga Kioyta
(1st Year)
178cm 65kg

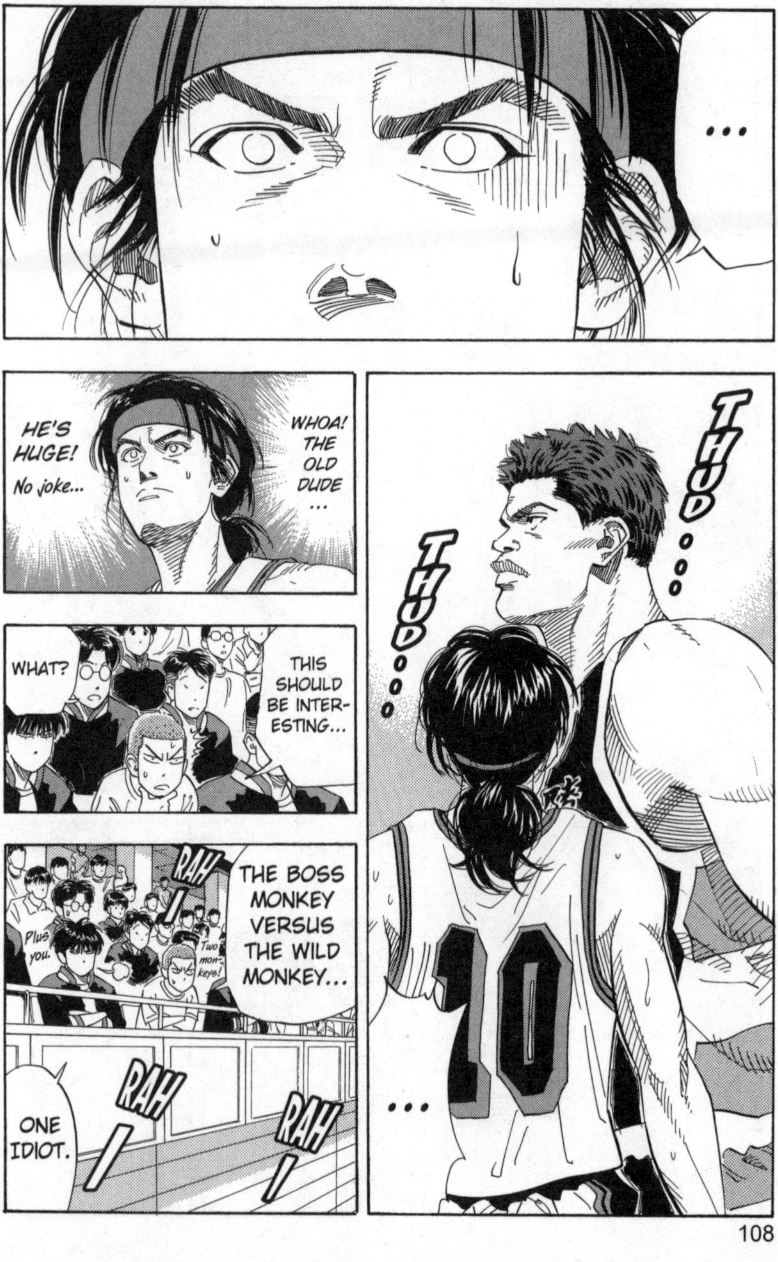
...
THUD...
THUD...
...
WHOA! THE OLD DUDE...
HE'S HUGE!
No joke...
THIS SHOULD BE INTERESTING...
WHAT?
RAH!
THE BOSS MONKEY VERSUS THE WILD MONKEY...
Two monkeys!
Plus you.
RAH!
RAH!
ONE IDIOT.

READ THIS WAY

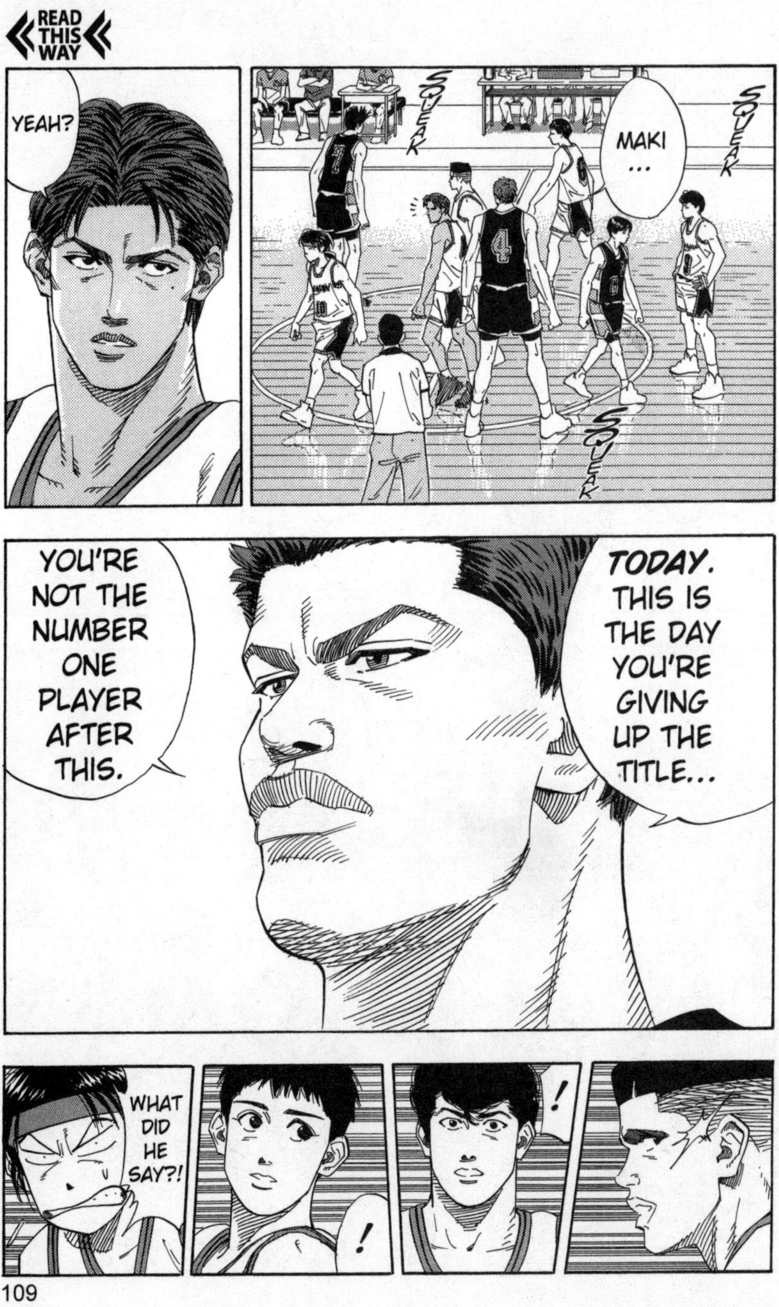
SQUEAK
MAKI ...
SQUEAK
SQUEAK
YEAH?
TODAY. THIS IS THE DAY YOU'RE GIVING UP THE TITLE...
YOU'RE NOT THE NUMBER ONE PLAYER AFTER THIS.
!
!
WHAT DID HE SAY?!

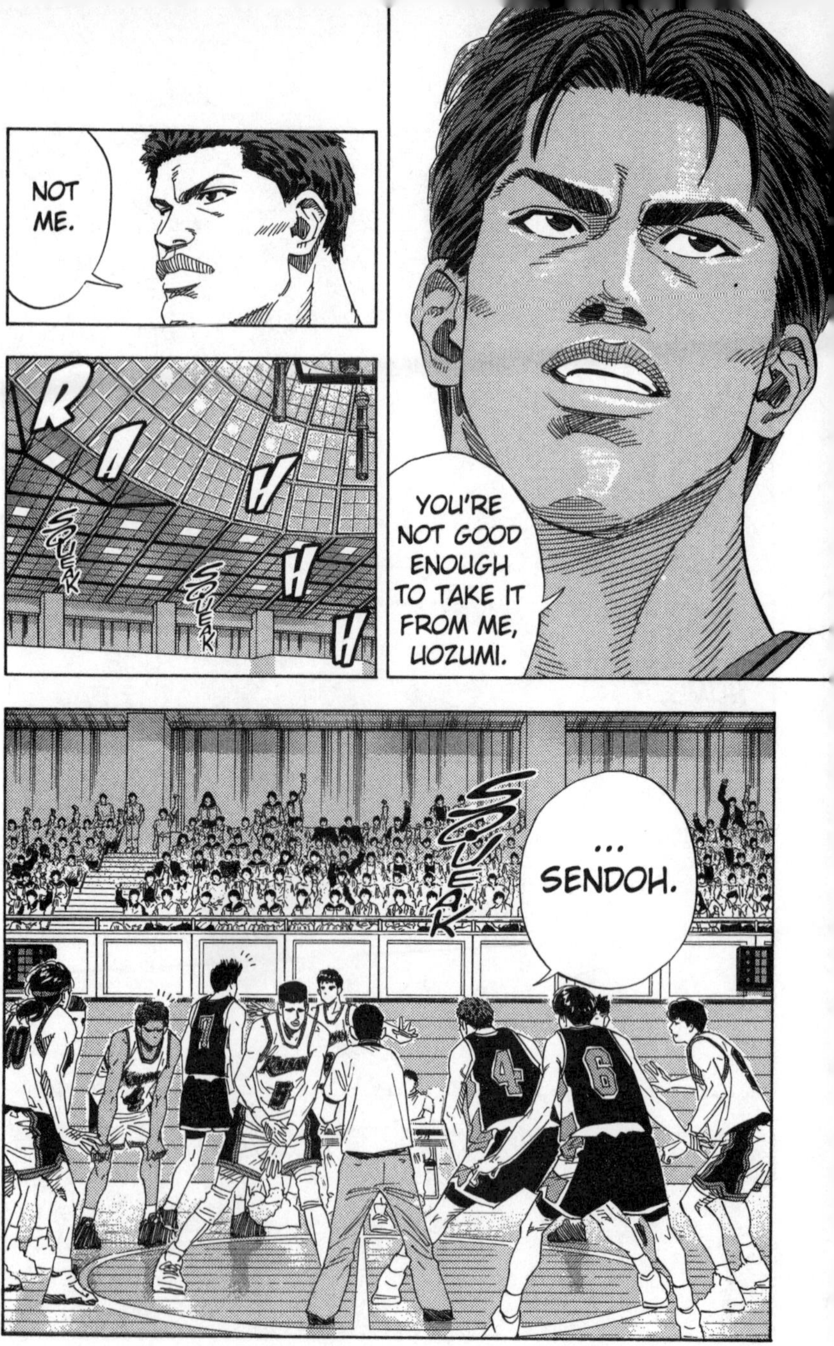
YOU'RE NOT GOOD ENOUGH TO TAKE IT FROM ME, UOZUMI.
NOT ME.
RAHHH
SQUEAK
SQUEAK
SQUEAK
... SENDOH.

«READ THIS WAY«

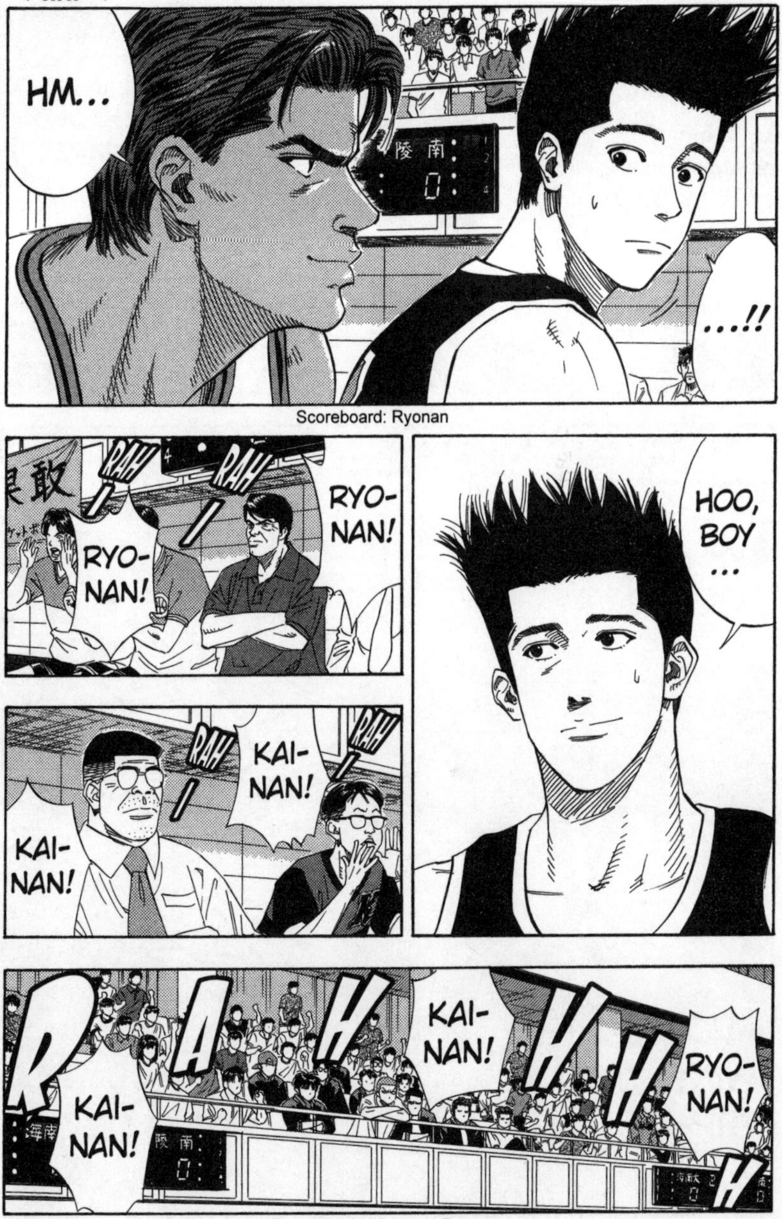
HM...
...!!
HOO, BOY...
RAH
RAH
RYO-NAN!
RYO-NAN!
RAH
KAI-NAN!
RAH
KAI-NAN!
RYO-NAN!
H
KAI-NAN!
H
H
H
A
R
KAI-NAN!

Scoreboard: Ryonan

Scoreboards: Kainan Ryonan

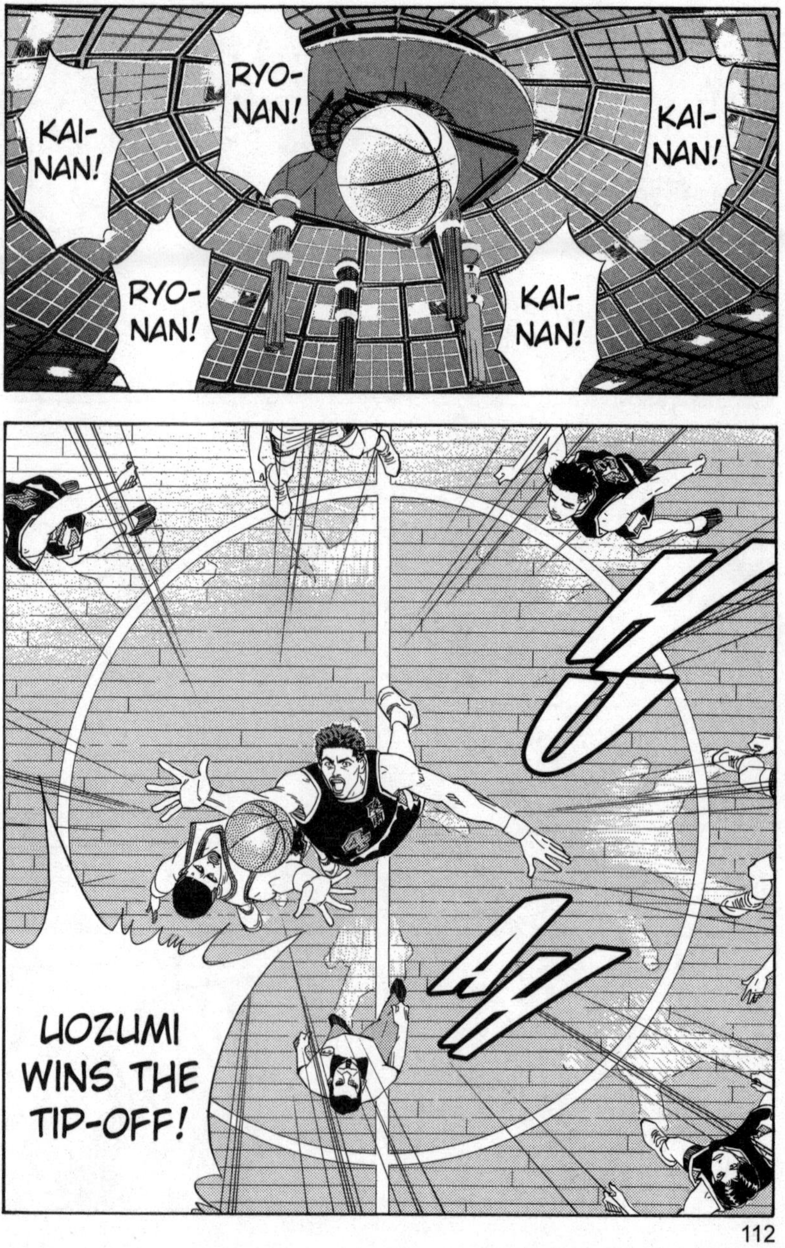
KAI-
NAN!
RYO-
NAN!
KAI-
NAN!
KAI-
NAN!
RYO-
NAN!
UOZUMI
WINS THE
TIP-OFF!

READ THIS WAY

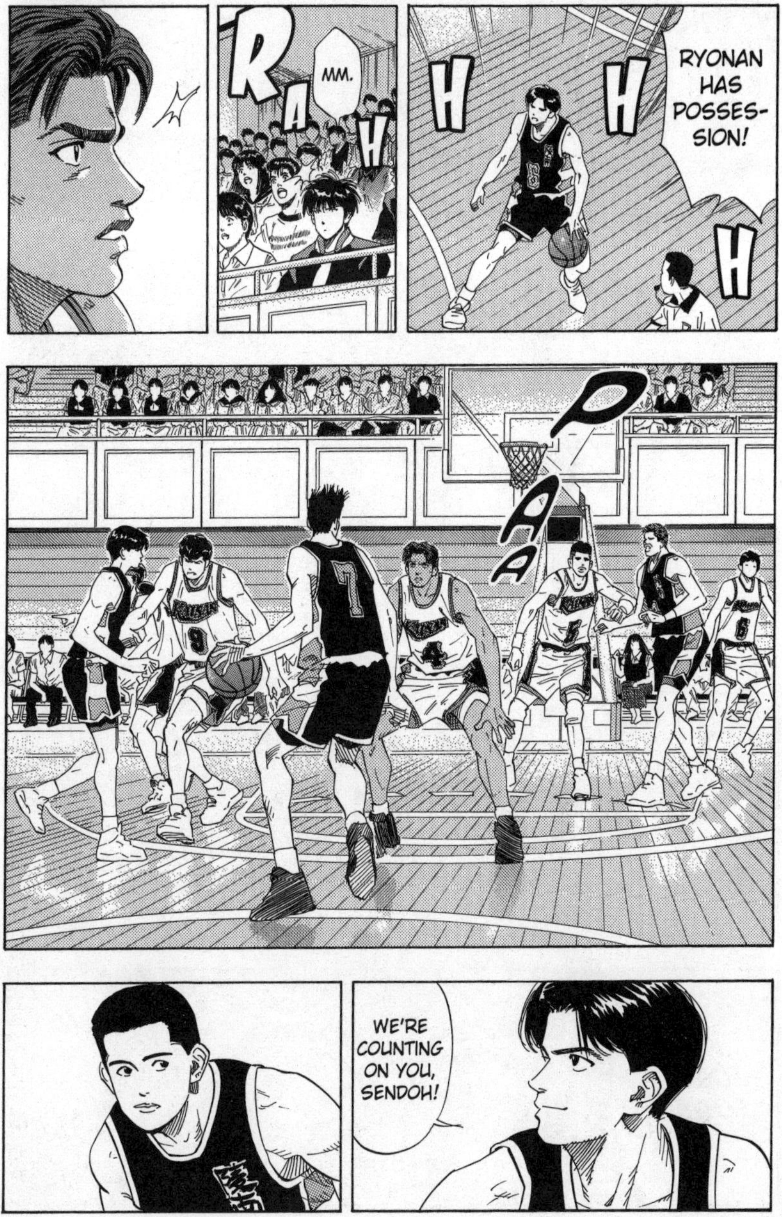

H
RYONAN HAS POSSESSION!
H
H
R
A
H
MM.
PAAA
WE'RE COUNTING ON YOU, SENDOH!

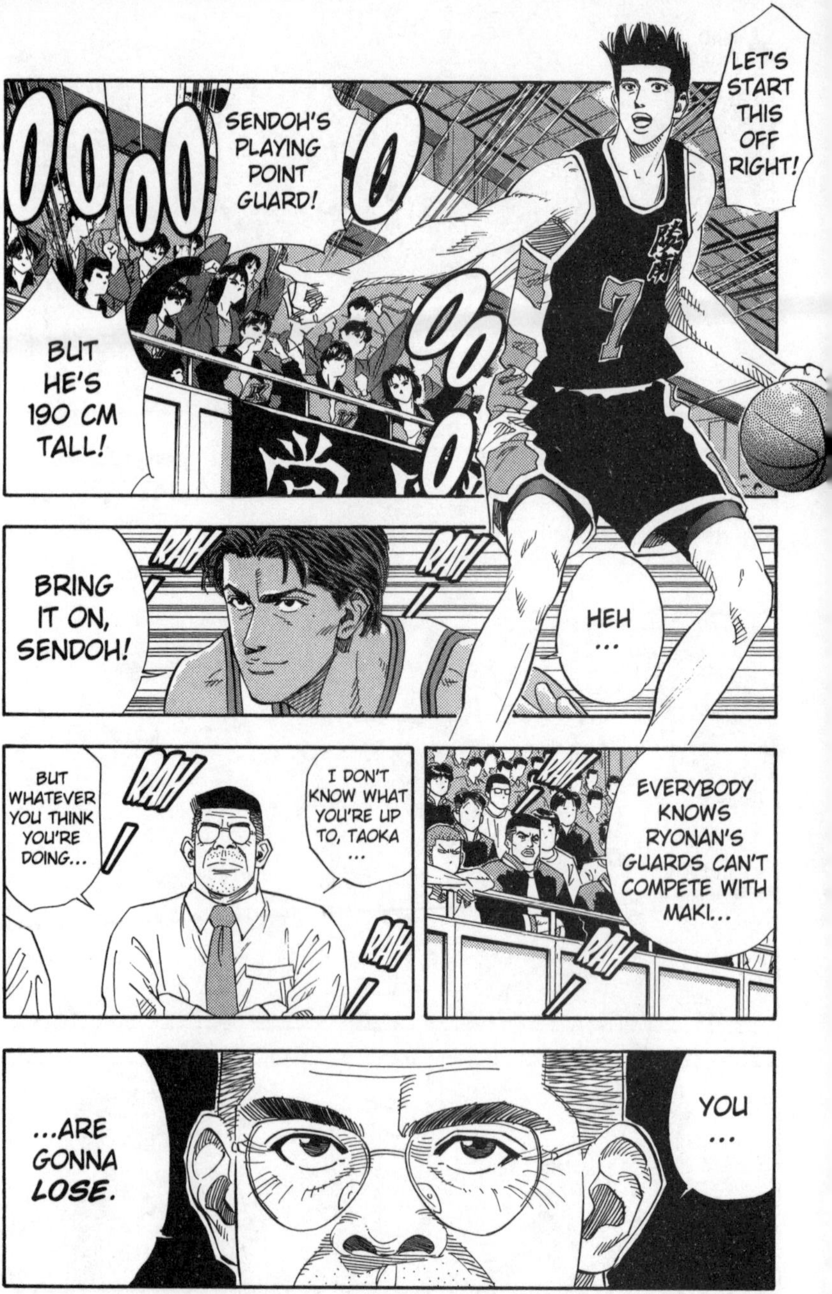
LET'S START THIS OFF RIGHT!
OOOOOO
SENDOH'S PLAYING POINT GUARD!
BUT HE'S 190 CM TALL!
OOO
HEH ...
RAH
RAH
BRING IT ON, SENDOH!
RAH
EVERYBODY KNOWS RYONAN'S GUARDS CAN'T COMPETE WITH MAKI...
RAH
RAH
RAH
I DON'T KNOW WHAT YOU'RE UP TO, TAOKA ...
BUT WHATEVER YOU THINK YOU'RE DOING...
YOU ...
...ARE GONNA LOSE.

READ THIS WAY

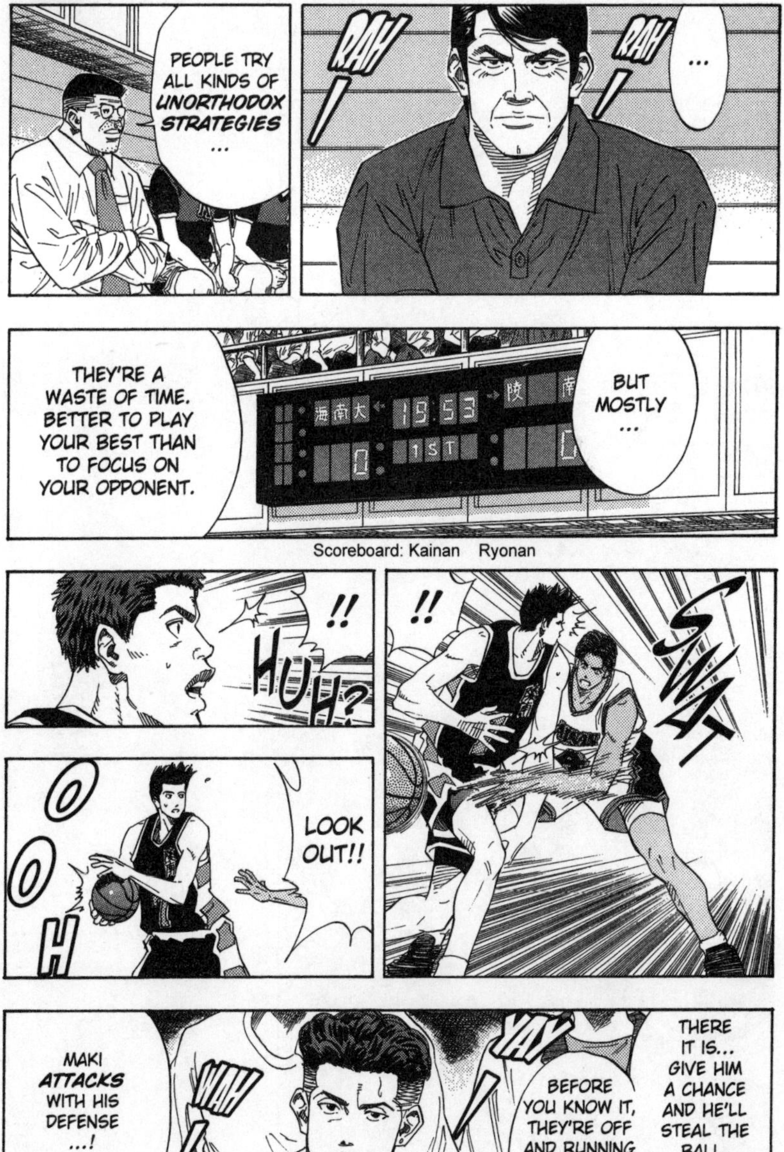

RAH
RAH
...
PEOPLE TRY ALL KINDS OF UNORTHODOX STRATEGIES ...
BUT MOSTLY ...
海南大 19:53 陵南
1ST
THEY'RE A WASTE OF TIME. BETTER TO PLAY YOUR BEST THAN TO FOCUS ON YOUR OPPONENT.
!!
SWAT
!!
HUH?
LOOK OUT!!
OOH
THERE IT IS... GIVE HIM A CHANCE AND HE'LL STEAL THE BALL.
BEFORE YOU KNOW IT, THEY'RE OFF AND RUNNING THE OTHER WAY.
YAY
WAH
MAKI ATTACKS WITH HIS DEFENSE ...!

Scoreboard: Kainan Ryonan

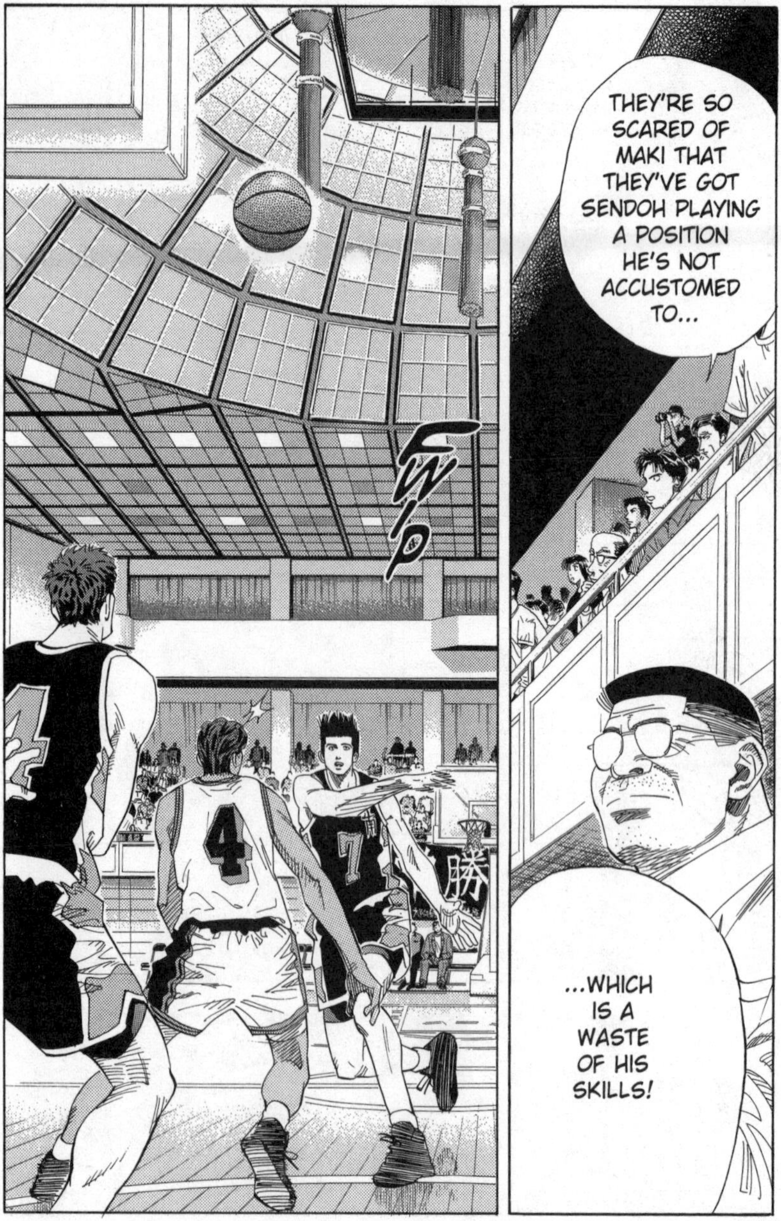
THEY'RE SO SCARED OF MAKI THAT THEY'VE GOT SENDOH PLAYING A POSITION HE'S NOT ACCUSTOMED TO...
...WHICH IS A WASTE OF HIS SKILLS!
FWIP

READ THIS WAY

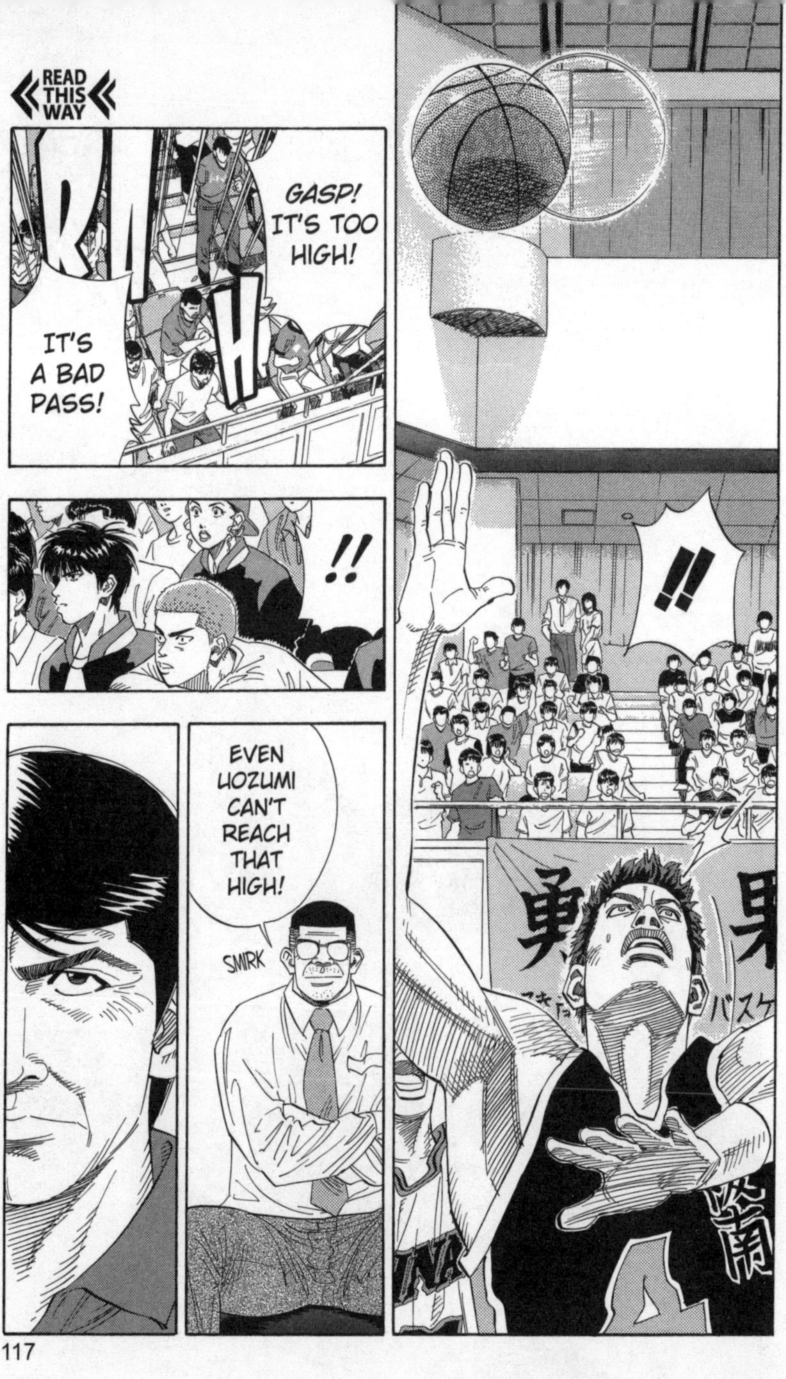
!!
GASP! IT'S TOO HIGH!
IT'S A BAD PASS!
!!
EVEN UOZUMI CAN'T REACH THAT HIGH!
SMIRK

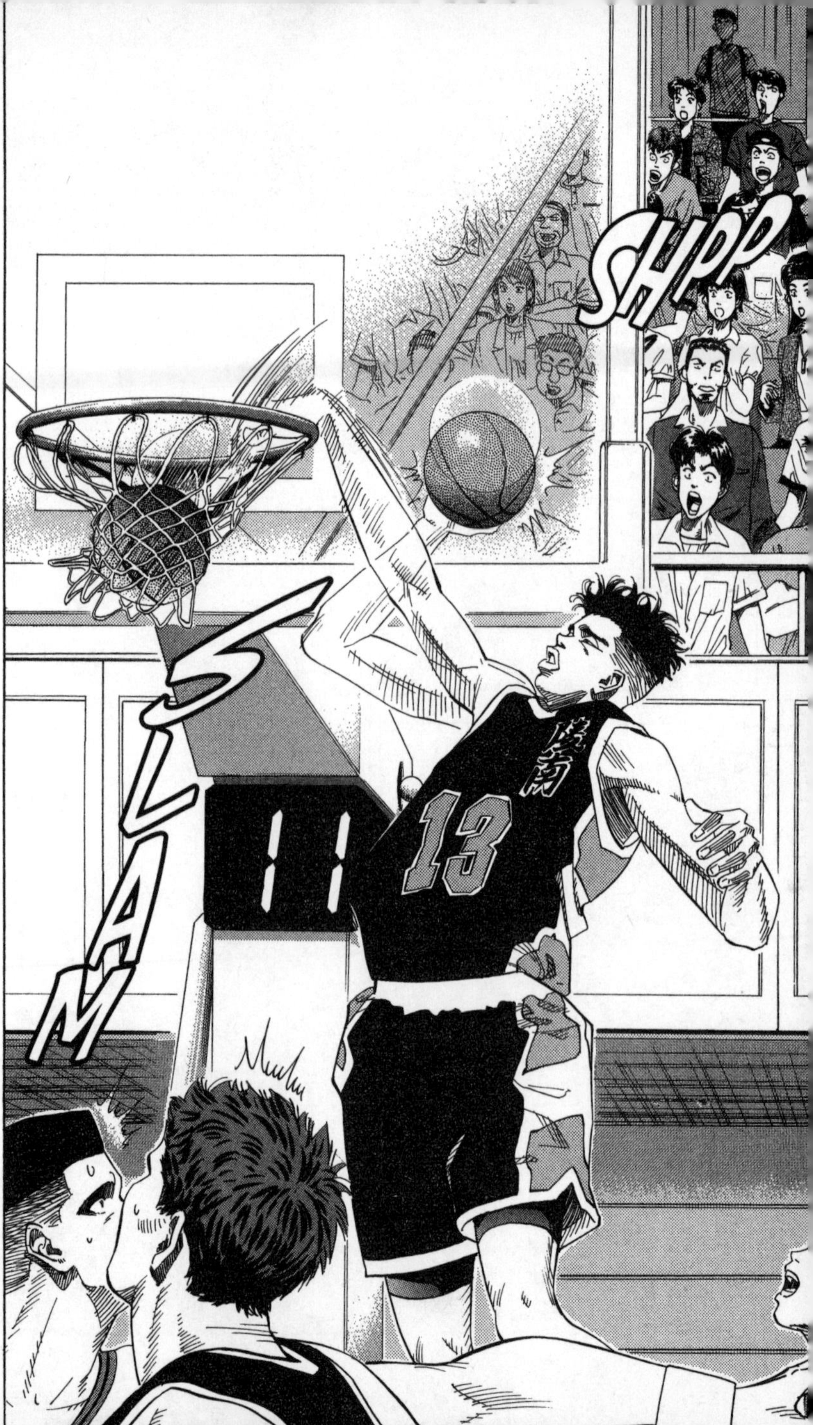
SHPP
SLAM

READ THIS WAY

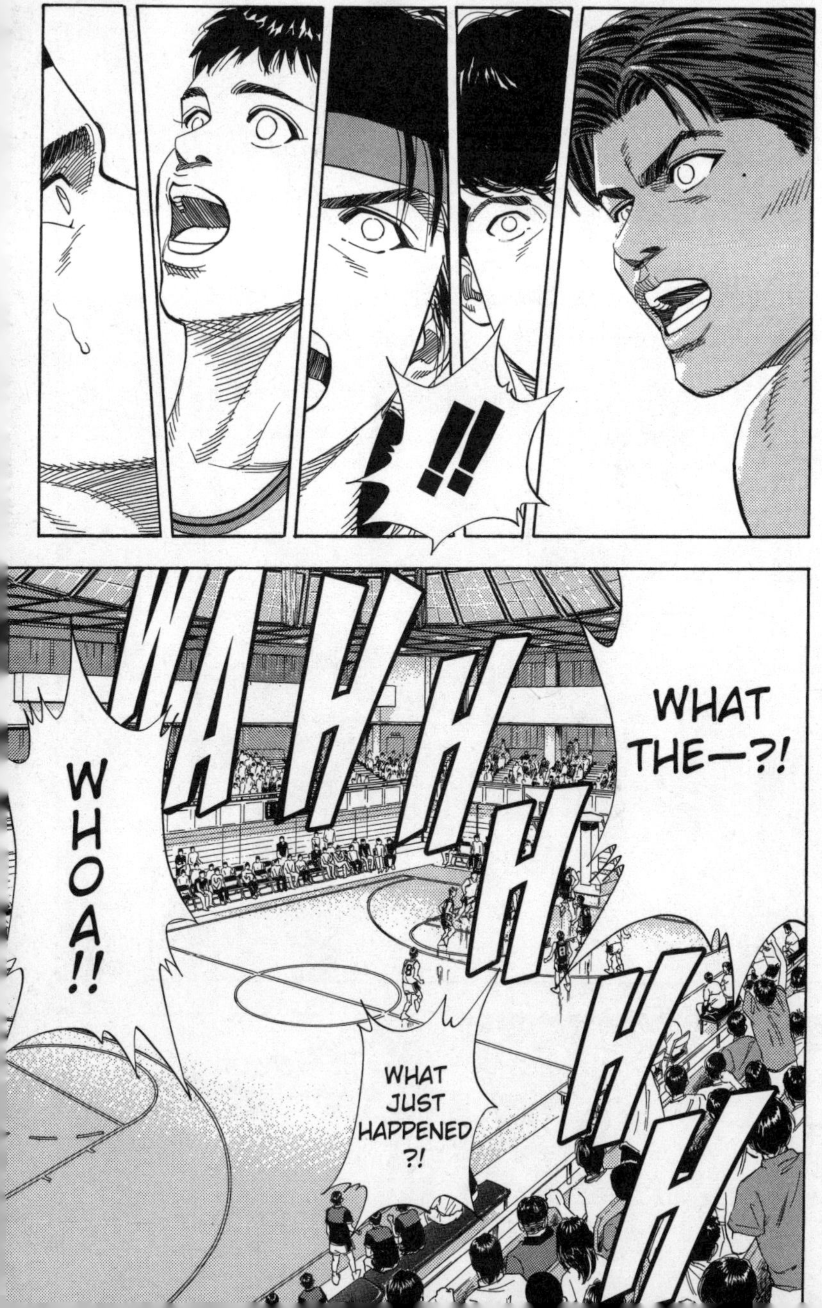
!!
WHAT THE—?!
WAHHHHHHHH
WHAT JUST HAPPENED ?!
WHOA!!

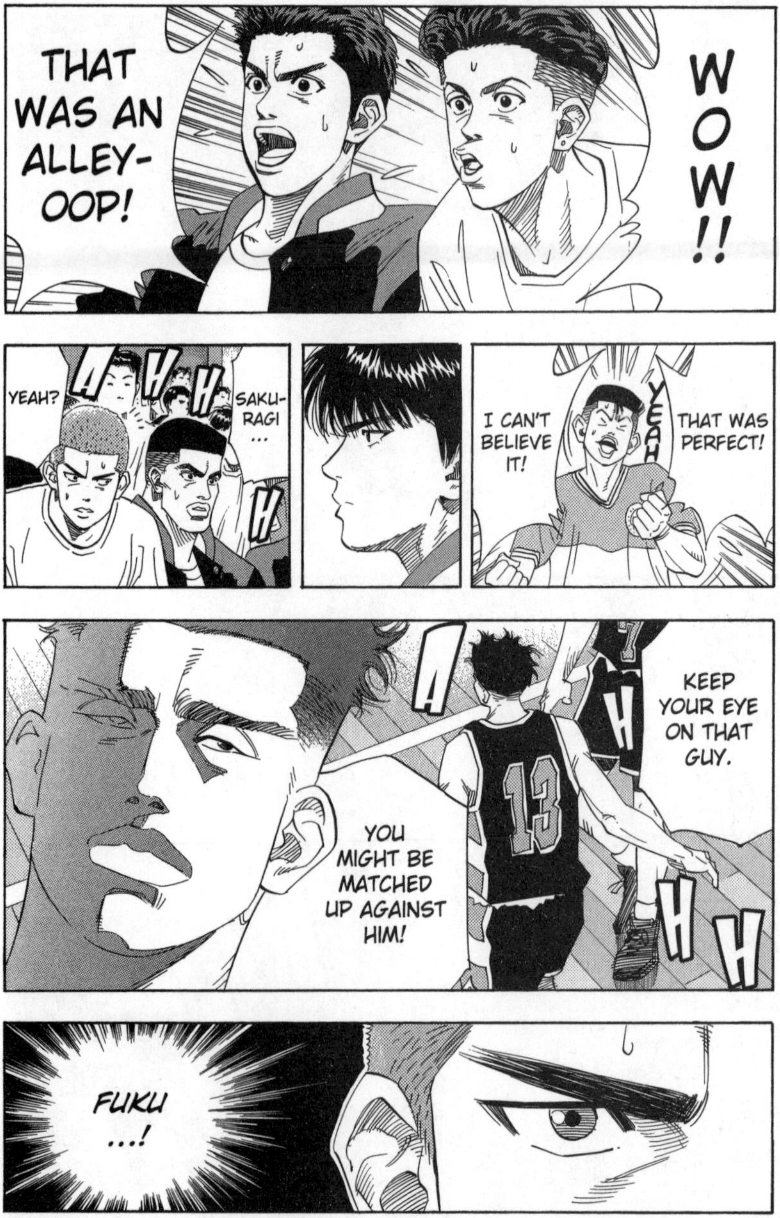
WOW!!
THAT WAS AN ALLEY-OOP!
THAT WAS PERFECT!
YEAH
I CAN'T BELIEVE IT!
SAKU-RAGI...
AHHH
YEAH?
H
KEEP YOUR EYE ON THAT GUY.
AH
YOU MIGHT BE MATCHED UP AGAINST HIM!
HH
FUKU...!

READ THIS WAY

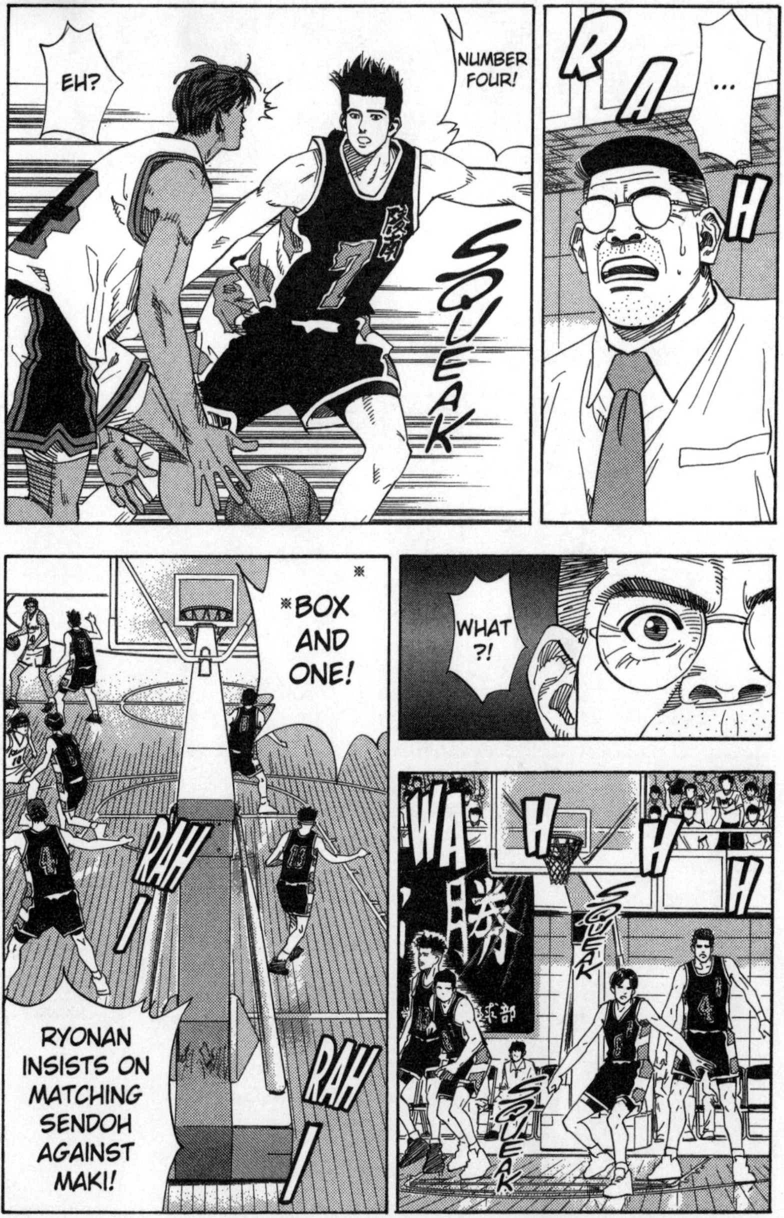

RA
...
H
NUMBER FOUR!
EH?
SQUEAK
WHAT?!
WA
H
H
H
SQUEAK
SQUEAK
※BOX AND ONE!
RAH
RAH
RYONAN INSISTS ON MATCHING SENDOH AGAINST MAKI!

※BOX AND ONE = ONE PLAYER DEFENDS AN OPPOSING PLAYER MAN-TO-MAN, WHILE THE REMAINING FOUR PLAYERS PLAY A ZONE COVERAGE.

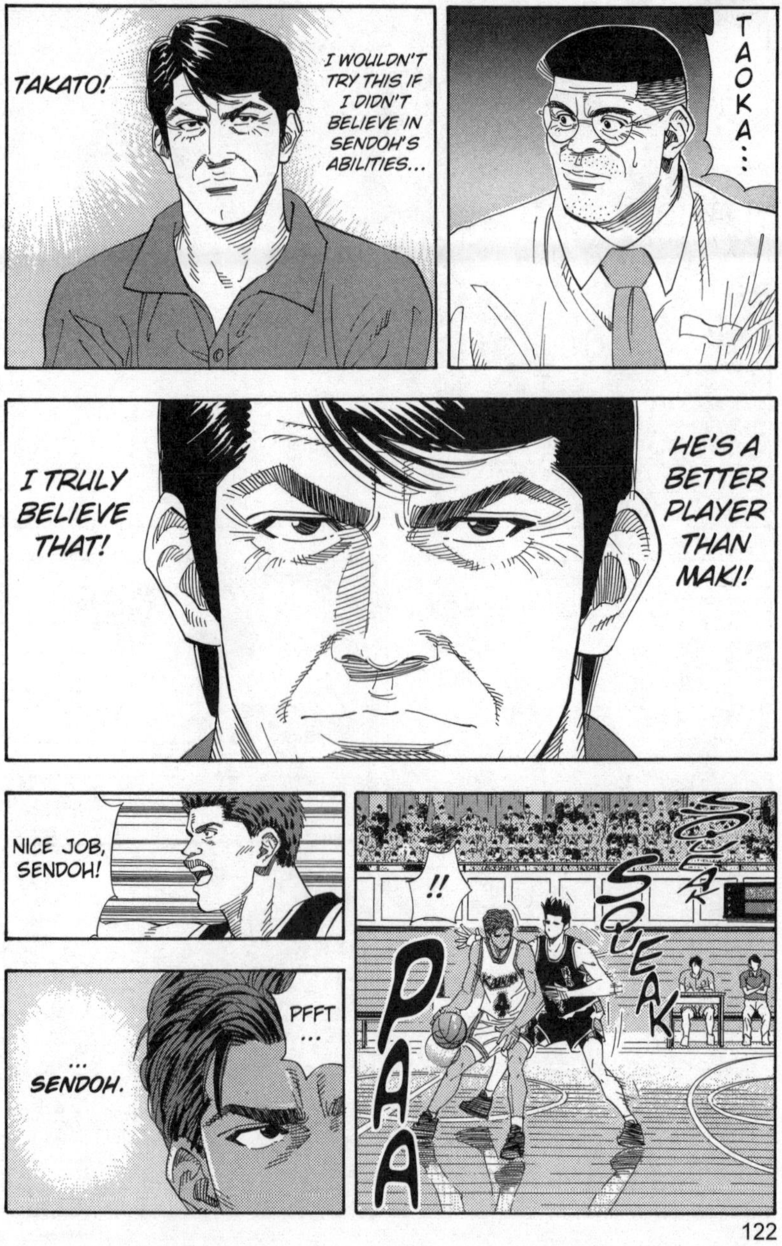
TAOKA...
I WOULDN'T TRY THIS IF I DIDN'T BELIEVE IN SENDOH'S ABILITIES...
TAKATO!
HE'S A BETTER PLAYER THAN MAKI!
I TRULY BELIEVE THAT!
SQUEAK
SQUEAK
!!
PAAA
NICE JOB, SENDOH!
PFFT ...
... SENDOH.

READ THIS WAY

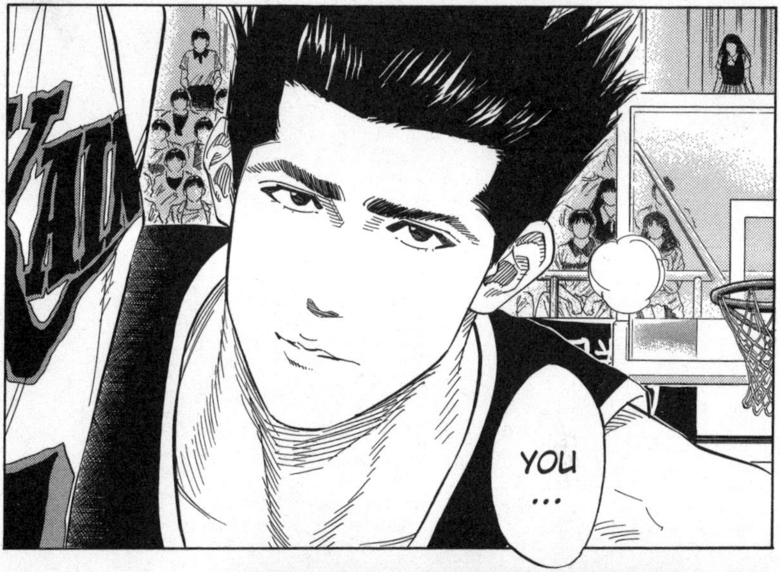
YOU ...

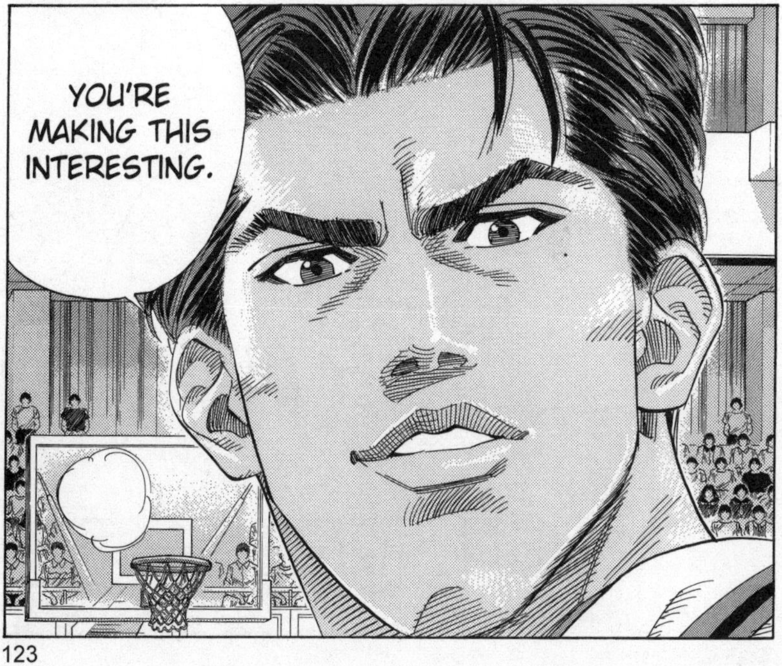
YOU'RE MAKING THIS INTERESTING.

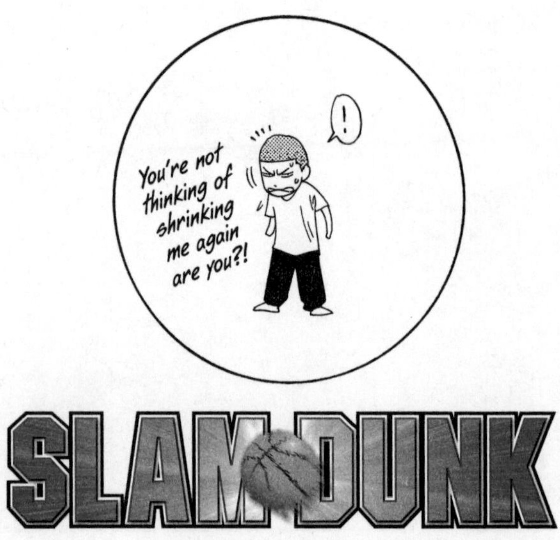
!
You're not thinking of shrinking me again are you?!

SLAM DUNK

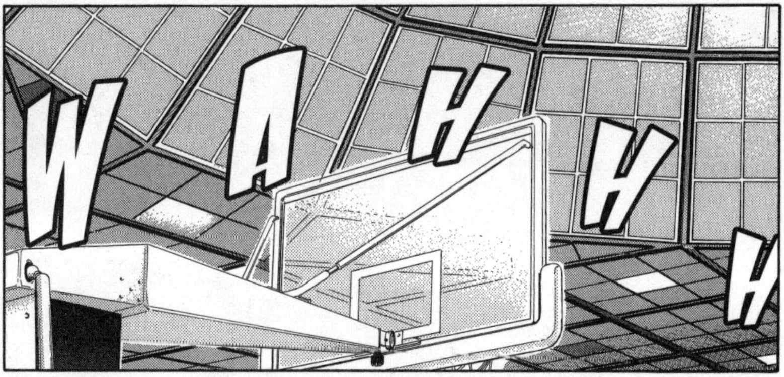
WAHHHH

#141 POINT GUARD

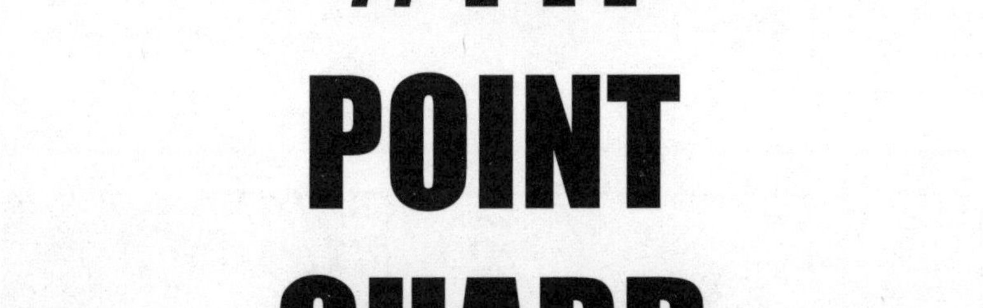
AIDA!
RAH!
RAH
RAH!
WHAT'S A POINT GUARD'S JOB?

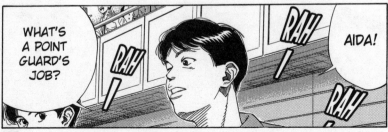

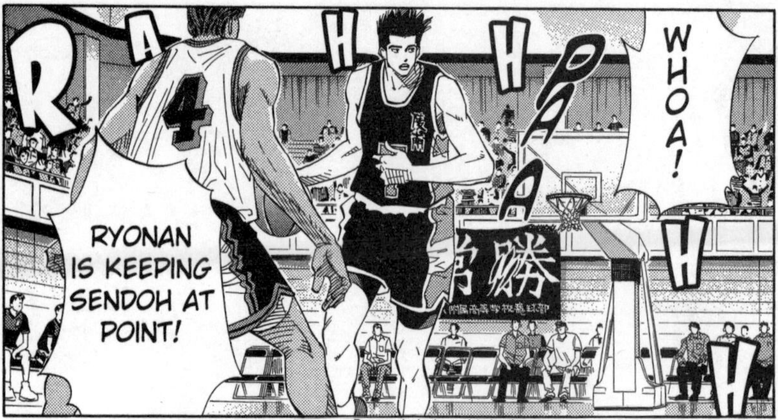
WHOA!
RAHHAAAAHHH
RYONAN IS KEEPING SENDOH AT POINT!
Banner: *Josho* (ever victorious)
Kainan Dai Fuzoku High School Basketball Team

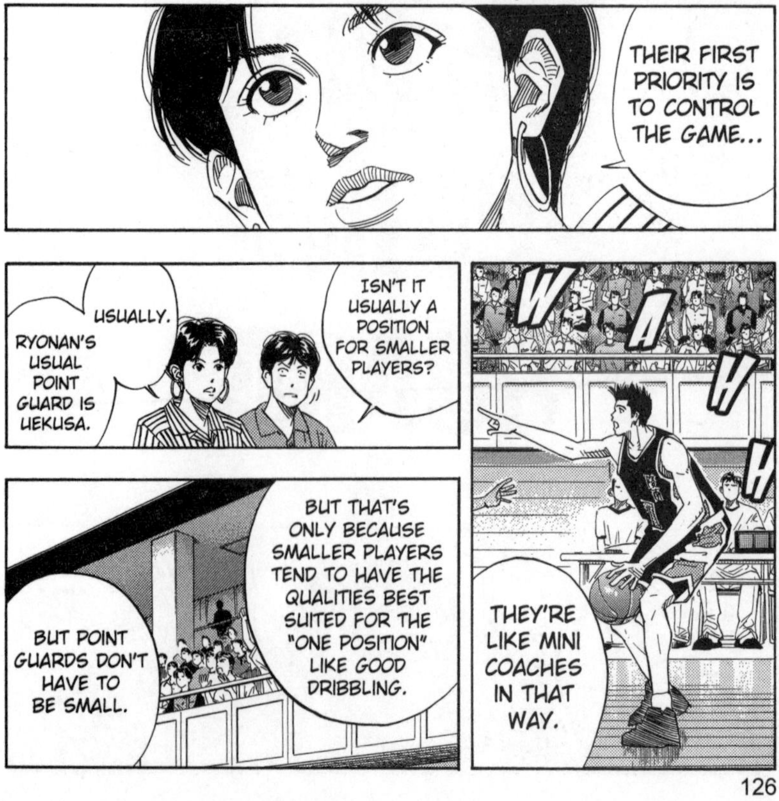
THEIR FIRST PRIORITY IS TO CONTROL THE GAME...
WAHHH
THEY'RE LIKE MINI COACHES IN THAT WAY.
ISN'T IT USUALLY A POSITION FOR SMALLER PLAYERS?
USUALLY.
RYONAN'S USUAL POINT GUARD IS UEKUSA.
BUT THAT'S ONLY BECAUSE SMALLER PLAYERS TEND TO HAVE THE QUALITIES BEST SUITED FOR THE "ONE POSITION" LIKE GOOD DRIBBLING.
BUT POINT GUARDS DON'T HAVE TO BE SMALL.

READ THIS WAY

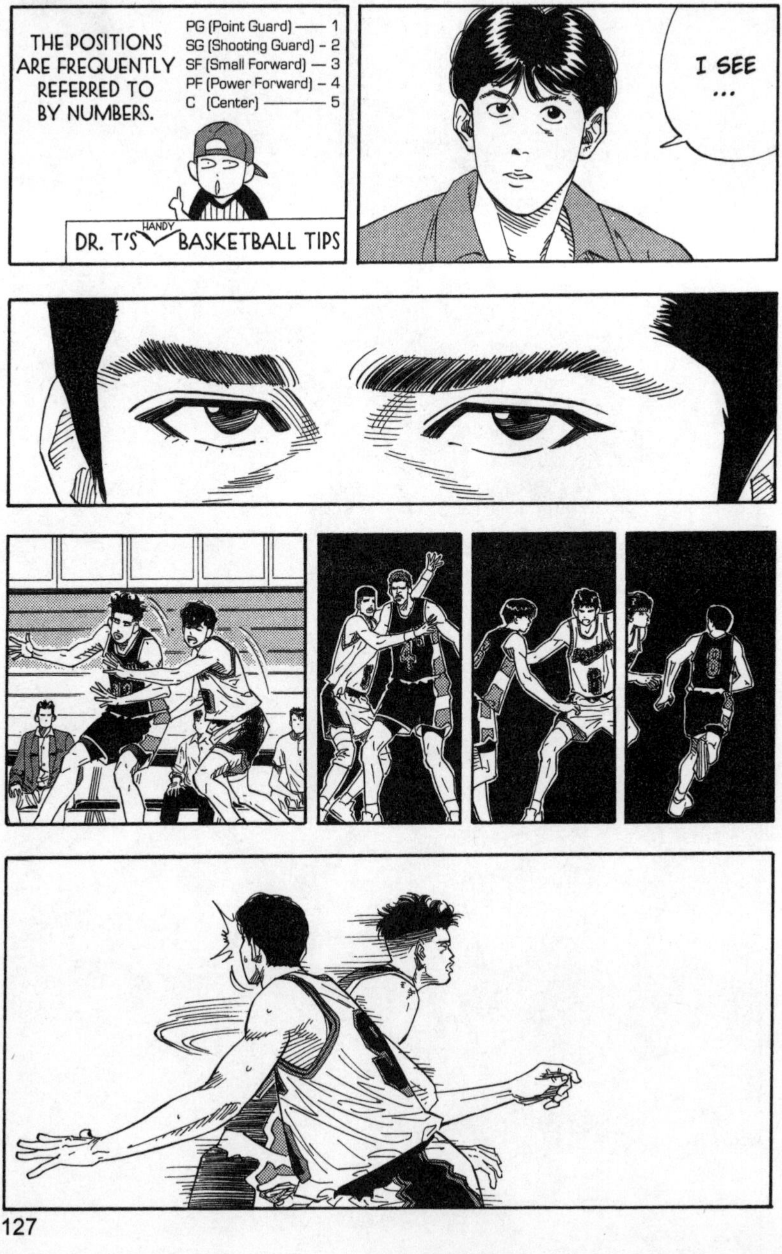
I SEE ...
THE POSITIONS ARE FREQUENTLY REFERRED TO BY NUMBERS.
PG (Point Guard) — 1
SG (Shooting Guard) - 2
SF (Small Forward) — 3
PF (Power Forward) – 4
C (Center) — 5
DR. T'S HANDY BASKETBALL TIPS

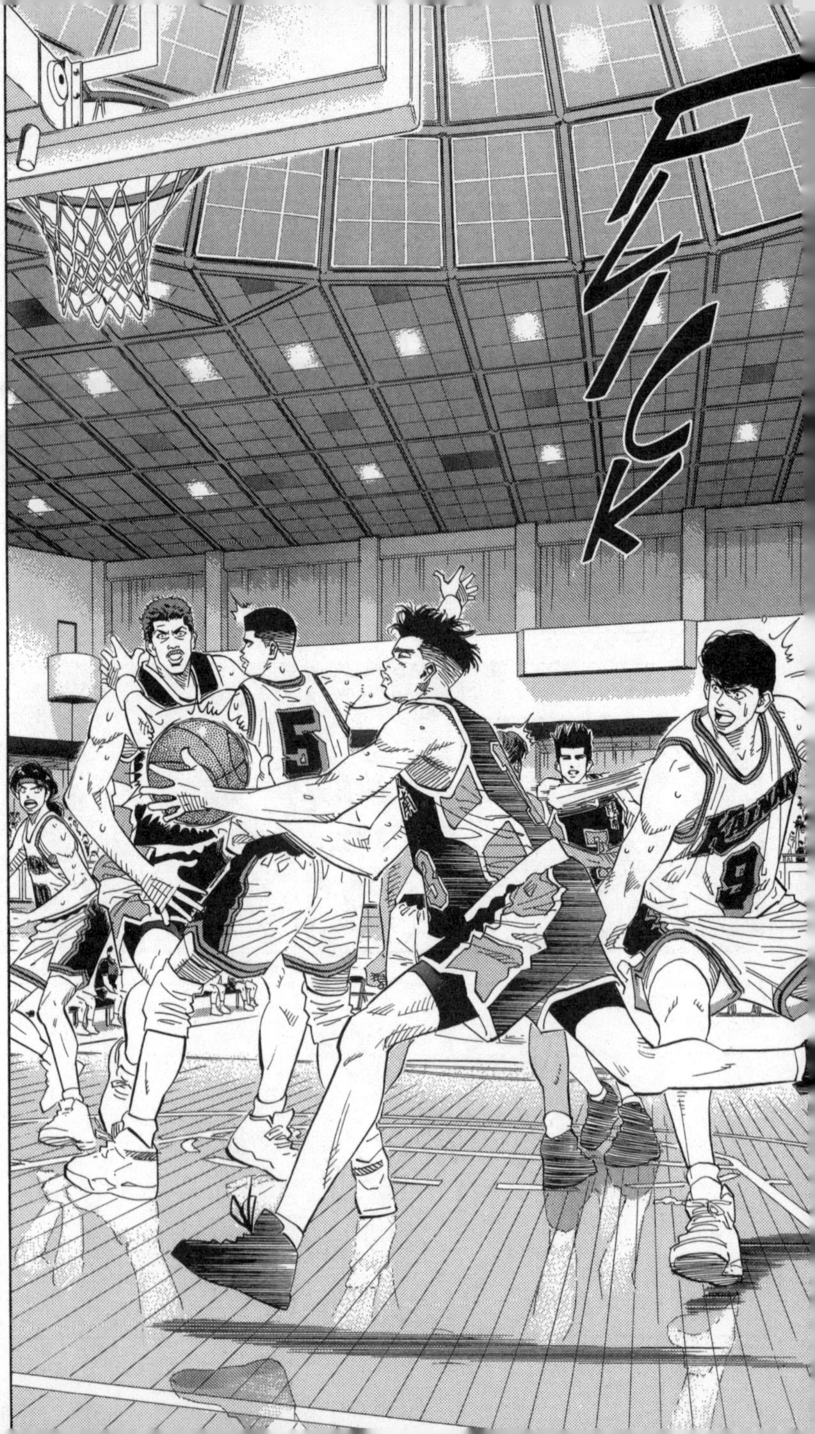
FLICK

READ THIS WAY

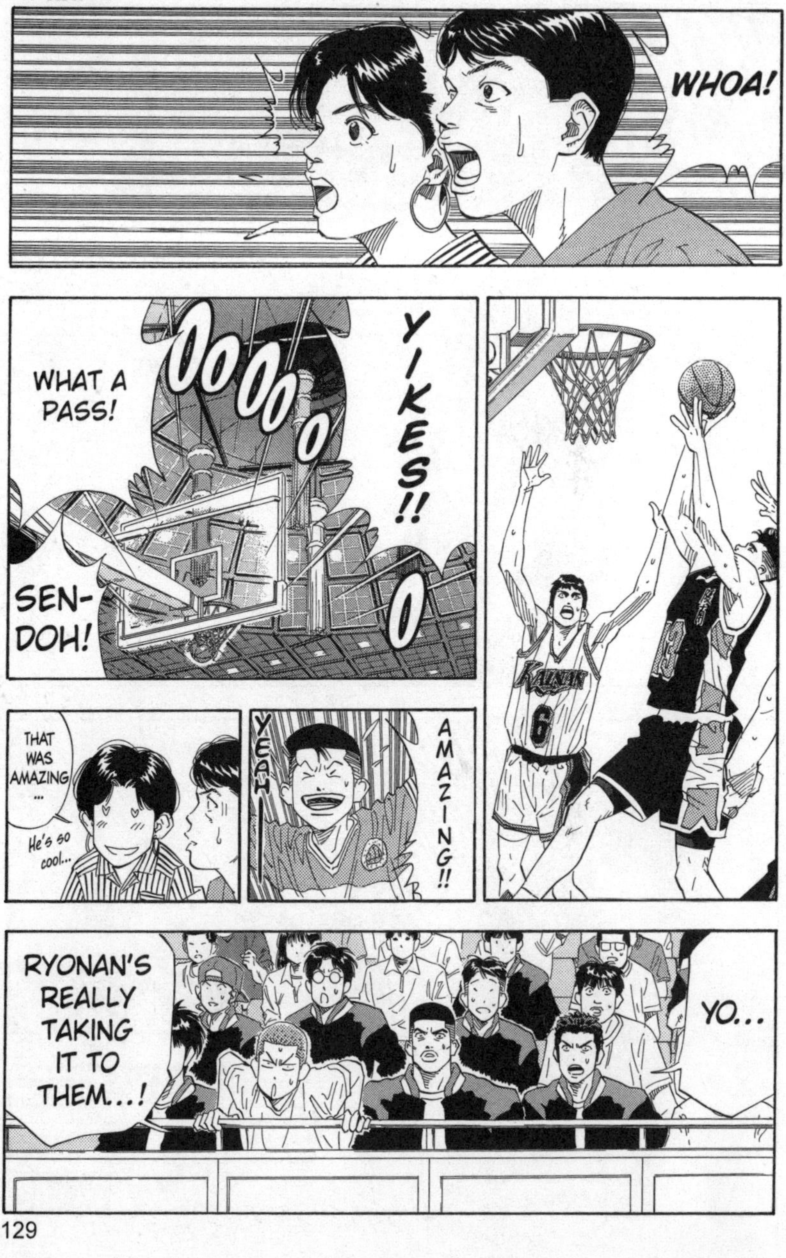
WHOA!
YIKES!!
OOOOOOO
WHAT A PASS!
SEN-DOH!
AMAZING!!
YEAH—
THAT WAS AMAZING...
He's so cool...
YO...
RYONAN'S REALLY TAKING IT TO THEM...!

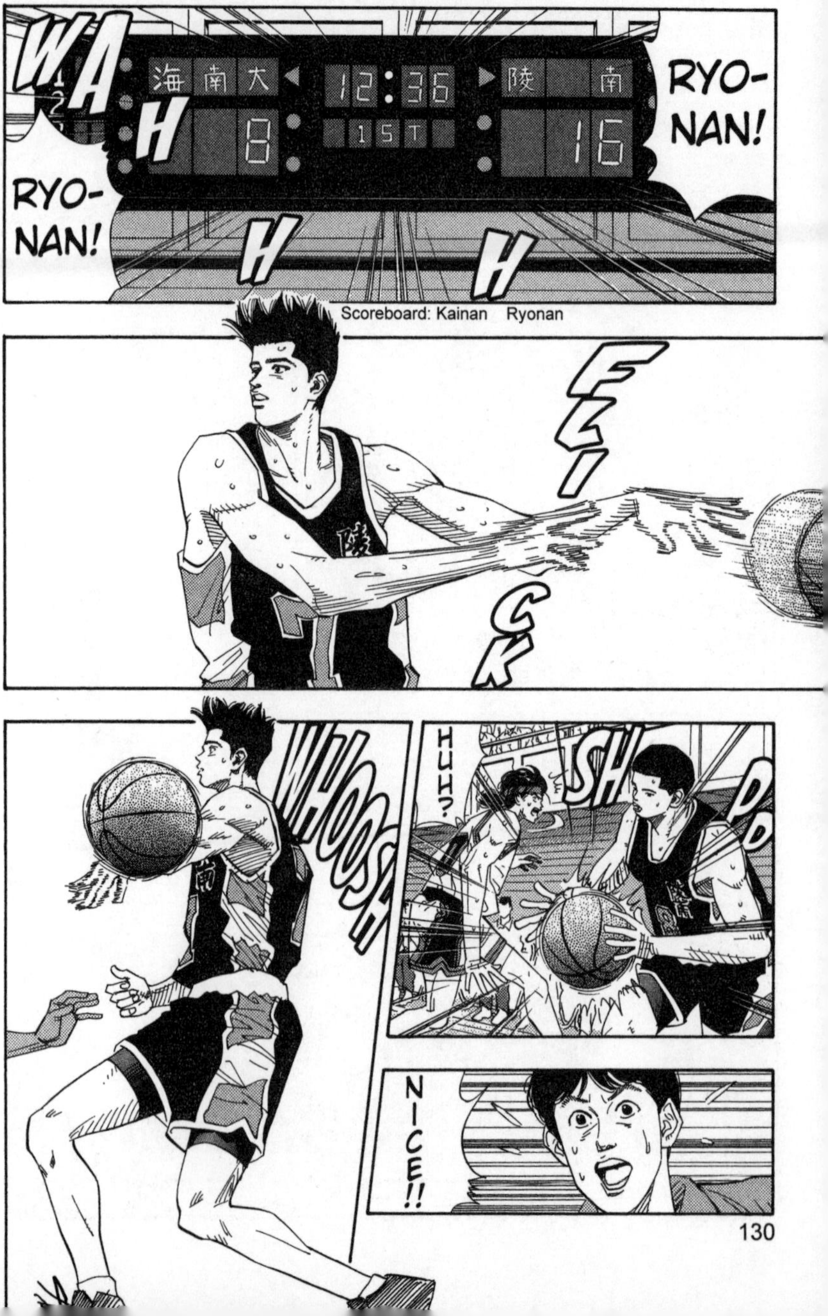
RYO-NAN!
WAH
RYO-NAN!
海南大 12:36 陵南
8 1ST 16
Scoreboard: Kainan Ryonan
FLICK
SHP
HUH?
NICE!!
WHOOSH

READ THIS WAY

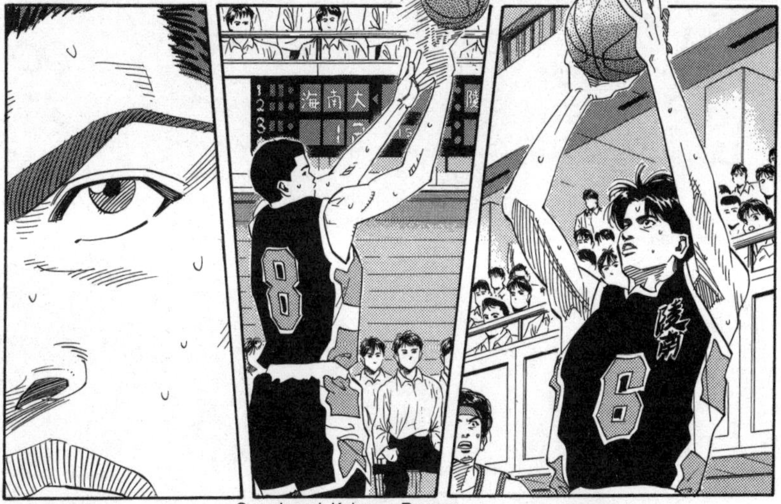
海南大
陵
Scoreboard: Kainan Ryonan

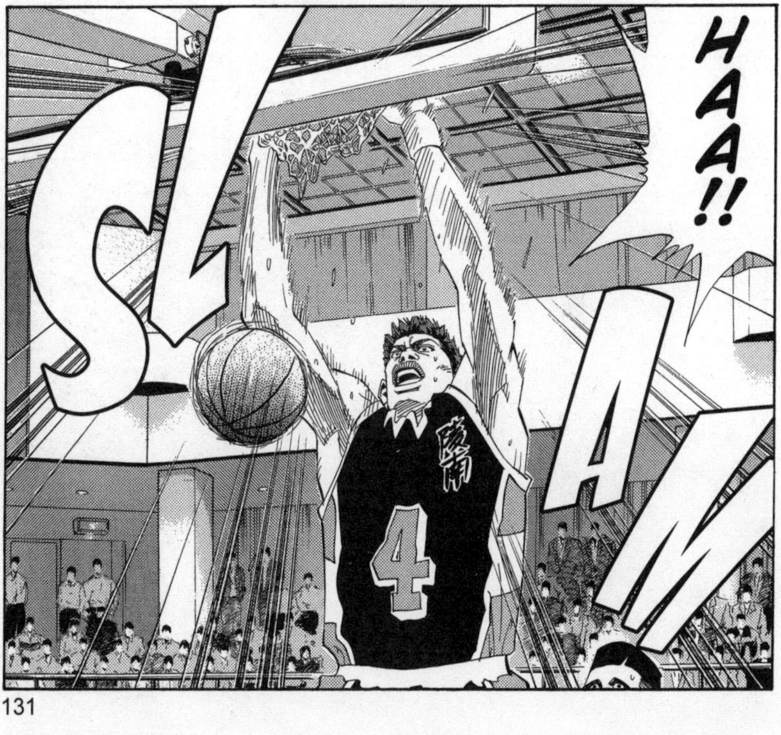
HAAA!!
SLAM

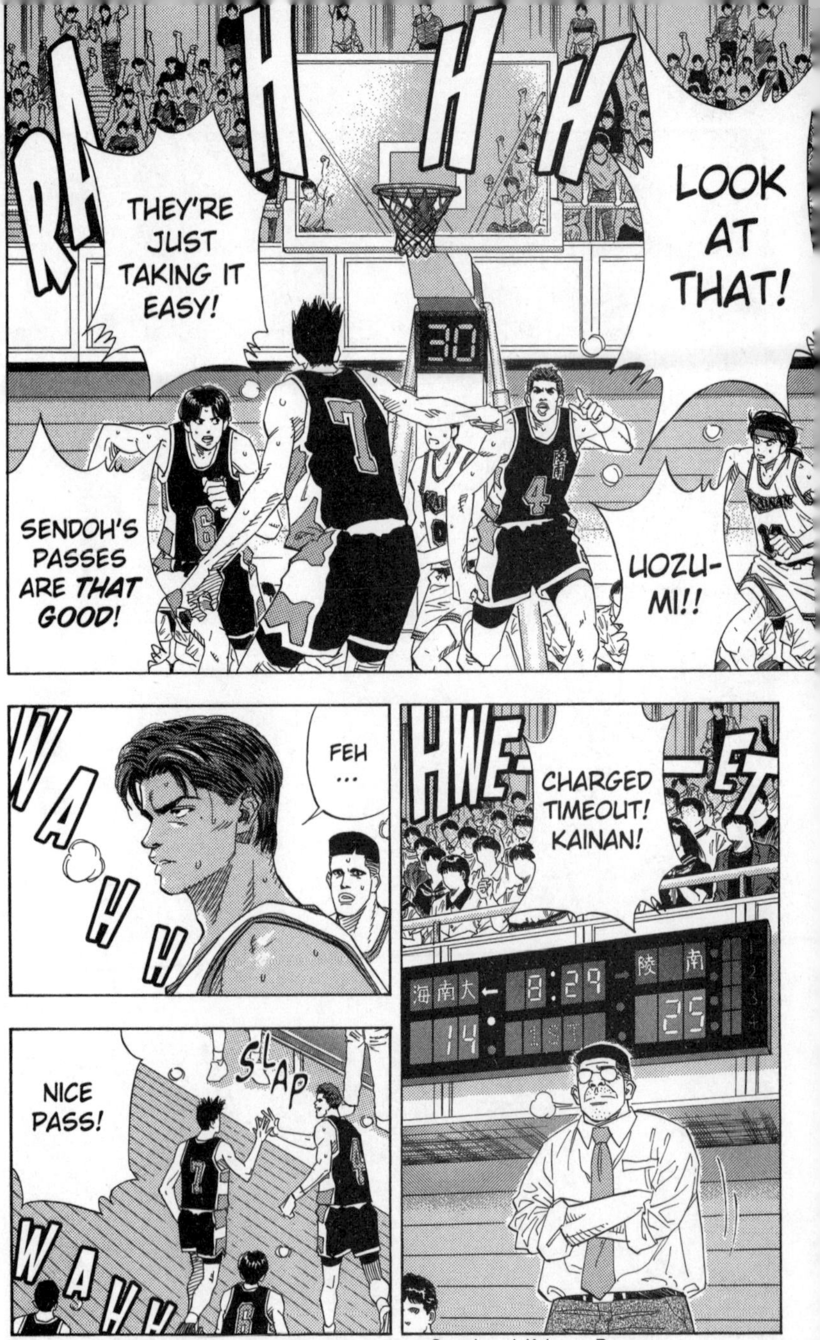
LOOK AT THAT!
RAHHHH
THEY'RE JUST TAKING IT EASY!
UOZUMI!!
SENDOH'S PASSES ARE *THAT* GOOD!
HWE-ET
CHARGED TIMEOUT! KAINAN!
海南大
8:29
陵南
14
25
FEH ...
WAHHH
NICE PASS!
SLAP
WAHHH

Scoreboard: Kainan Ryonan

READ THIS WAY

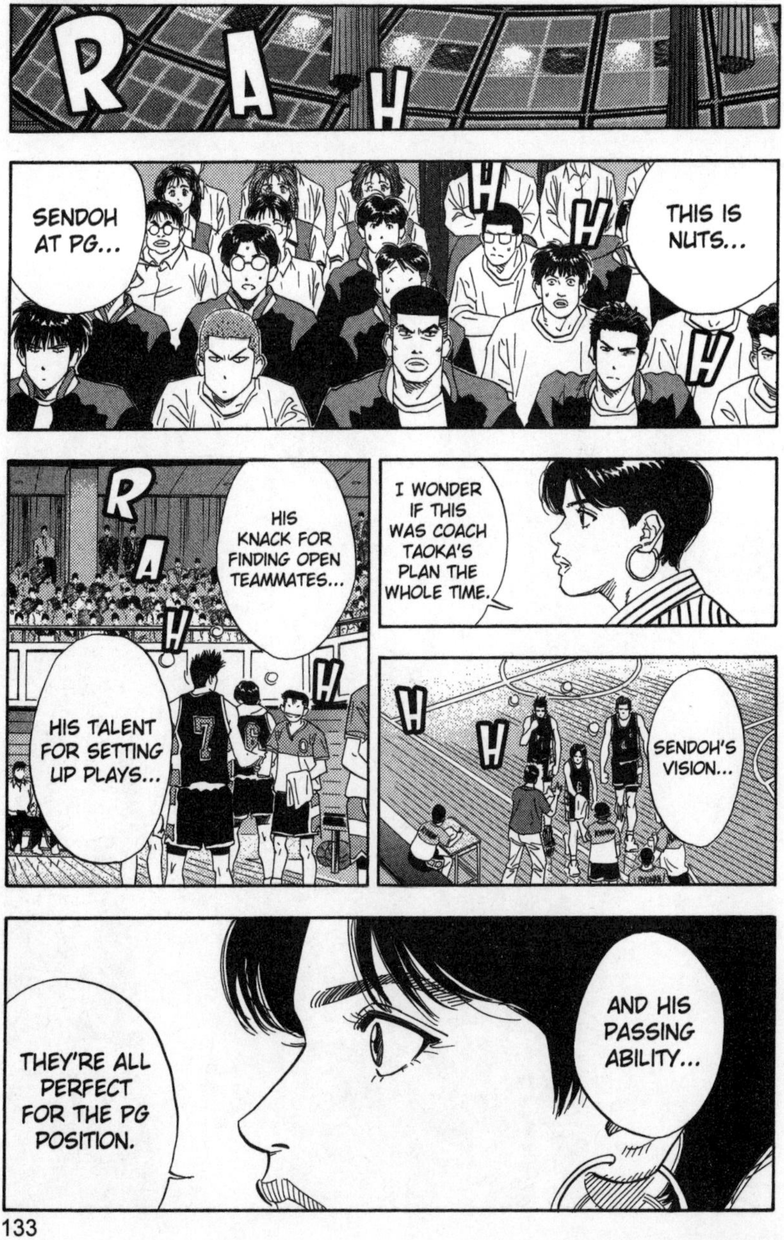
RAH
HHHH
THIS IS NUTS...
SENDOH AT PG...
I WONDER IF THIS WAS COACH TAOKA'S PLAN THE WHOLE TIME.
HH
SENDOH'S VISION...
RAHH
HIS KNACK FOR FINDING OPEN TEAMMATES...
HIS TALENT FOR SETTING UP PLAYS...
AND HIS PASSING ABILITY...
THEY'RE ALL PERFECT FOR THE PG POSITION.

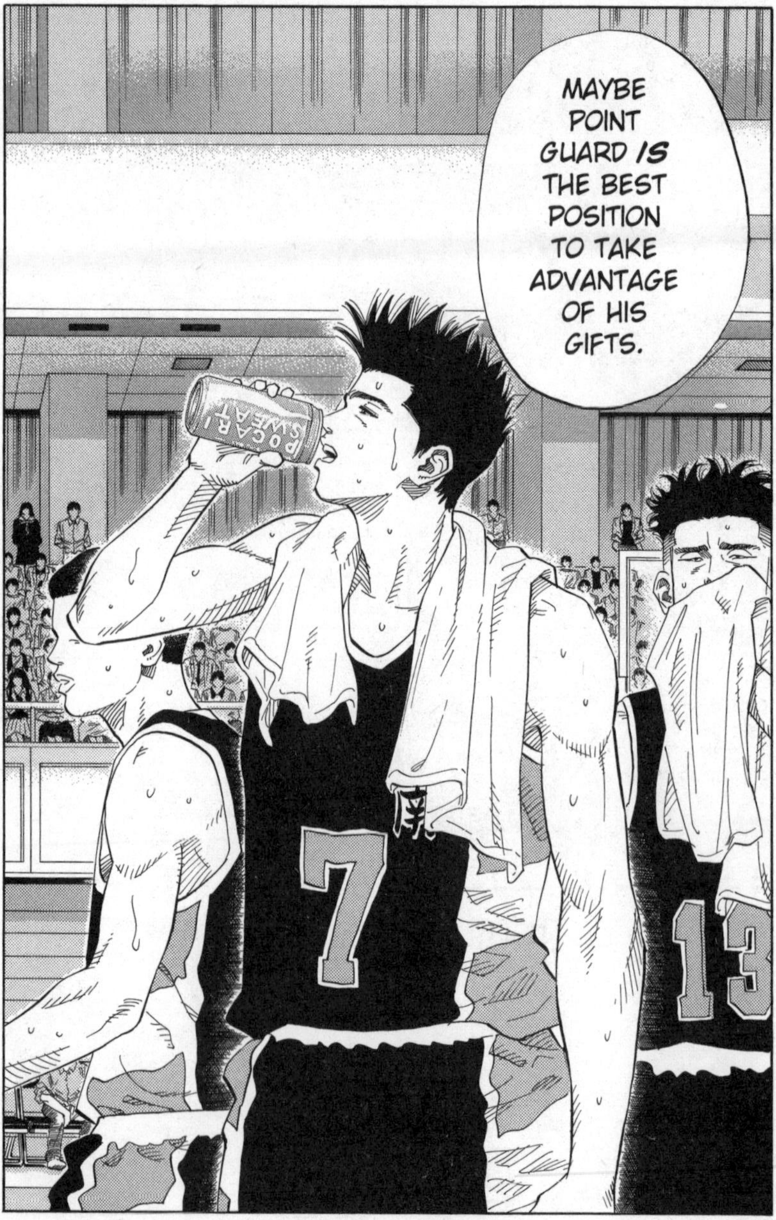
MAYBE POINT GUARD *IS* THE BEST POSITION TO TAKE ADVANTAGE OF HIS GIFTS.
POCARI SWEAT

READ THIS WAY

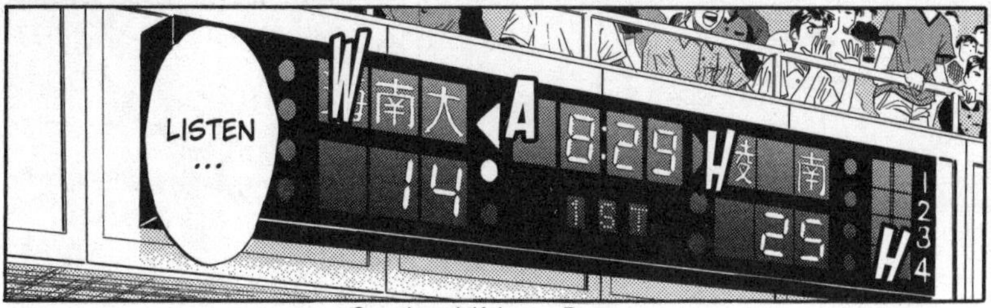
LISTEN ...

Scoreboard: Kainan Ryonan

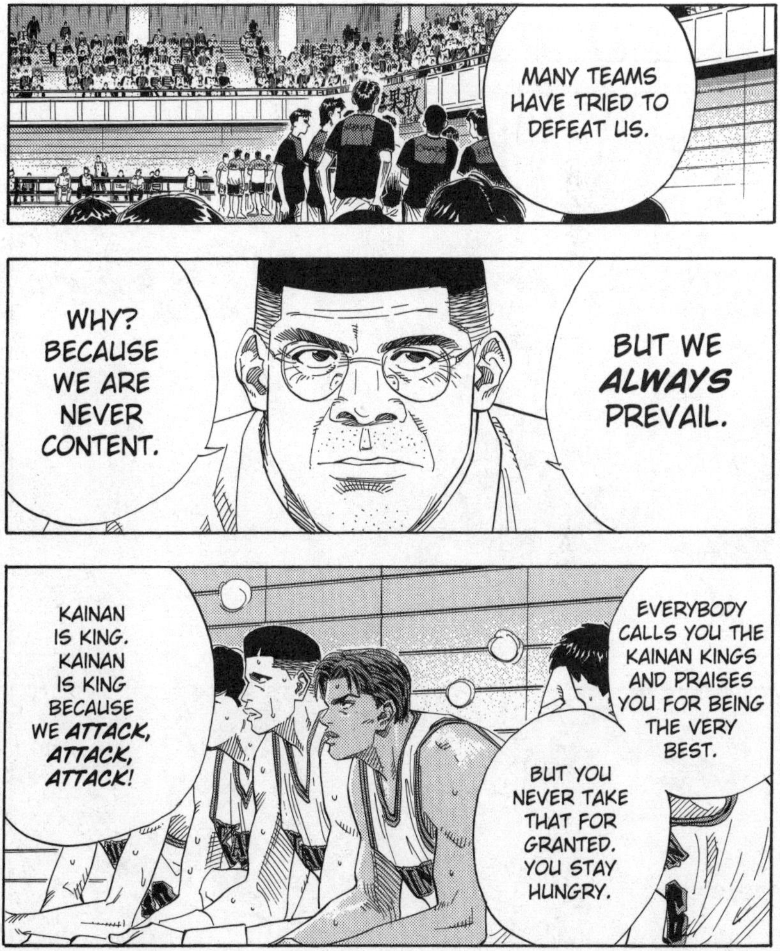
MANY TEAMS HAVE TRIED TO DEFEAT US.
BUT WE ***ALWAYS*** PREVAIL.
WHY? BECAUSE WE ARE NEVER CONTENT.
EVERYBODY CALLS YOU THE KAINAN KINGS AND PRAISES YOU FOR BEING THE VERY BEST.
BUT YOU NEVER TAKE THAT FOR GRANTED. YOU STAY HUNGRY.
KAINAN IS KING. KAINAN IS KING BECAUSE WE ***ATTACK, ATTACK, ATTACK!***

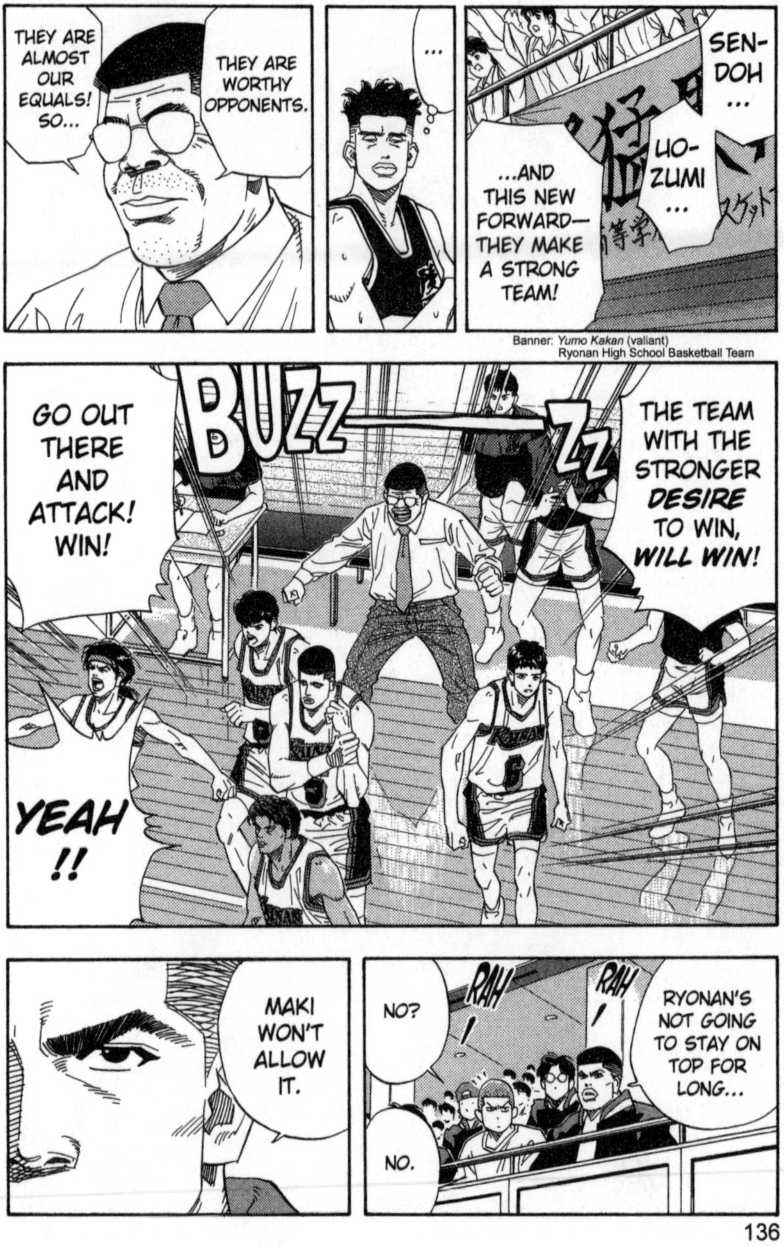
SEN-DOH ...
UO-ZUMI ...
...AND THIS NEW FORWARD— THEY MAKE A STRONG TEAM!
...
THEY ARE WORTHY OPPONENTS.
THEY ARE ALMOST OUR EQUALS! SO...
Banner: *Yumo Kakan* (valiant)
Ryonan High School Basketball Team
BUZZ ZZ
THE TEAM WITH THE STRONGER ***DESIRE*** TO WIN, ***WILL WIN!***
GO OUT THERE AND ATTACK! WIN!
YEAH !!
RYONAN'S NOT GOING TO STAY ON TOP FOR LONG...
RAH!
RAH!
NO?
NO.
MAKI WON'T ALLOW IT.

READ THIS WAY

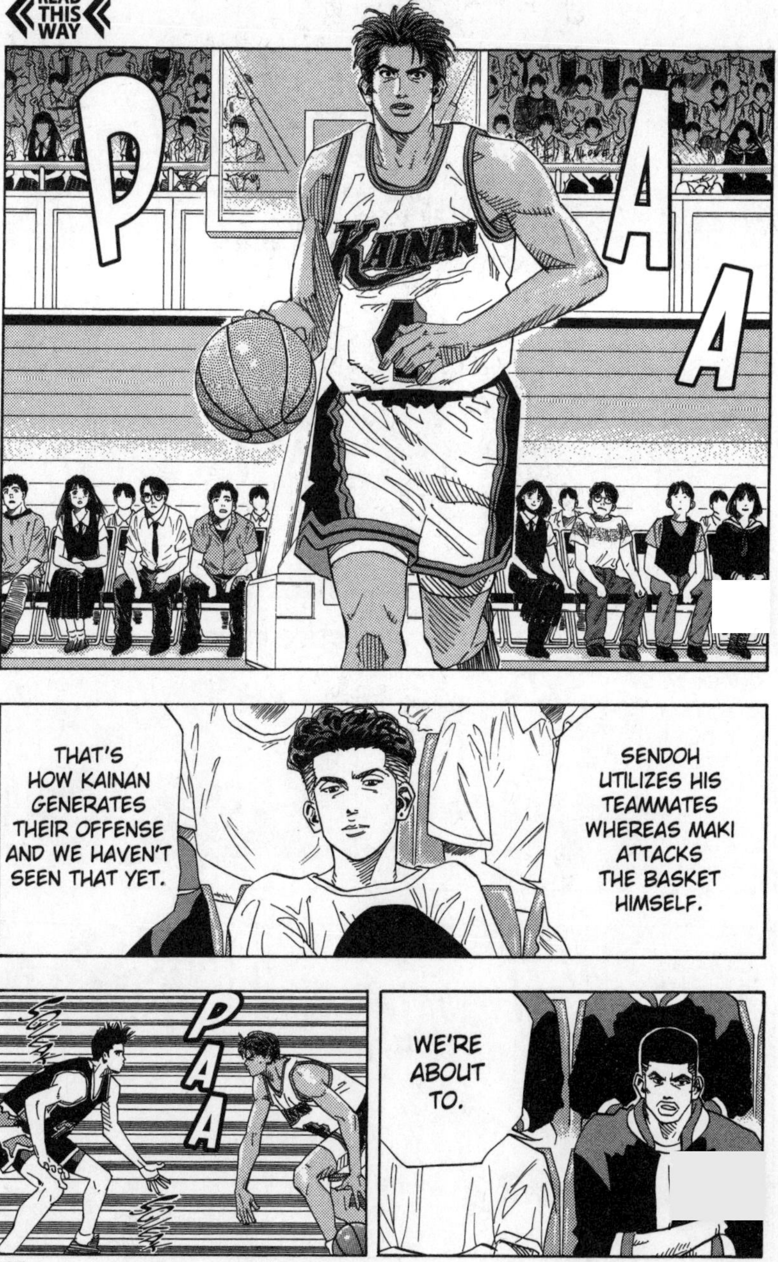
P
A
A
SENDOH UTILIZES HIS TEAMMATES WHEREAS MAKI ATTACKS THE BASKET HIMSELF.
THAT'S HOW KAINAN GENERATES THEIR OFFENSE AND WE HAVEN'T SEEN THAT YET.
WE'RE ABOUT TO.
PAA

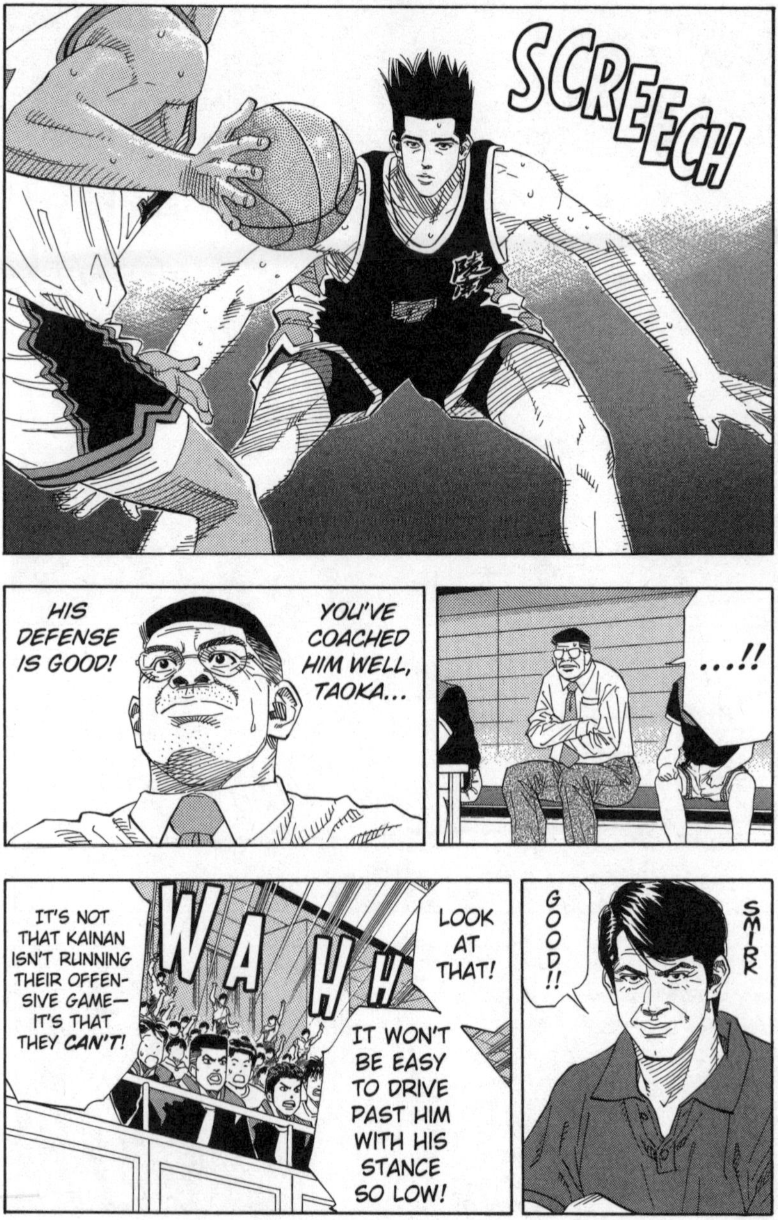
SCREECH
...!!
YOU'VE COACHED HIM WELL, TAOKA...
HIS DEFENSE IS GOOD!
SMIRK
GOOD!!
LOOK AT THAT!
IT WON'T BE EASY TO DRIVE PAST HIM WITH HIS STANCE SO LOW!
WAHH
IT'S NOT THAT KAINAN ISN'T RUNNING THEIR OFFEN-SIVE GAME— IT'S THAT THEY CAN'T!

READ THIS WAY

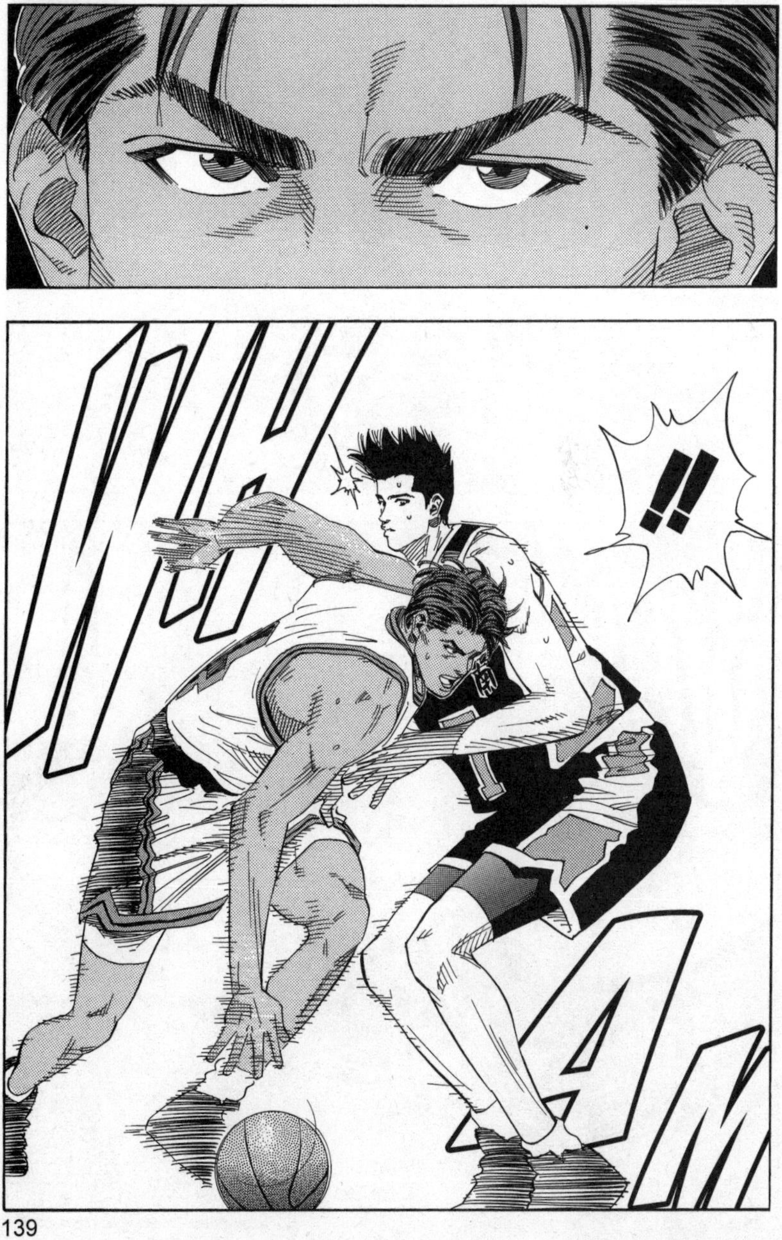
WHAM
!!

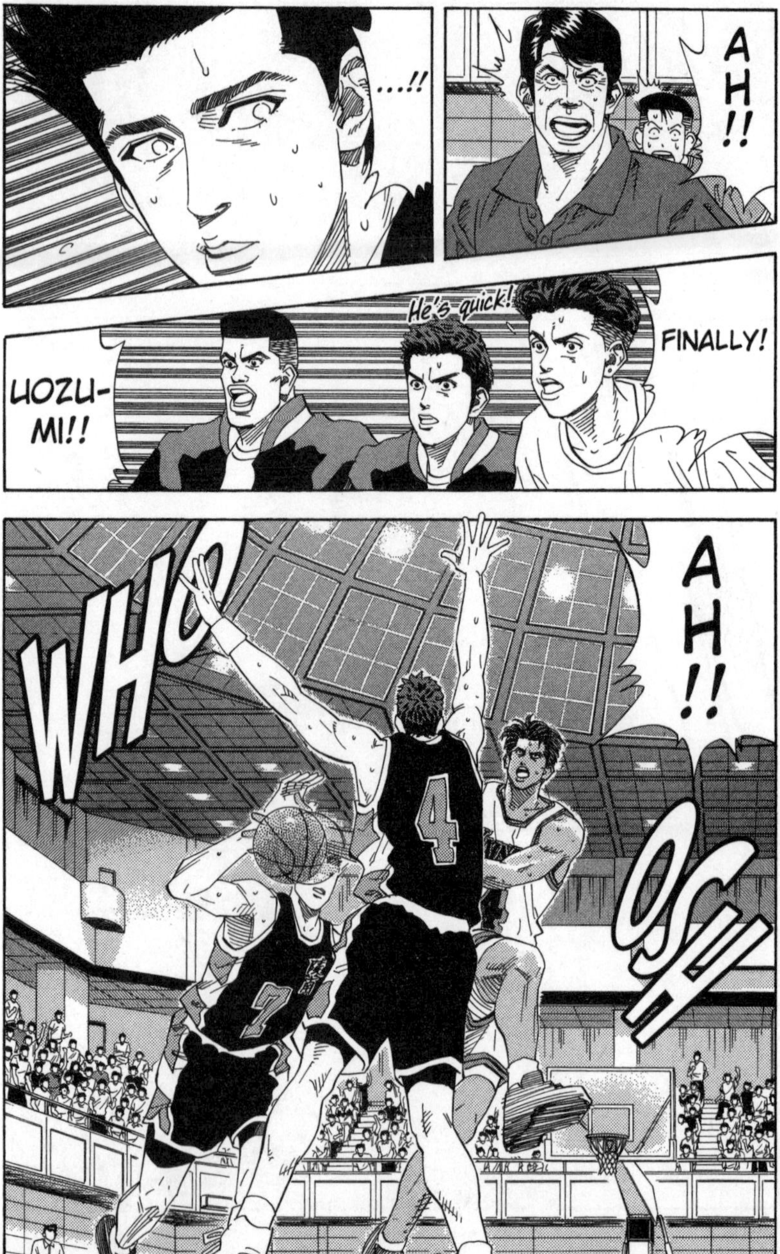
AH!!
...!!
FINALLY!
He's quick!
UOZUMI!!
AH!!
WHOOSH

READ THIS WAY

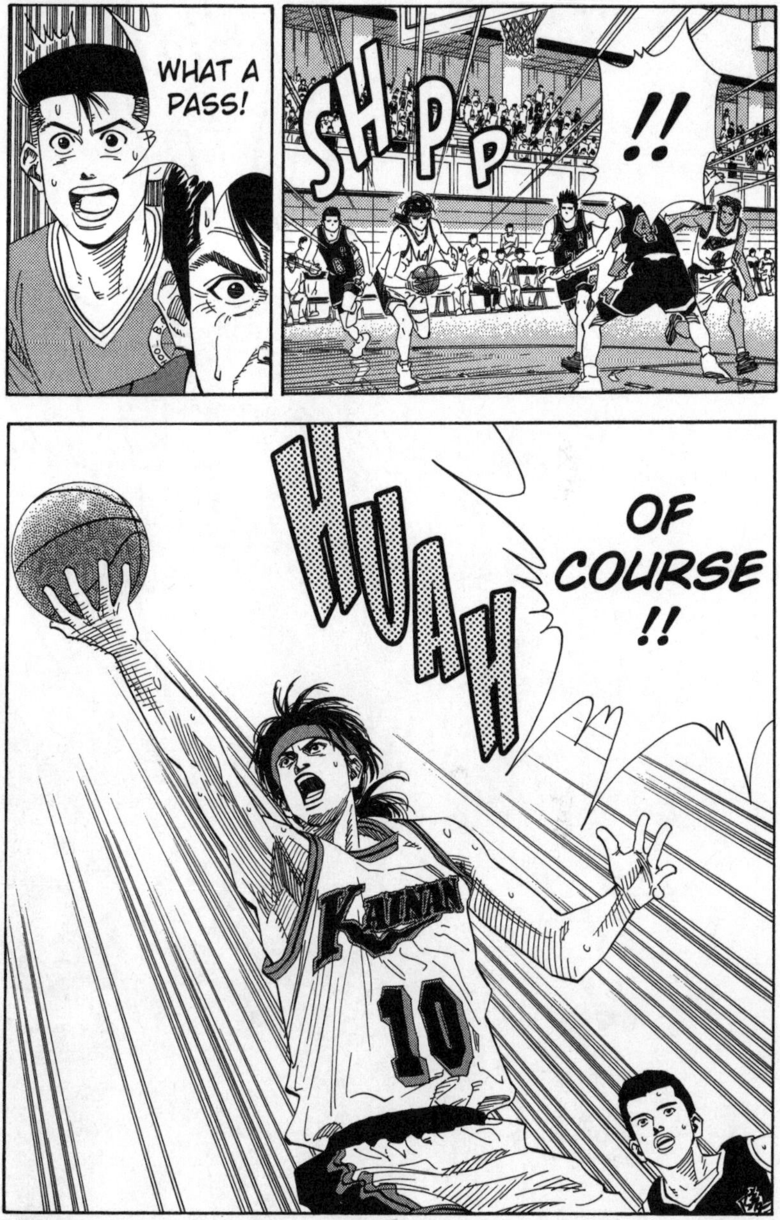
SHPP
!!
WHAT A PASS!
HUAH
OF COURSE!!

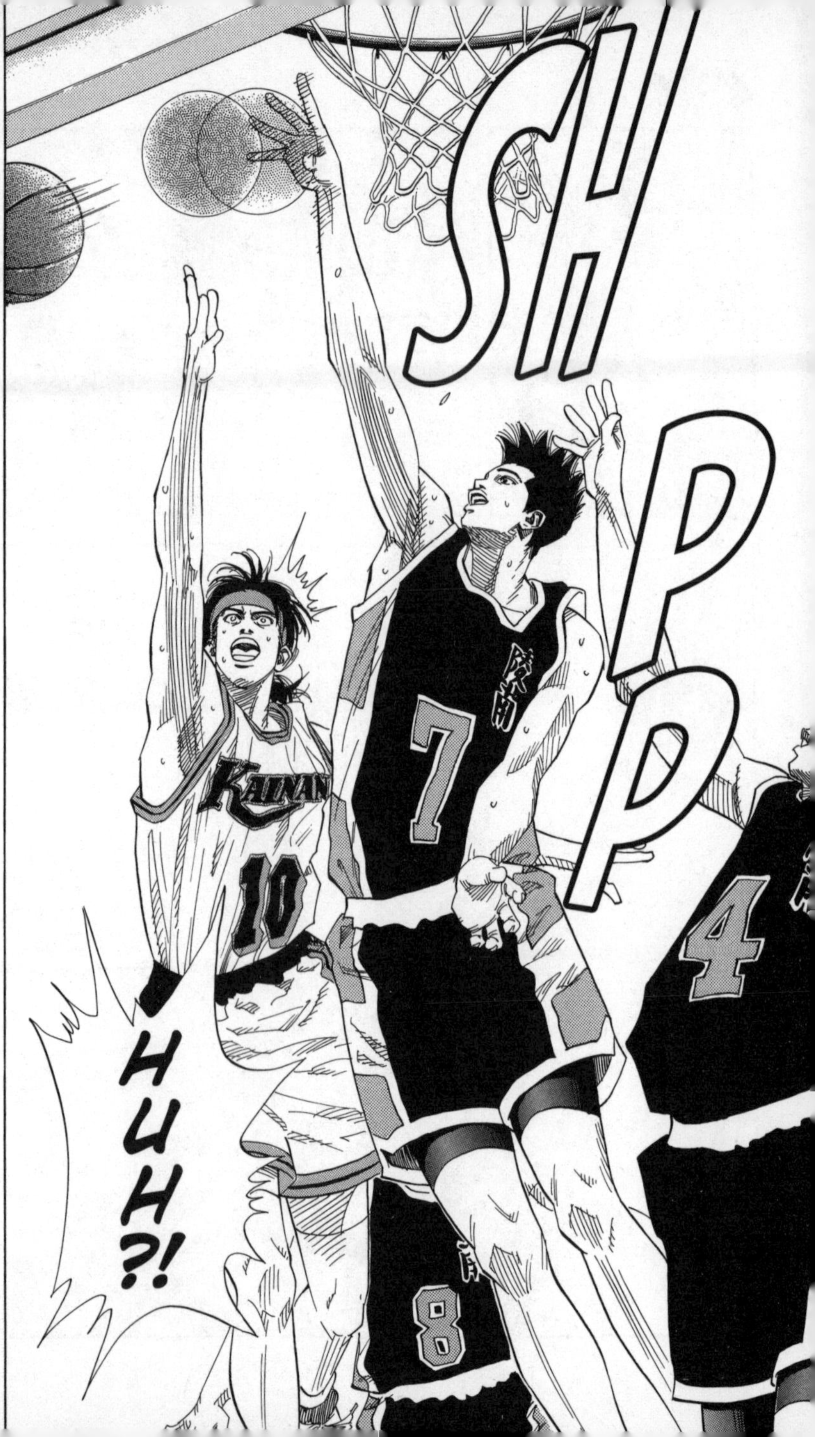
SHPP
HUH?!

READ THIS WAY

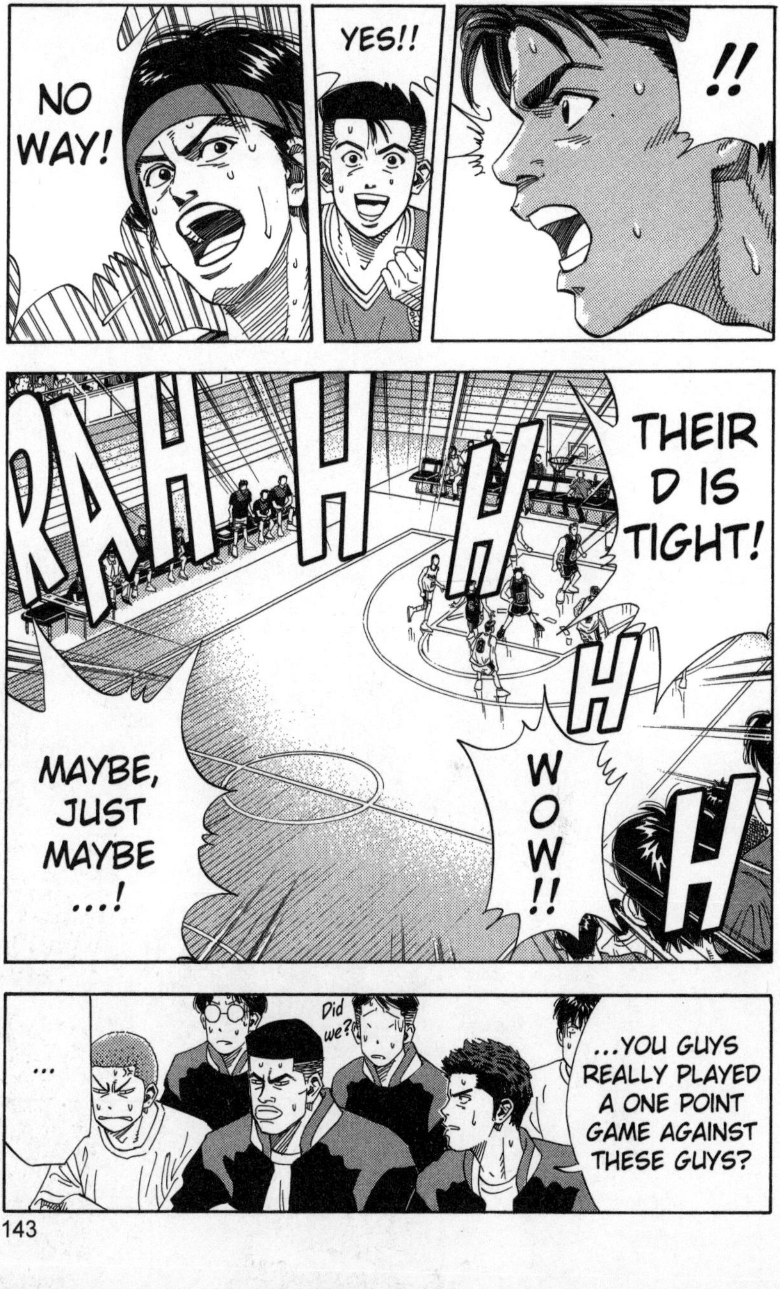
!!
YES!!
NO WAY!
THEIR D IS TIGHT!
RAHHHHHH
WOW!!
MAYBE, JUST MAYBE ...!
...YOU GUYS REALLY PLAYED A ONE POINT GAME AGAINST THESE GUYS?
Did we?
...

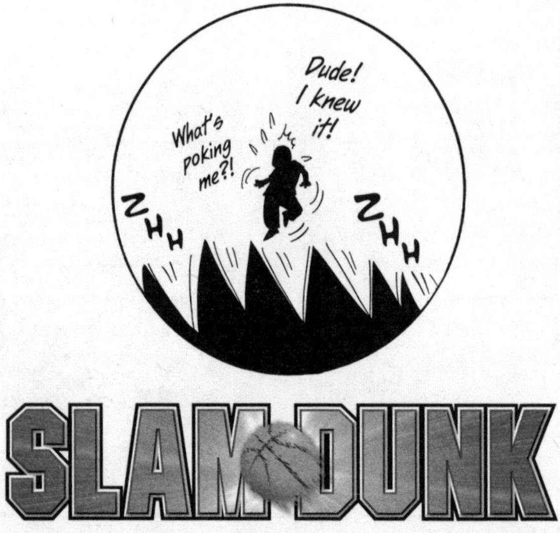
Dude! I knew it!
What's poking me?!
ZHH
ZHH

SLAM DUNK

#142 FUKUDA'S SECRET

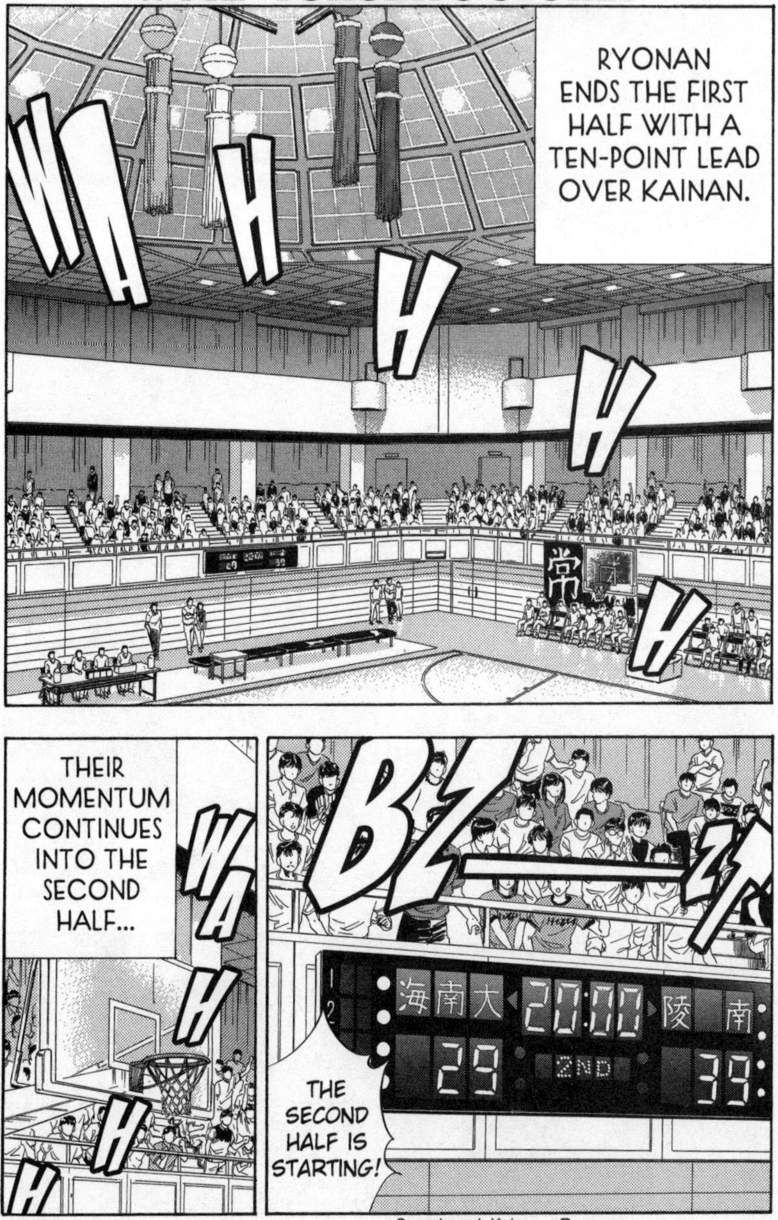

RYONAN ENDS THE FIRST HALF WITH A TEN-POINT LEAD OVER KAINAN.
WAAHHHH
BZZZT
海南大 20:00 陵南
29 2ND 39
THE SECOND HALF IS STARTING!
THEIR MOMENTUM CONTINUES INTO THE SECOND HALF...
WAHHHH

Scoreboard: Kainan Ryonan

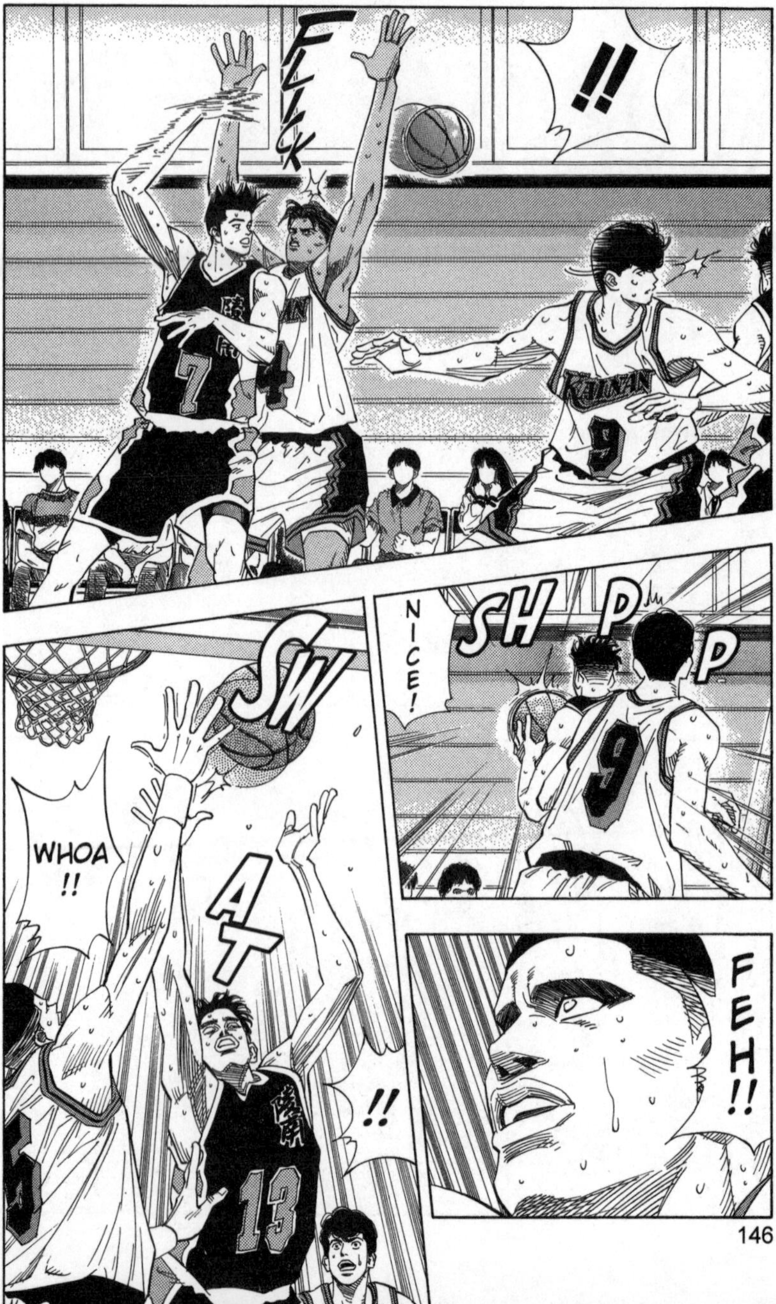
!!
FLICK
NICE!
SHPP
FEH!!
SWAT
!!
WHOA!!

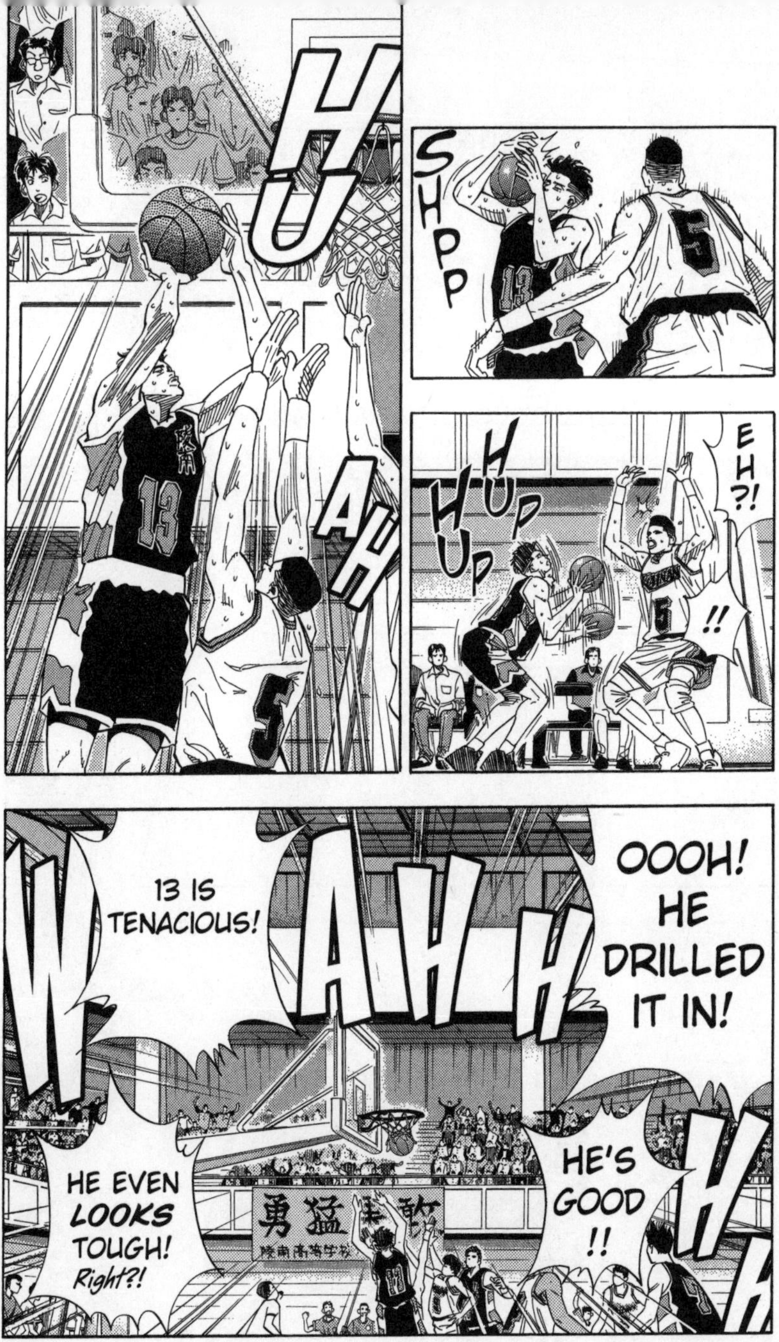

SHPP
HUP
HUP
EH?!
!!
HU
AH
OOOH! HE DRILLED IT IN!
WAHHH
13 IS TENACIOUS!
HE'S GOOD !!
HE EVEN **LOOKS** TOUGH! *Right?!*

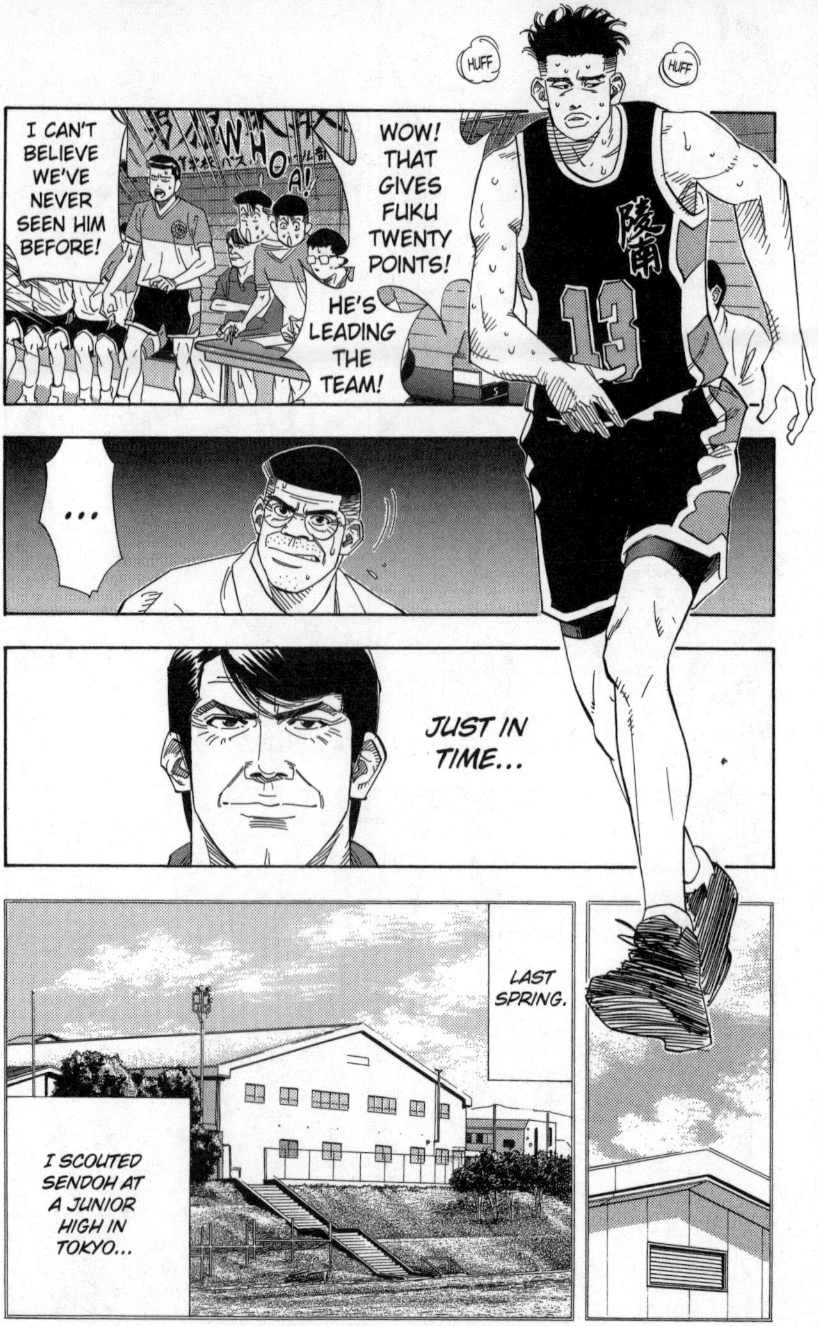
HUFF
HUFF
WOW! THAT GIVES FUKU TWENTY POINTS!
HE'S LEADING THE TEAM!
WHOA!
I CAN'T BELIEVE WE'VE NEVER SEEN HIM BEFORE!
...
JUST IN TIME...
LAST SPRING.
I SCOUTED SENDOH AT A JUNIOR HIGH IN TOKYO...

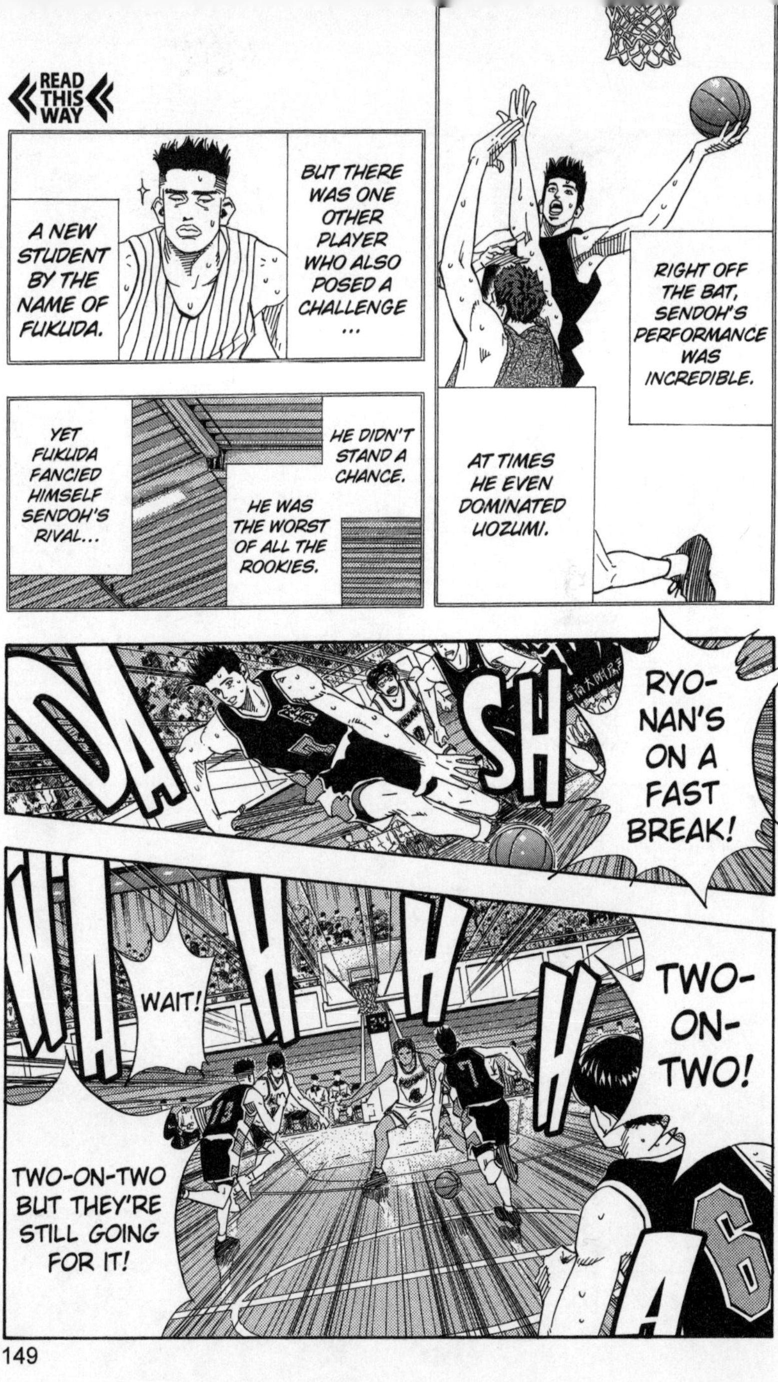
READ THIS WAY
RIGHT OFF THE BAT, SENDOH'S PERFORMANCE WAS INCREDIBLE.
AT TIMES HE EVEN DOMINATED UOZUMI.
BUT THERE WAS ONE OTHER PLAYER WHO ALSO POSED A CHALLENGE...
A NEW STUDENT BY THE NAME OF FUKUDA.
HE DIDN'T STAND A CHANCE.
HE WAS THE WORST OF ALL THE ROOKIES.
YET FUKUDA FANCIED HIMSELF SENDOH'S RIVAL...
DASH
RYO-NAN'S ON A FAST BREAK!
WAHHHH
TWO-ON-TWO!
WAIT!
TWO-ON-TWO BUT THEY'RE STILL GOING FOR IT!

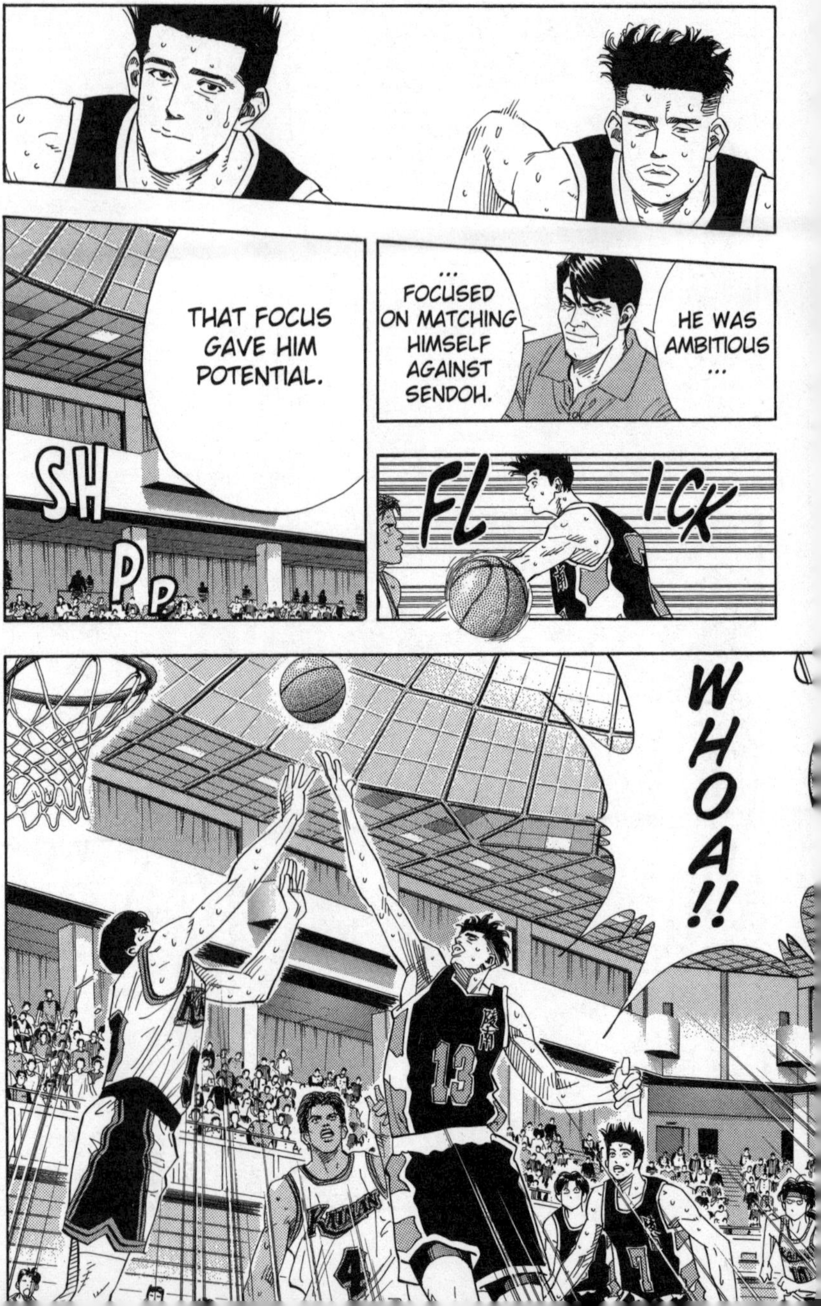
HE WAS AMBITIOUS ...
... FOCUSED ON MATCHING HIMSELF AGAINST SENDOH.
FLICK
THAT FOCUS GAVE HIM POTENTIAL.
SHPP
WHOA!!

READ THIS WAY

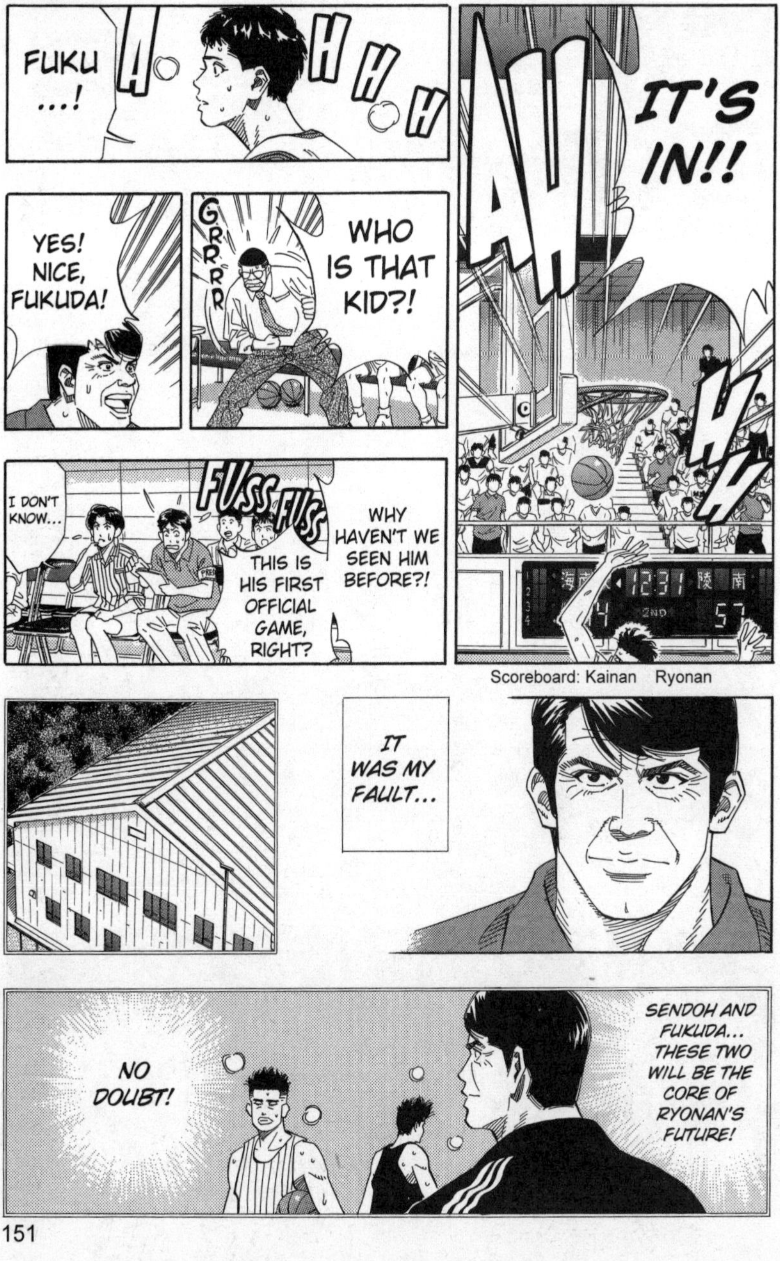

AH
IT'S IN!!
HH
FUKU ...!
HHHH
WHO IS THAT KID?!
GRRRR
YES! NICE, FUKUDA!
WHY HAVEN'T WE SEEN HIM BEFORE?!
THIS IS HIS FIRST OFFICIAL GAME, RIGHT?
FUSS FUSS
I DON'T KNOW...
Scoreboard: Kainan Ryonan
IT WAS MY FAULT...
SENDOH AND FUKUDA... THESE TWO WILL BE THE CORE OF RYONAN'S FUTURE!
NO DOUBT!

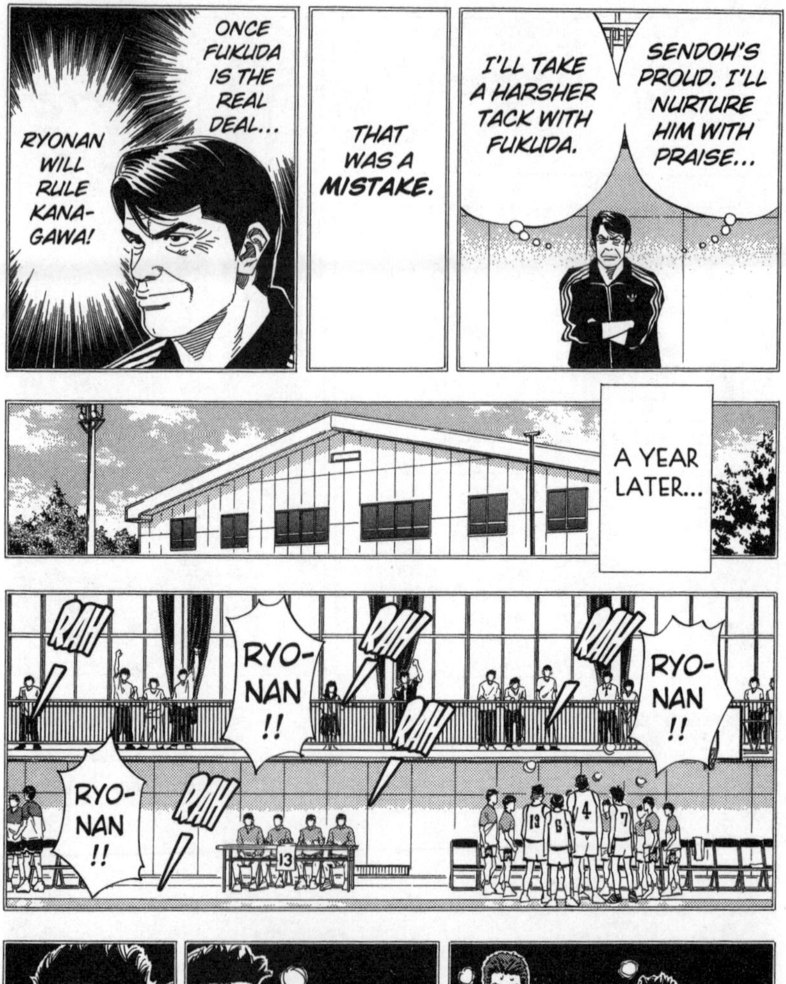
SENDOH'S PROUD. I'LL NURTURE HIM WITH PRAISE...
I'LL TAKE A HARSHER TACK WITH FUKUDA.
THAT WAS A MISTAKE.
ONCE FUKUDA IS THE REAL DEAL...
RYONAN WILL RULE KANA-GAWA!
A YEAR LATER...
RYO-NAN !!
RAH
RAH
RYO-NAN !!
RAH
RAH
RAH
RYO-NAN !!
13

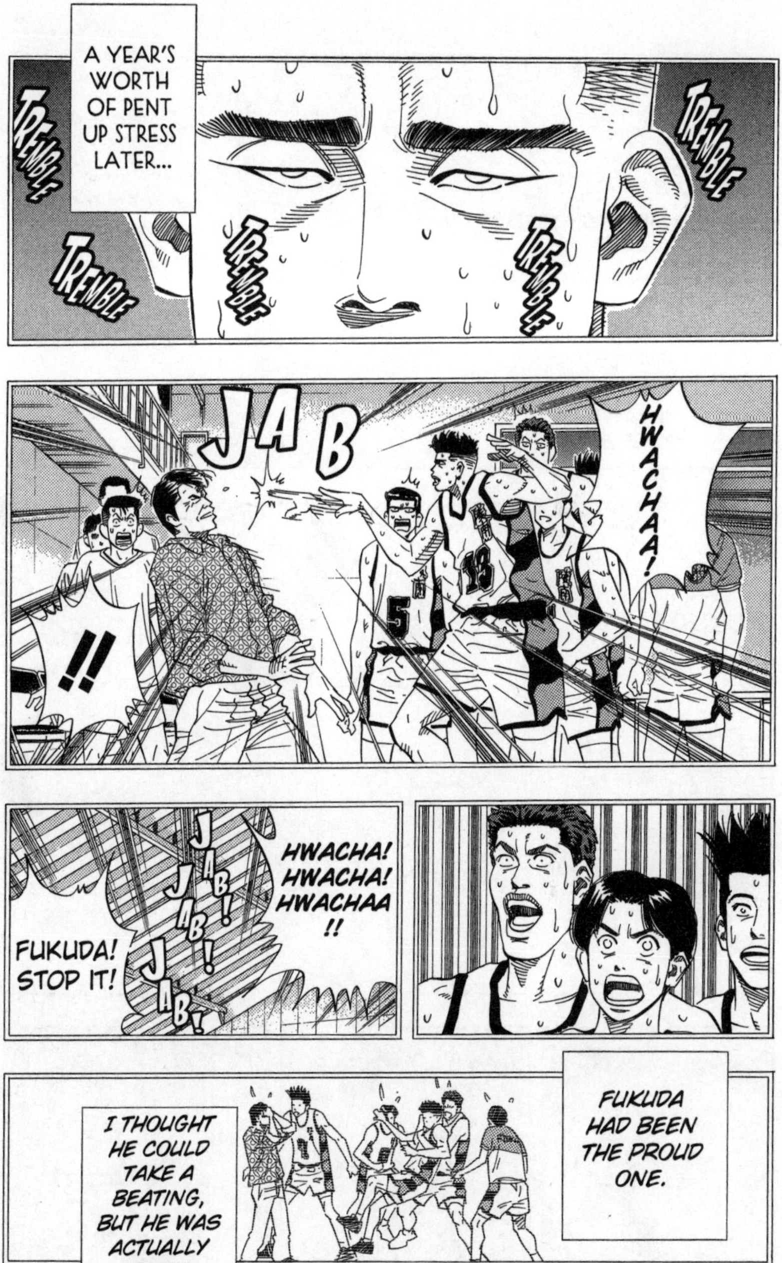

TREMBLE
A YEAR'S WORTH OF PENT UP STRESS LATER...
TREMBLE
TREMBLE
TREMBLE
TREMBLE
HWACHAA!
JAB
!!
HWACHA! HWACHA! HWACHAA !!
JAB!
JAB!
JAB!
FUKUDA! STOP IT!
FUKUDA HAD BEEN THE PROUD ONE.
I THOUGHT HE COULD TAKE A BEATING, BUT HE WAS ACTUALLY QUITE SENSITIVE.

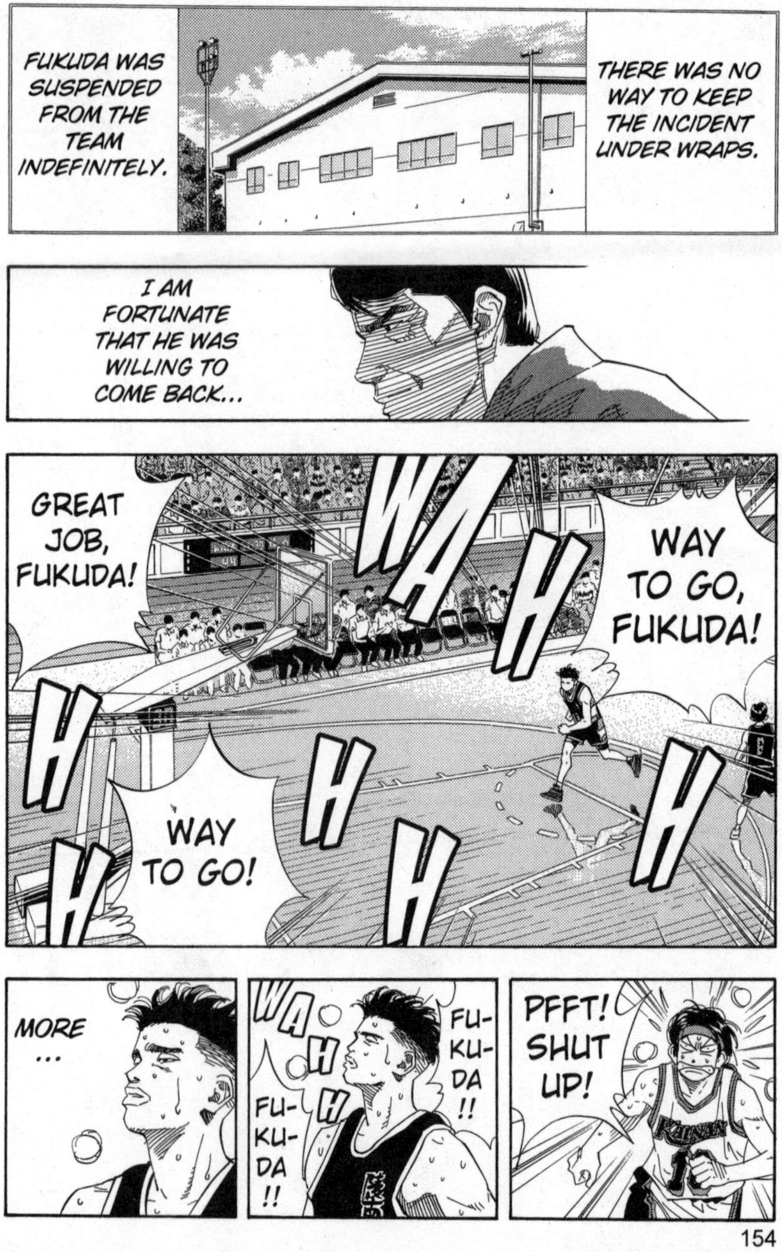
THERE WAS NO WAY TO KEEP THE INCIDENT UNDER WRAPS.
FUKUDA WAS SUSPENDED FROM THE TEAM INDEFINITELY.
I AM FORTUNATE THAT HE WAS WILLING TO COME BACK...
WAY TO GO, FUKUDA!
WAHHHHHHH
GREAT JOB, FUKUDA!
WAY TO GO!
PFFT! SHUT UP!
FU-KU-DA!!
WAHH
FU-KU-DA!!
MORE ...

READ THIS WAY

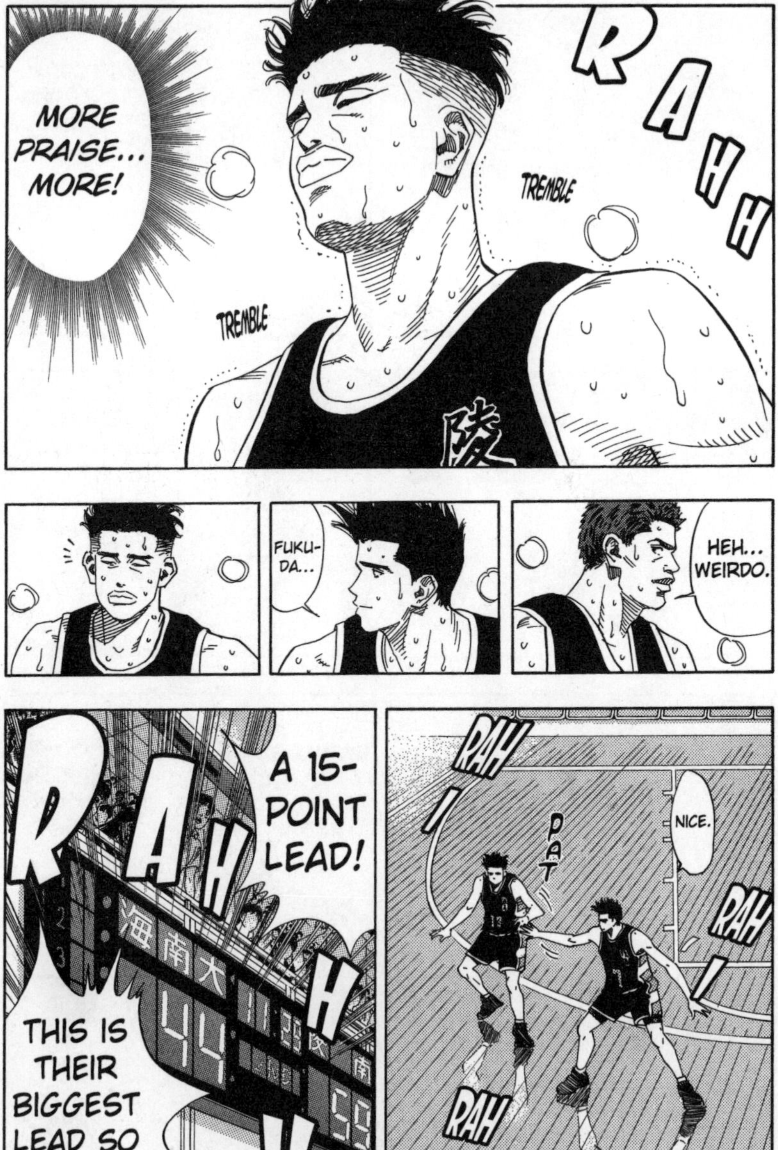
MORE PRAISE... MORE!
RAHH
TREMBLE
TREMBLE
HEH... WEIRDO.
FUKU-DA...
RAH!
PAT
NICE.
RAH!
RAH!
RAHHH
A 15-POINT LEAD!
THIS IS THEIR BIGGEST LEAD SO FAR!

Scoreboard: Kainan Ryonan

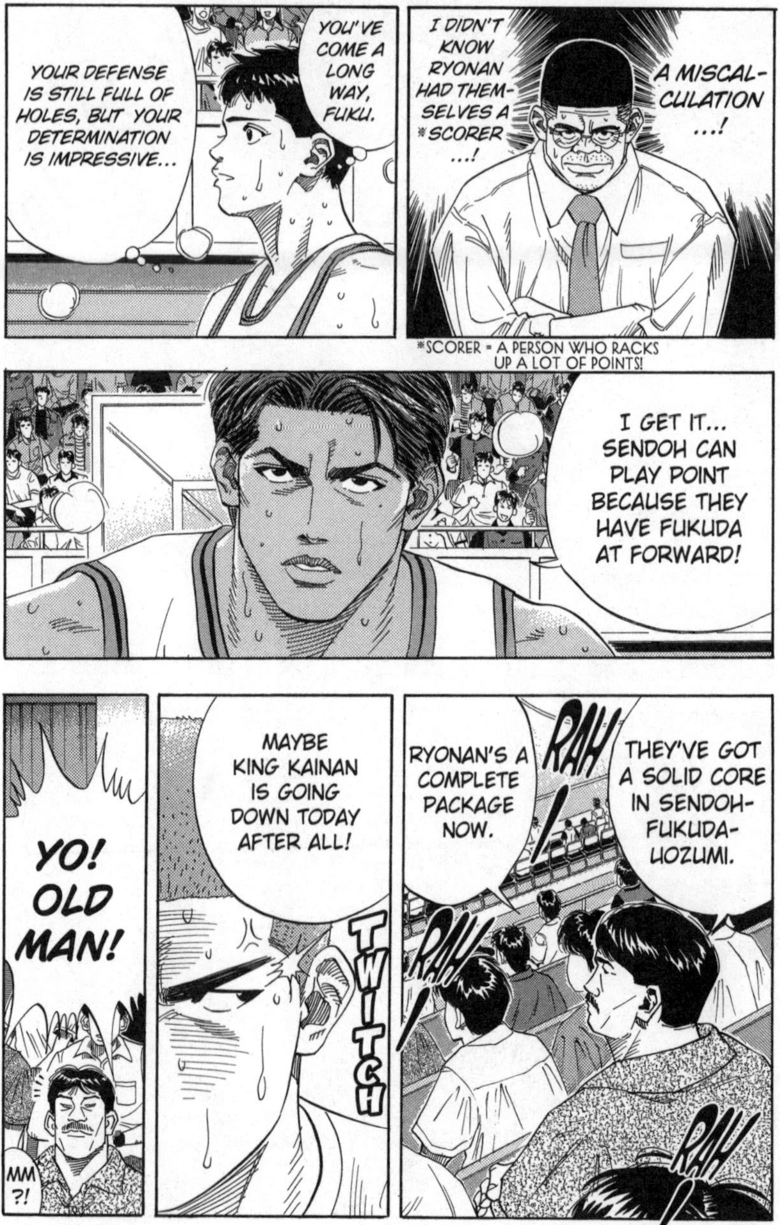
A MISCALCULATION...!
I DIDN'T KNOW RYONAN HAD THEMSELVES A *SCORER ...!
YOU'VE COME A LONG WAY, FUKU.
YOUR DEFENSE IS STILL FULL OF HOLES, BUT YOUR DETERMINATION IS IMPRESSIVE...
*SCORER = A PERSON WHO RACKS UP A LOT OF POINTS!
I GET IT... SENDOH CAN PLAY POINT BECAUSE THEY HAVE FUKUDA AT FORWARD!
THEY'VE GOT A SOLID CORE IN SENDOH-FUKUDA-UOZUMI.
RAH!
RYONAN'S A COMPLETE PACKAGE NOW.
RAH!
RAH!
MAYBE KING KAINAN IS GOING DOWN TODAY AFTER ALL!
TWITCH
YO! OLD MAN!
MM?!

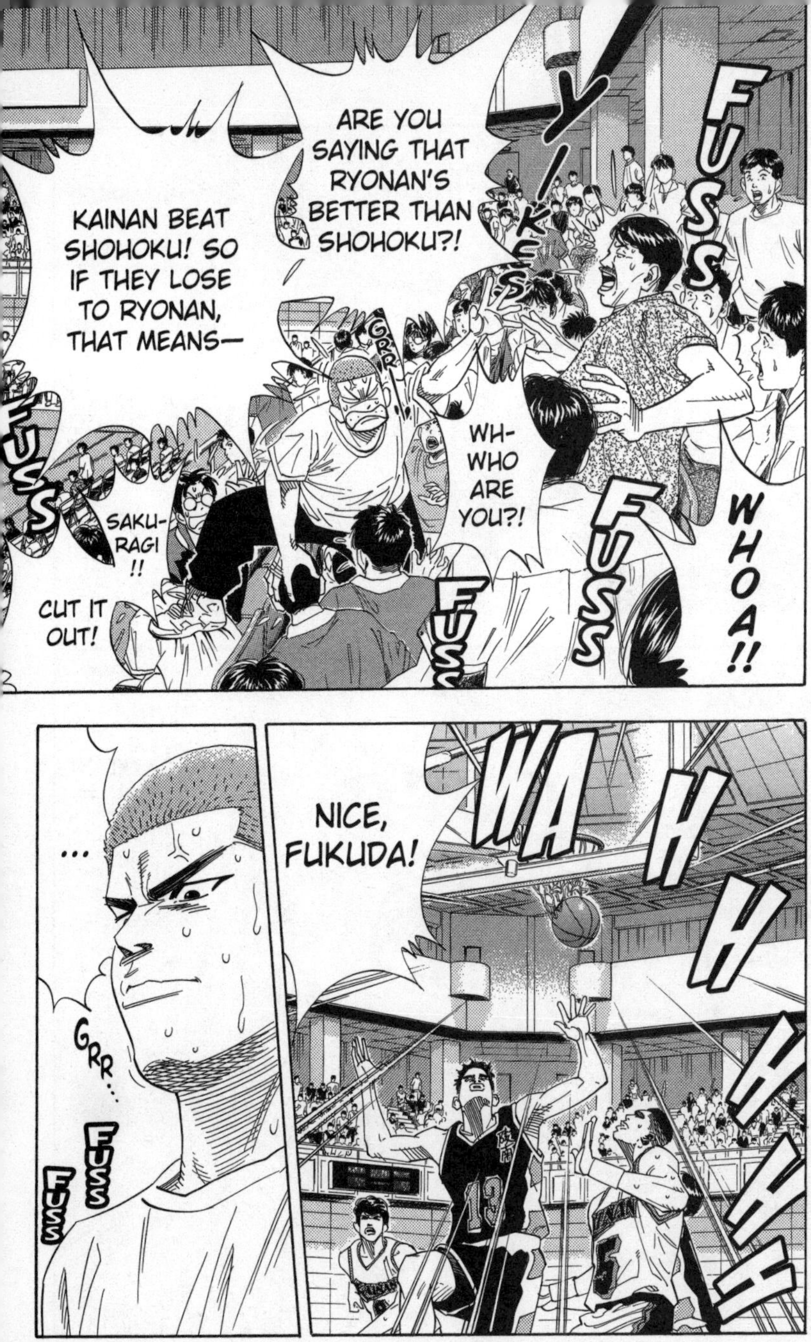

YIKES
FUSS
ARE YOU SAYING THAT RYONAN'S BETTER THAN SHOHOKU?!
KAINAN BEAT SHOHOKU! SO IF THEY LOSE TO RYONAN, THAT MEANS—
GRR
WH- WHO ARE YOU?!
WHOA!!
FUSS
FUSS
SAKURAGI!!
CUT IT OUT!
FUSS
WAHHHHHH
NICE, FUKUDA!
...
GRR...
FUSS
FUSS

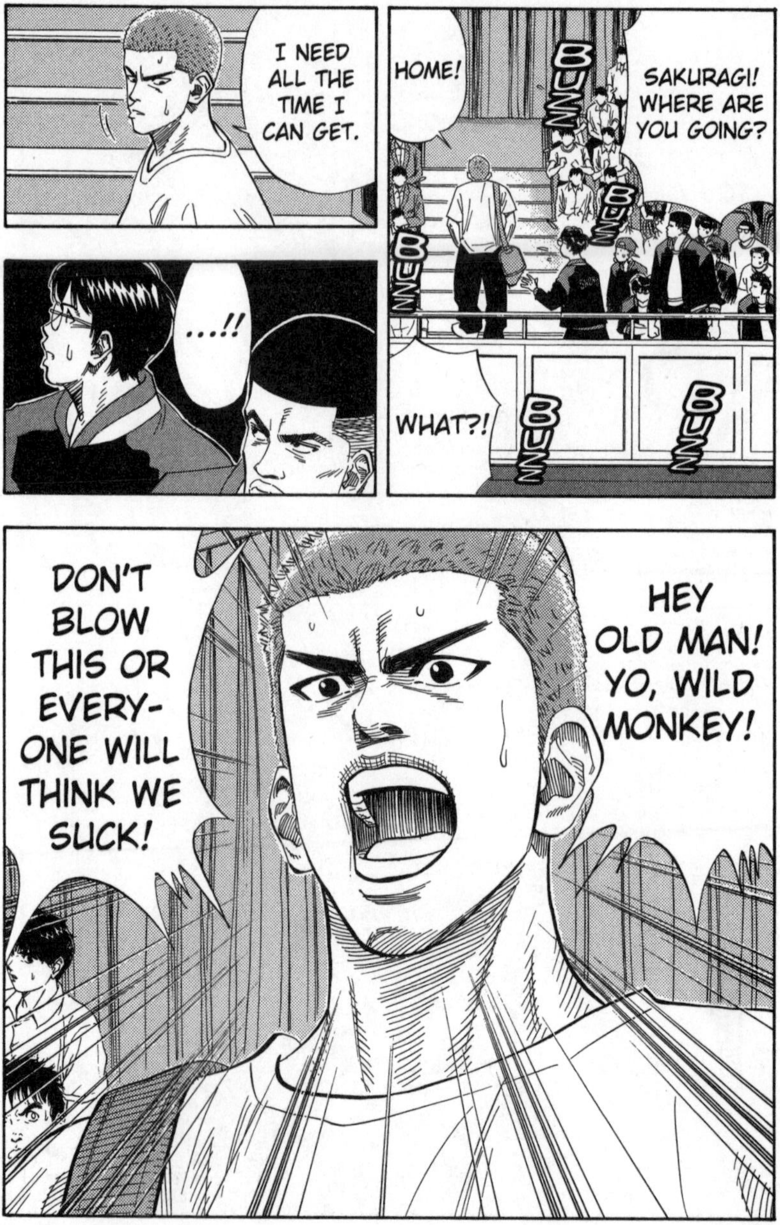
SAKURAGI! WHERE ARE YOU GOING?
HOME!
BUZZ
BUZZ
BUZZ
WHAT?!
BUZZ
BUZZ
I NEED ALL THE TIME I CAN GET.
...!!
HEY OLD MAN! YO, WILD MONKEY!
DON'T BLOW THIS OR EVERY-ONE WILL THINK WE SUCK!

READ THIS WAY

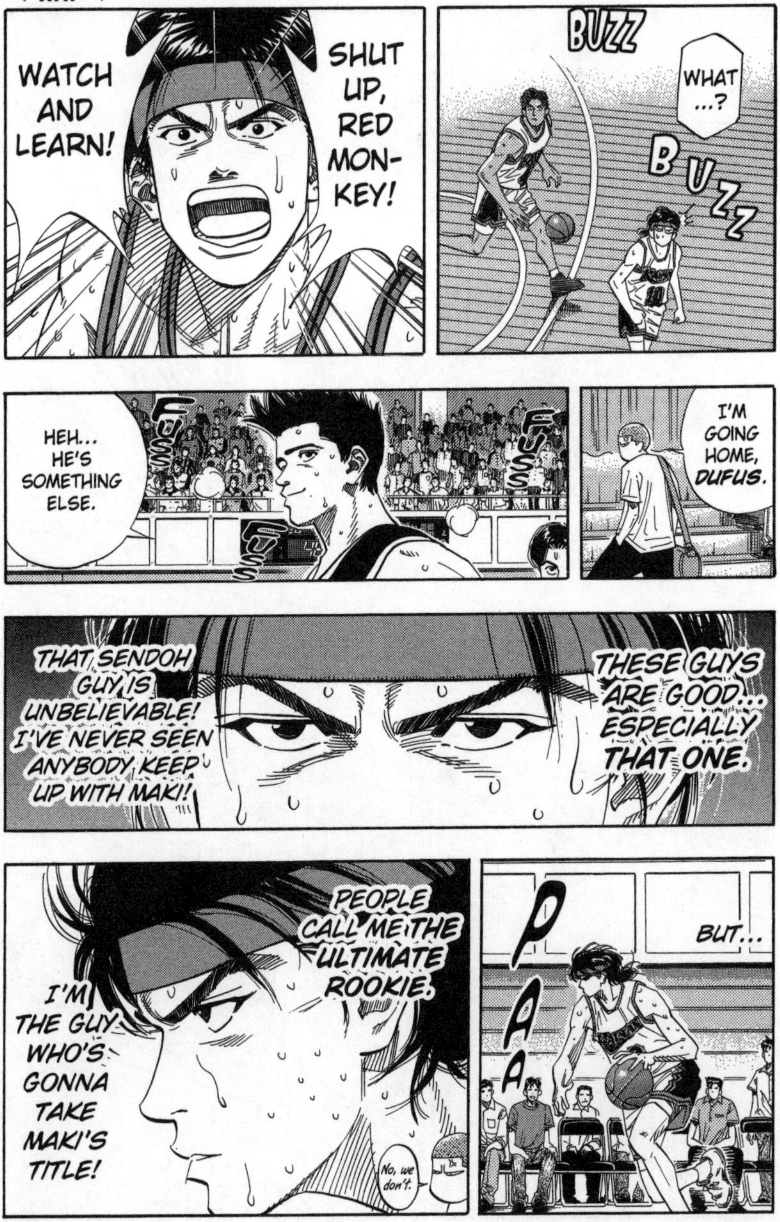

BUZZ
WHAT ...?
BUZZ
SHUT UP, RED MONKEY!
WATCH AND LEARN!
I'M GOING HOME, DUFUS.
FUSS
HEH... HE'S SOMETHING ELSE.
FUSS
FUSS
THESE GUYS ARE GOOD... ESPECIALLY THAT ONE.
THAT SENDOH GUY IS UNBELIEVABLE! I'VE NEVER SEEN ANYBODY KEEP UP WITH MAKI!
BUT...
PAAA
PEOPLE CALL ME THE ULTIMATE ROOKIE.
I'M THE GUY WHO'S GONNA TAKE MAKI'S TITLE!
No, we don't.

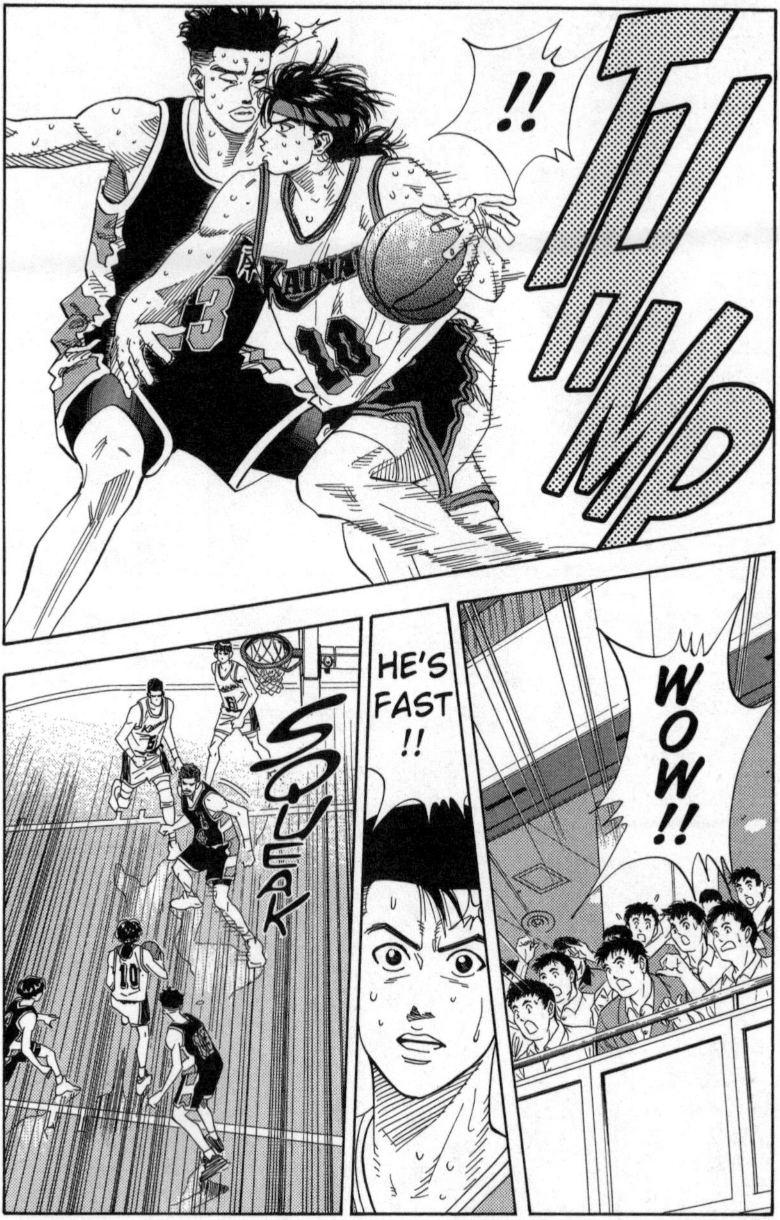
THUMP
!!
WOW!!
HE'S FAST !!
SQUEAK

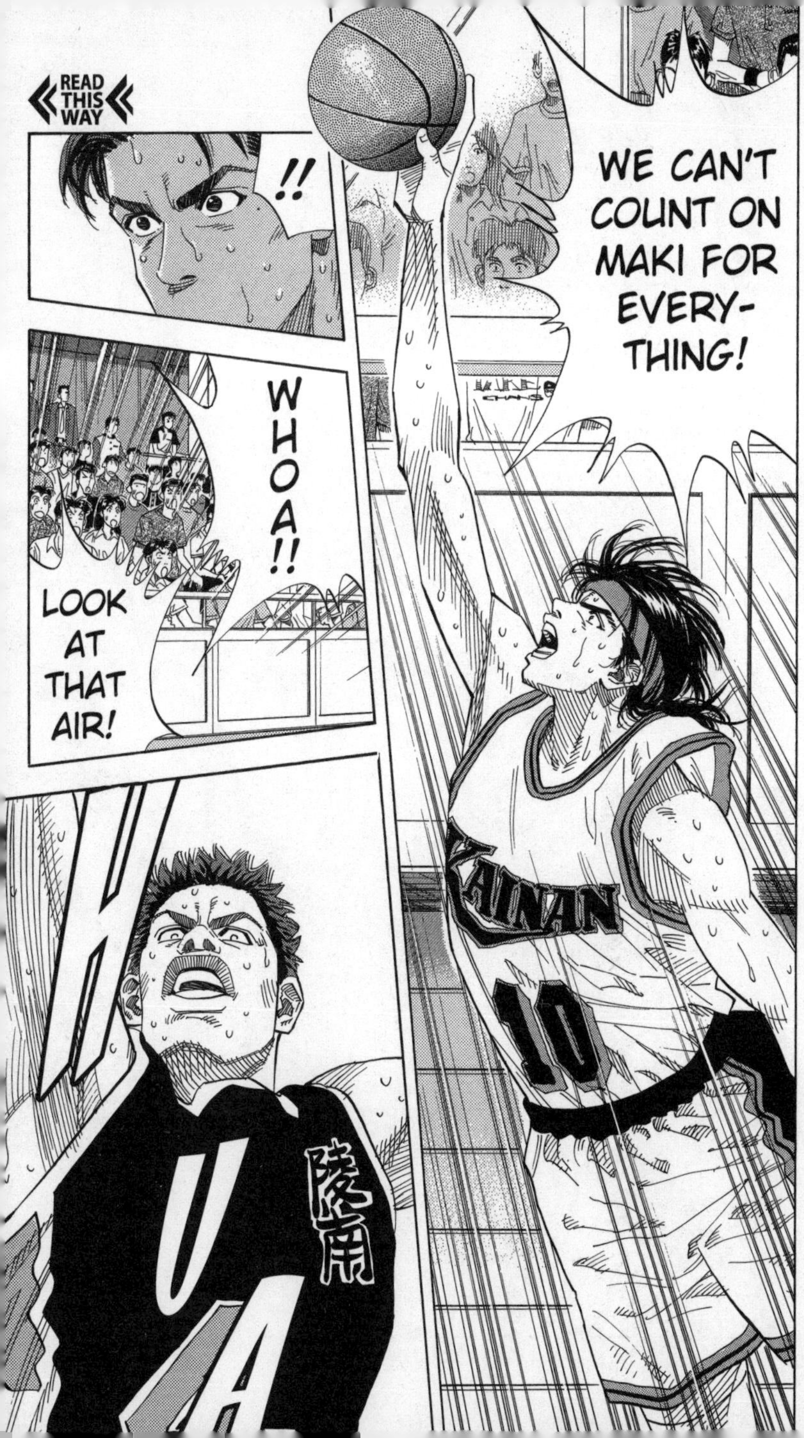
READ THIS WAY
WE CAN'T COUNT ON MAKI FOR EVERY-THING!
!!
WHOA!!
LOOK AT THAT AIR!
KAINAN
10
陵南

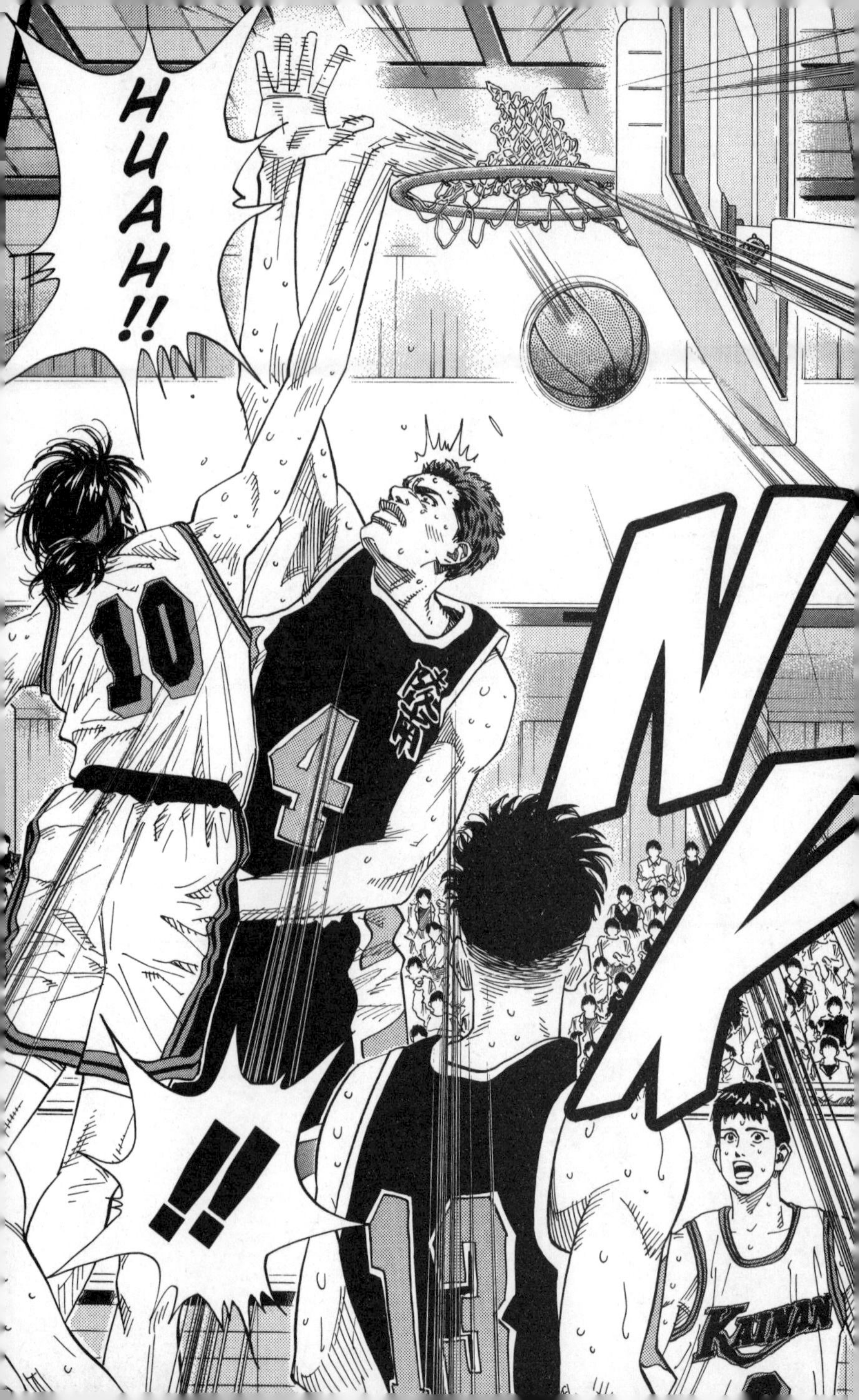
HUAH!!
NK
KAINAN
!!

READ THIS WAY

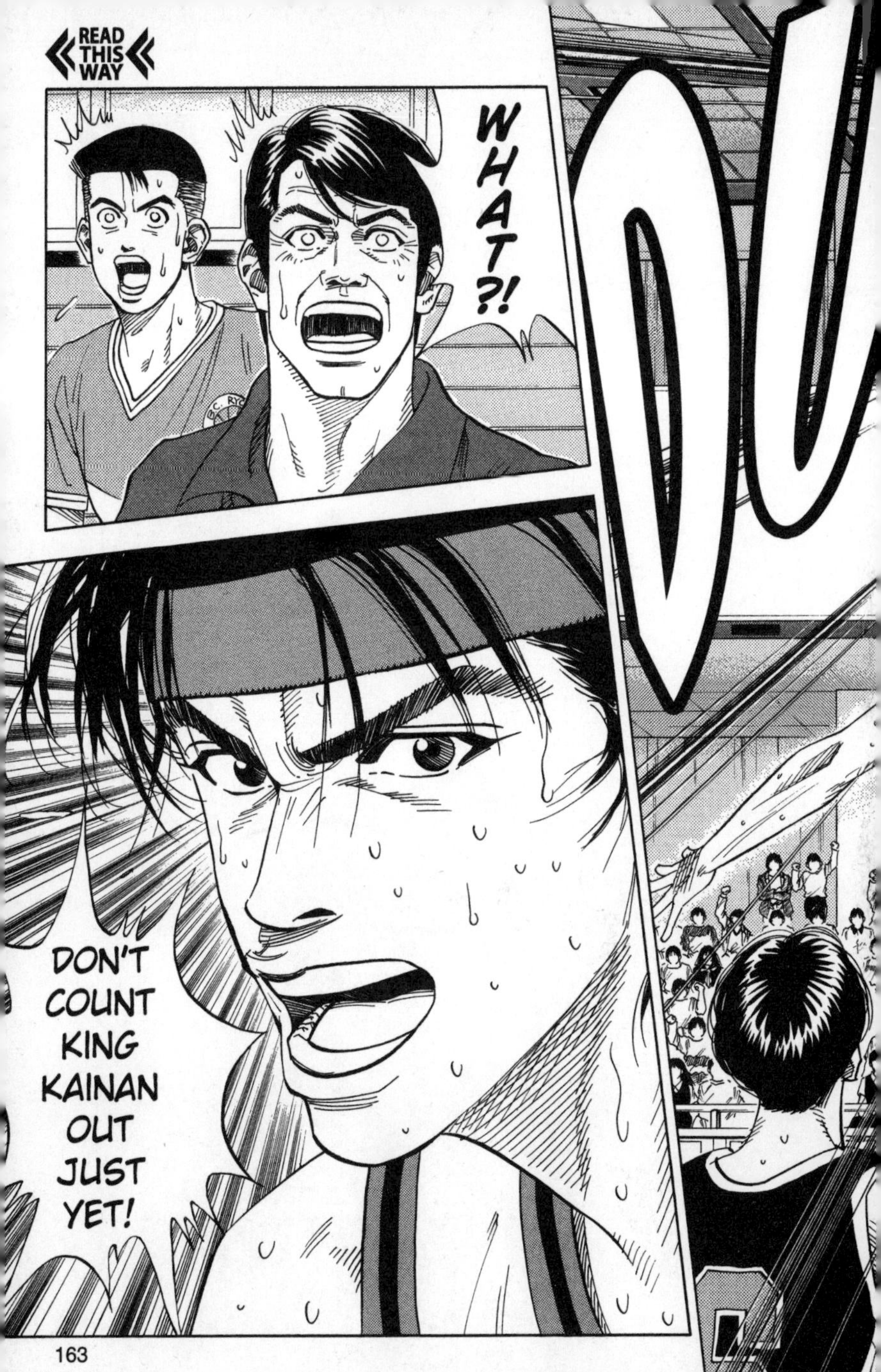
WHAT?!
DON'T COUNT KING KAINAN OUT JUST YET!

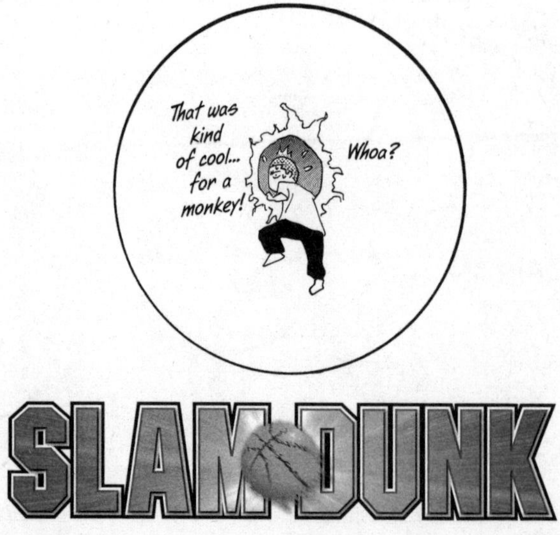
Whoa?
That was kind of cool... for a monkey!

SLAM DUNK

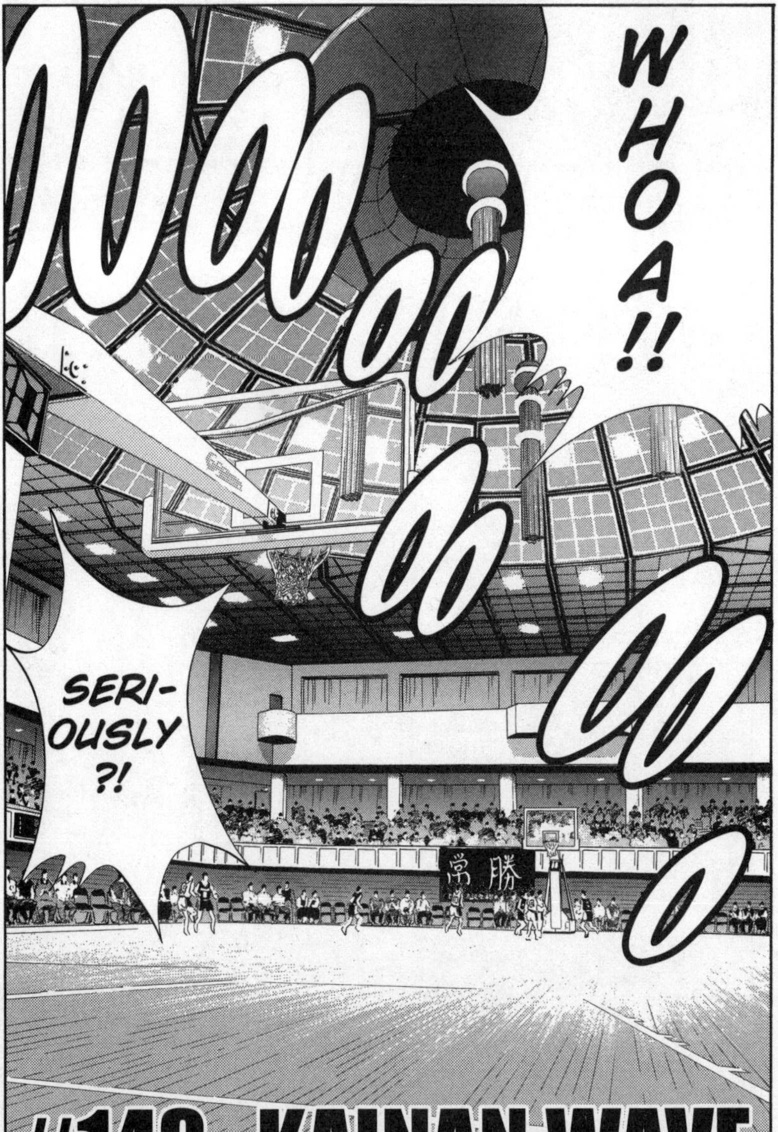
WHOA!!
OOOOOOOOOOOOOOOOO
SERI-OUSLY?!
常勝

#143 KAINAN WAVE

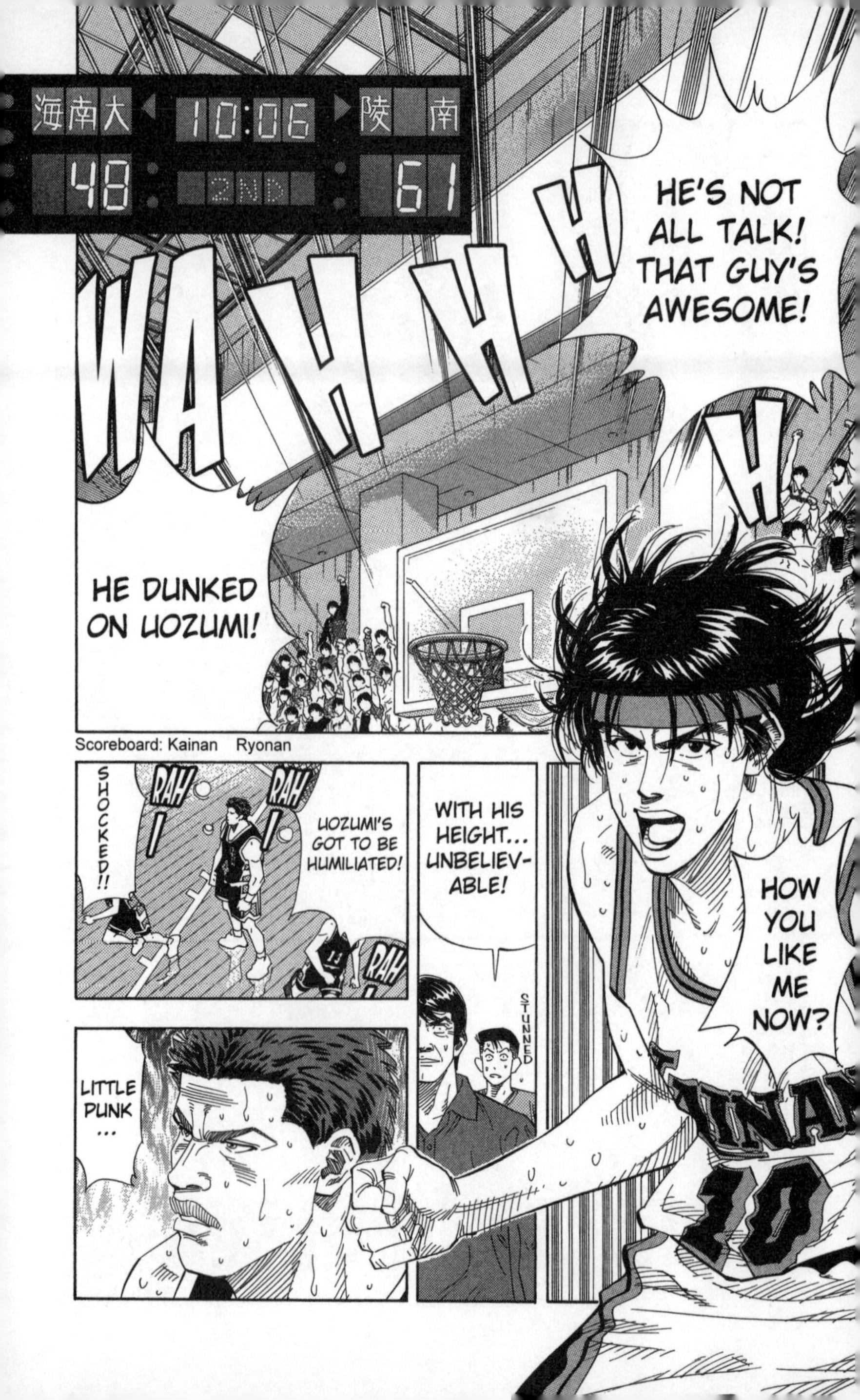
海南大
10:06
陵南
48
2ND
61
WAHHHH
HE'S NOT ALL TALK! THAT GUY'S AWESOME!
HE DUNKED ON UOZUMI!
HOW YOU LIKE ME NOW?
WITH HIS HEIGHT... UNBELIEVABLE!
STUNNED
RAH
RAH
SHOCKED!!
UOZUMI'S GOT TO BE HUMILIATED!
RAH
LITTLE PUNK...
Scoreboard: Kainan Ryonan

READ THIS WAY

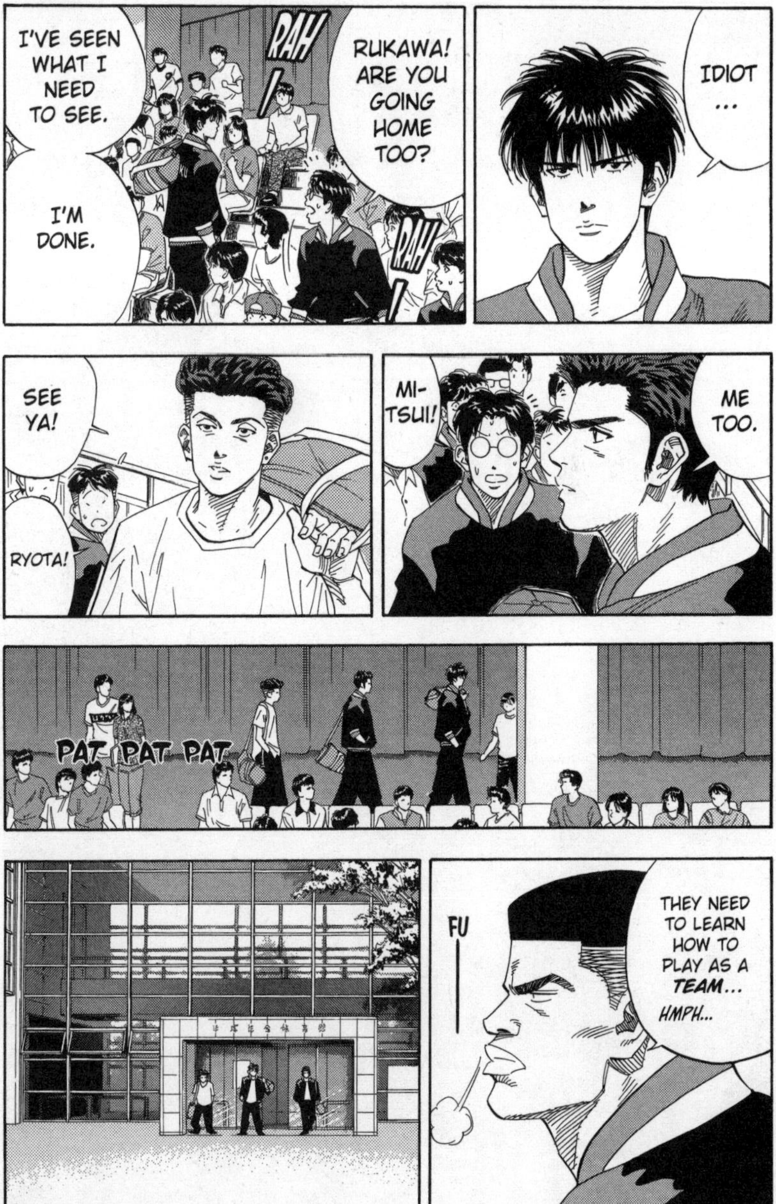
IDIOT ...
RUKAWA! ARE YOU GOING HOME TOO?
RAH!
I'VE SEEN WHAT I NEED TO SEE.
I'M DONE.
RAH!
ME TOO.
MI-TSUI!
SEE YA!
RYOTA!
PAT PAT PAT
THEY NEED TO LEARN HOW TO PLAY AS A *TEAM*...
FU—
HMPH...

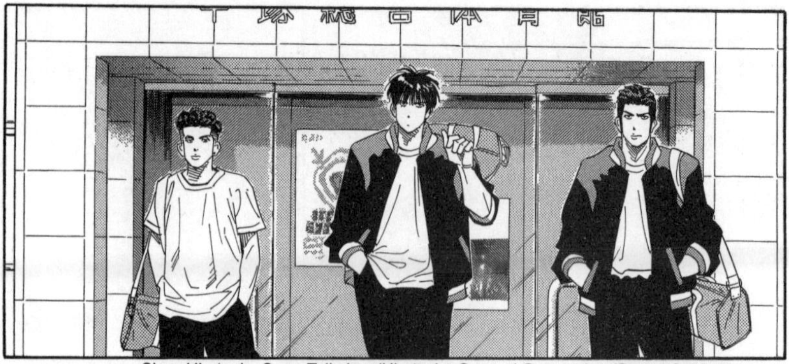

Sign: *Hiratsuka Sogo Taikukan* (Hiratsuka General Gymnasium/Sports Center)

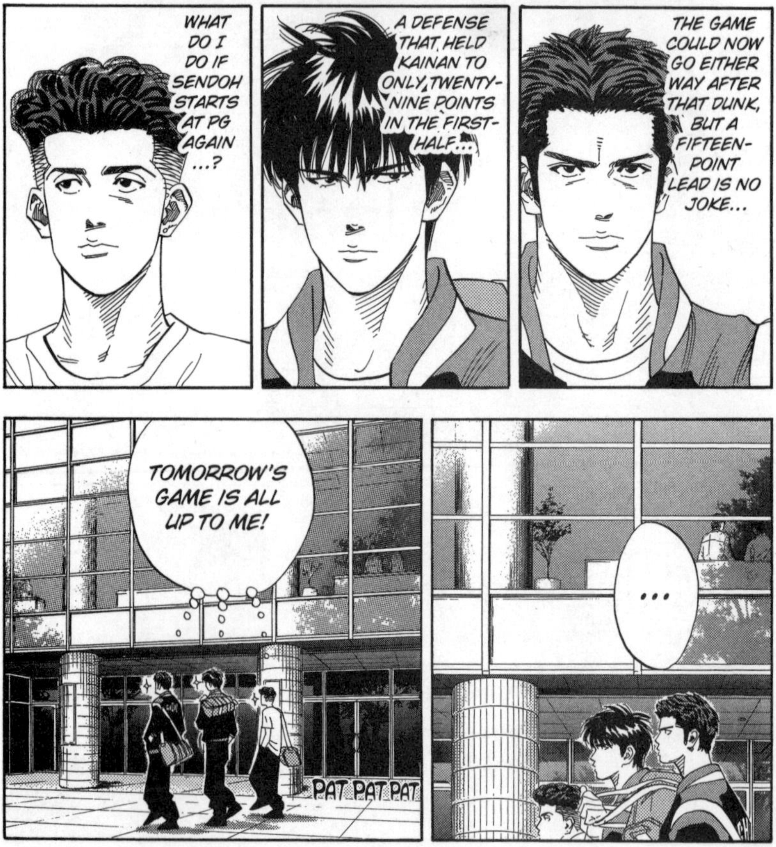
THE GAME COULD NOW GO EITHER WAY AFTER THAT DUNK, BUT A FIFTEEN-POINT LEAD IS NO JOKE...
A DEFENSE THAT HELD KAINAN TO ONLY TWENTY-NINE POINTS IN THE FIRST-HALF...
WHAT DO I DO IF SENDOH STARTS AT PG AGAIN...?
...
TOMORROW'S GAME IS ALL UP TO ME!
PAT PAT PAT

READ THIS WAY

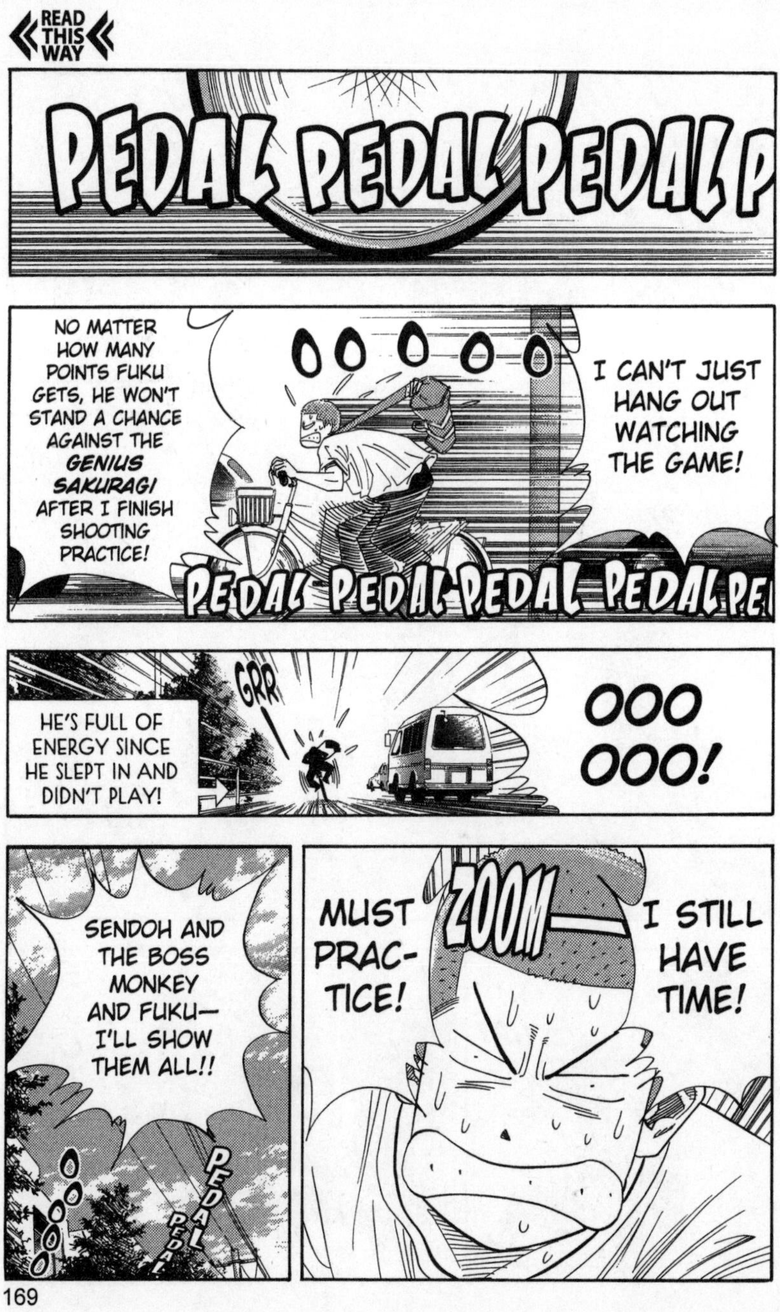

PEDAL PEDAL PEDAL P
I CAN'T JUST HANG OUT WATCHING THE GAME!
OOOOO
NO MATTER HOW MANY POINTS FUKU GETS, HE WON'T STAND A CHANCE AGAINST THE *GENIUS SAKURAGI* AFTER I FINISH SHOOTING PRACTICE!
PEDAL PEDAL PEDAL PEDAL PE
OOO OOO!
GRR
HE'S FULL OF ENERGY SINCE HE SLEPT IN AND DIDN'T PLAY!
I STILL HAVE TIME!
ZOOM
MUST PRAC-TICE!
SENDOH AND THE BOSS MONKEY AND FUKU— I'LL SHOW THEM ALL!!
PEDAL PEDAL PEDAL
OOOO

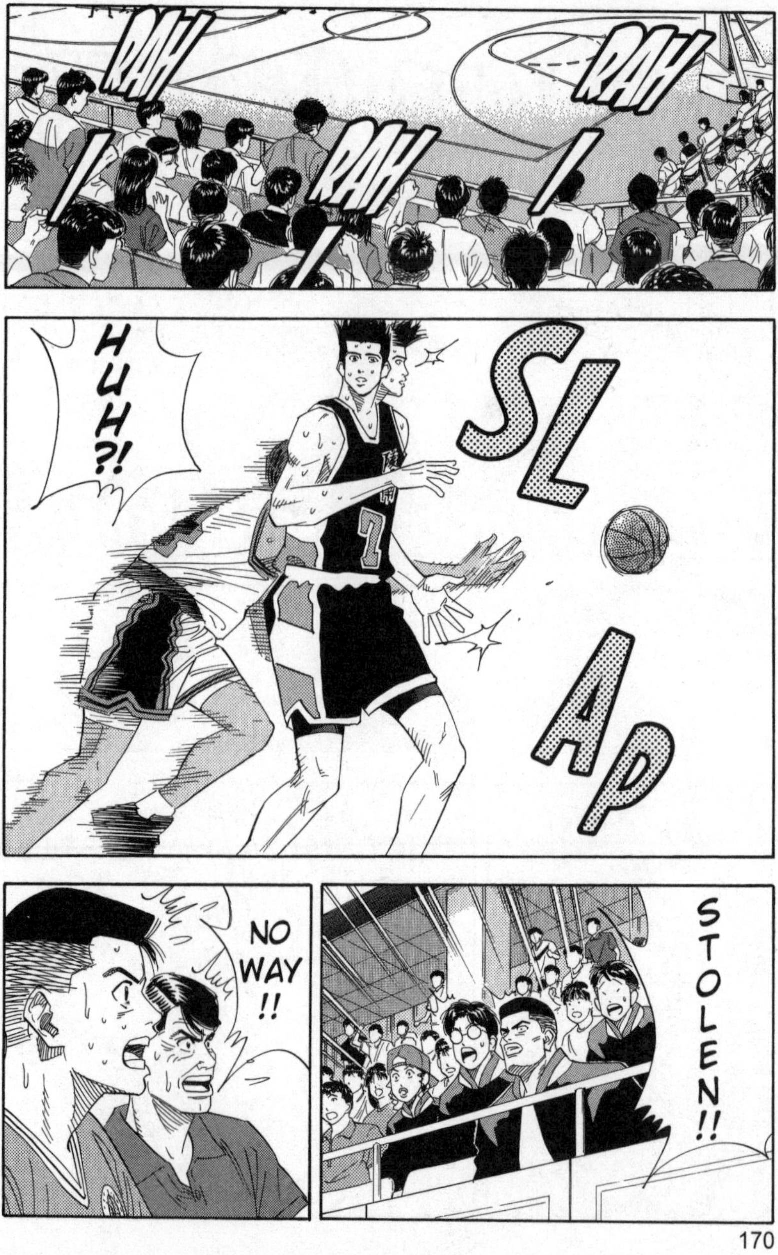
RAH
RAH
RAH
SLAP
HUH?!
STOLEN!!
NO WAY!!

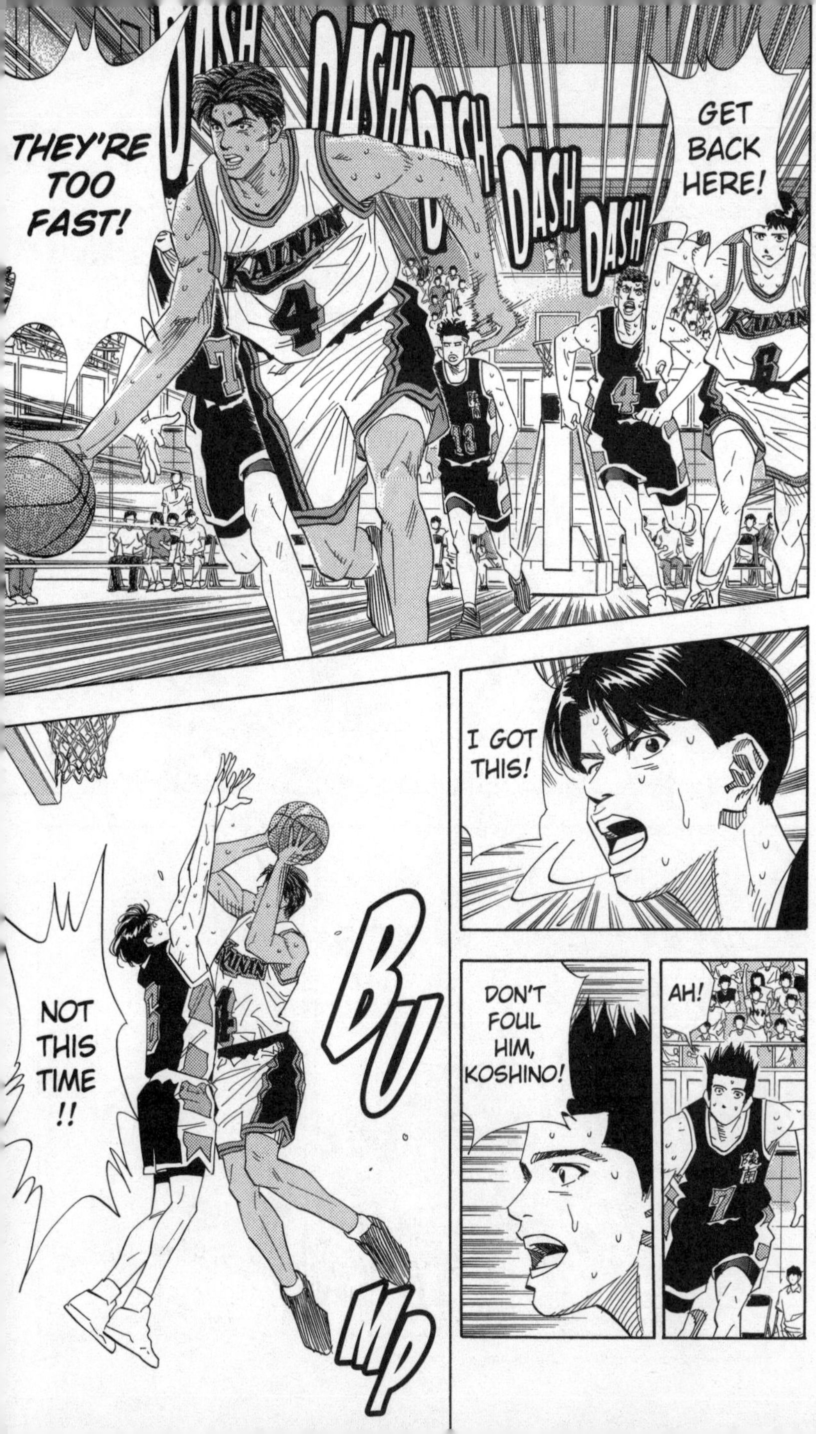
GET BACK HERE!
DASH DASH DASH DASH DASH
THEY'RE TOO FAST!
I GOT THIS!
AH!
DON'T FOUL HIM, KOSHINO!
BUMP
NOT THIS TIME !!

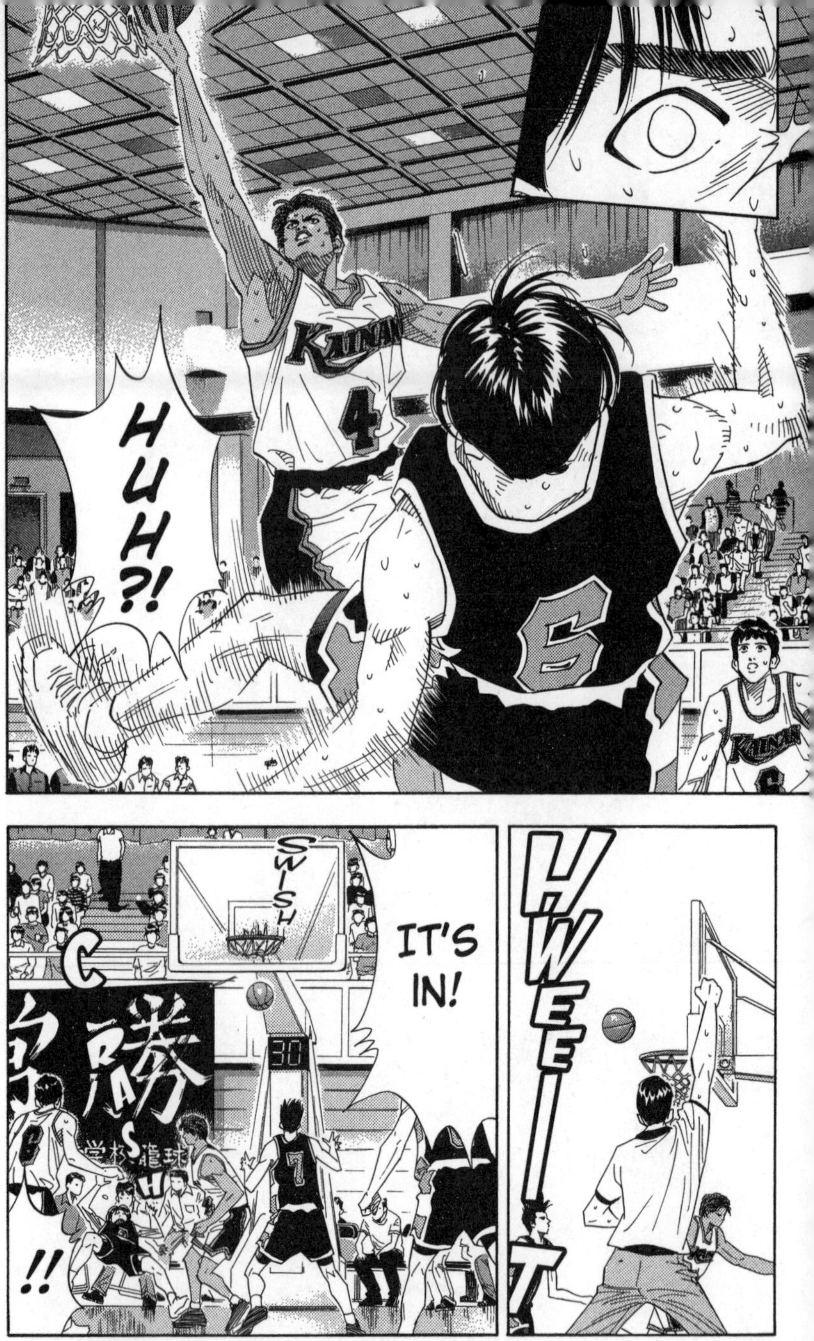
HUH?!
HWEEET
SWISH
IT'S IN!
!!

Banner: *Josho* (ever victorious)
Kainan Dai Fuzoku High School Basketball Team

READ THIS WAY

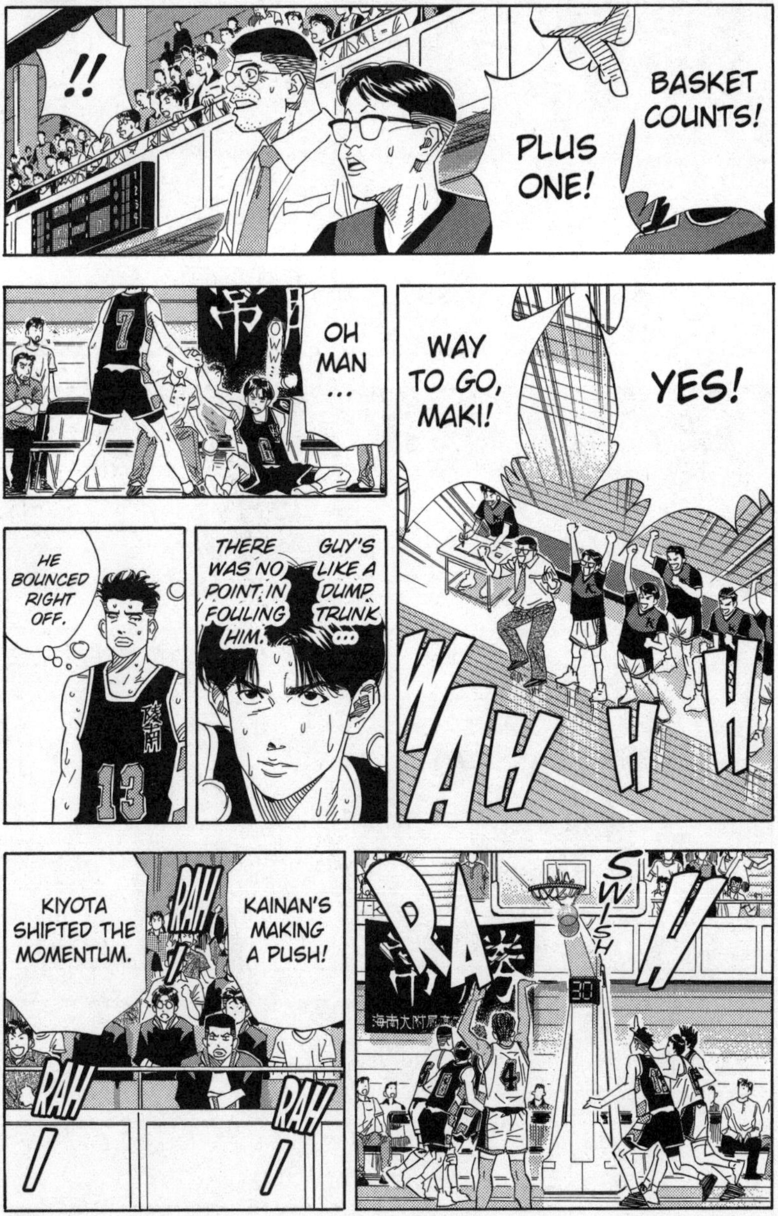

BASKET COUNTS!
PLUS ONE!
!!
YES!
WAY TO GO, MAKI!
WAHHH
OH MAN ...
GUY'S LIKE A DUMP TRUNK ...
THERE WAS NO POINT IN FOULING HIM.
HE BOUNCED RIGHT OFF.
SWISH
RAHH
KAINAN'S MAKING A PUSH!
KIYOTA SHIFTED THE MOMENTUM.
RAH!
RAH!
RAH!

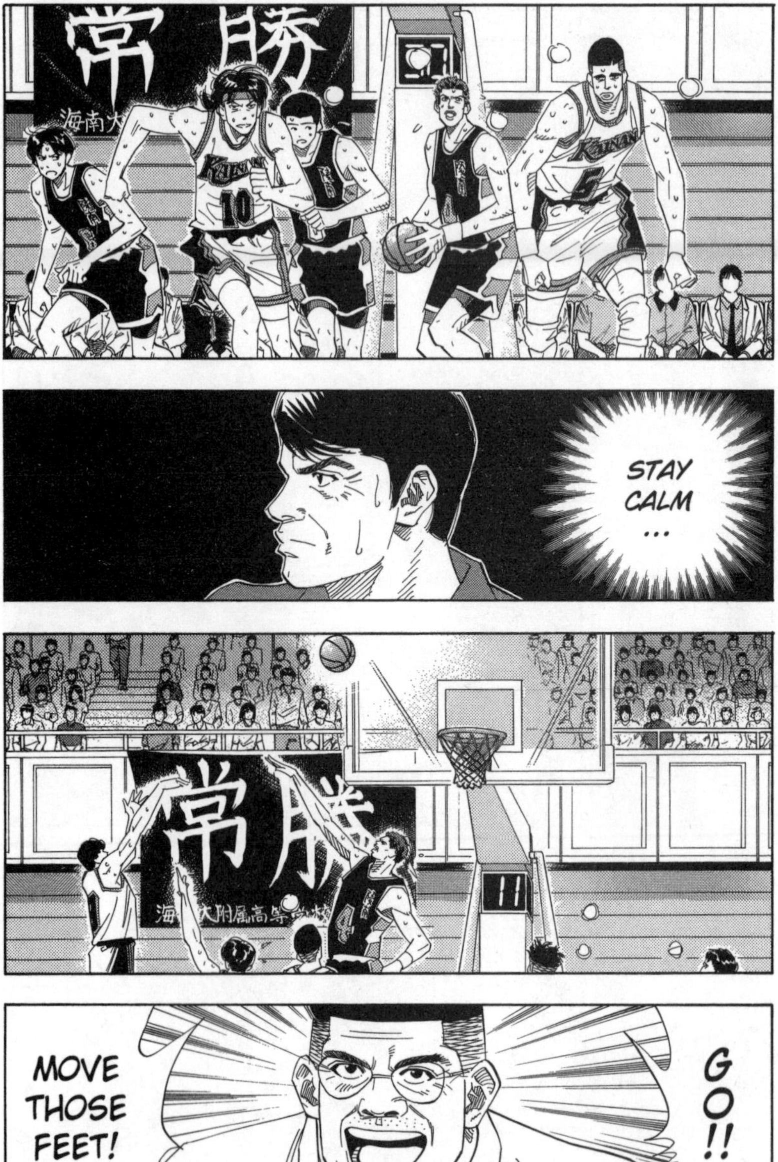

STAY CALM ...
GO!!
MOVE THOSE FEET!

READ THIS WAY

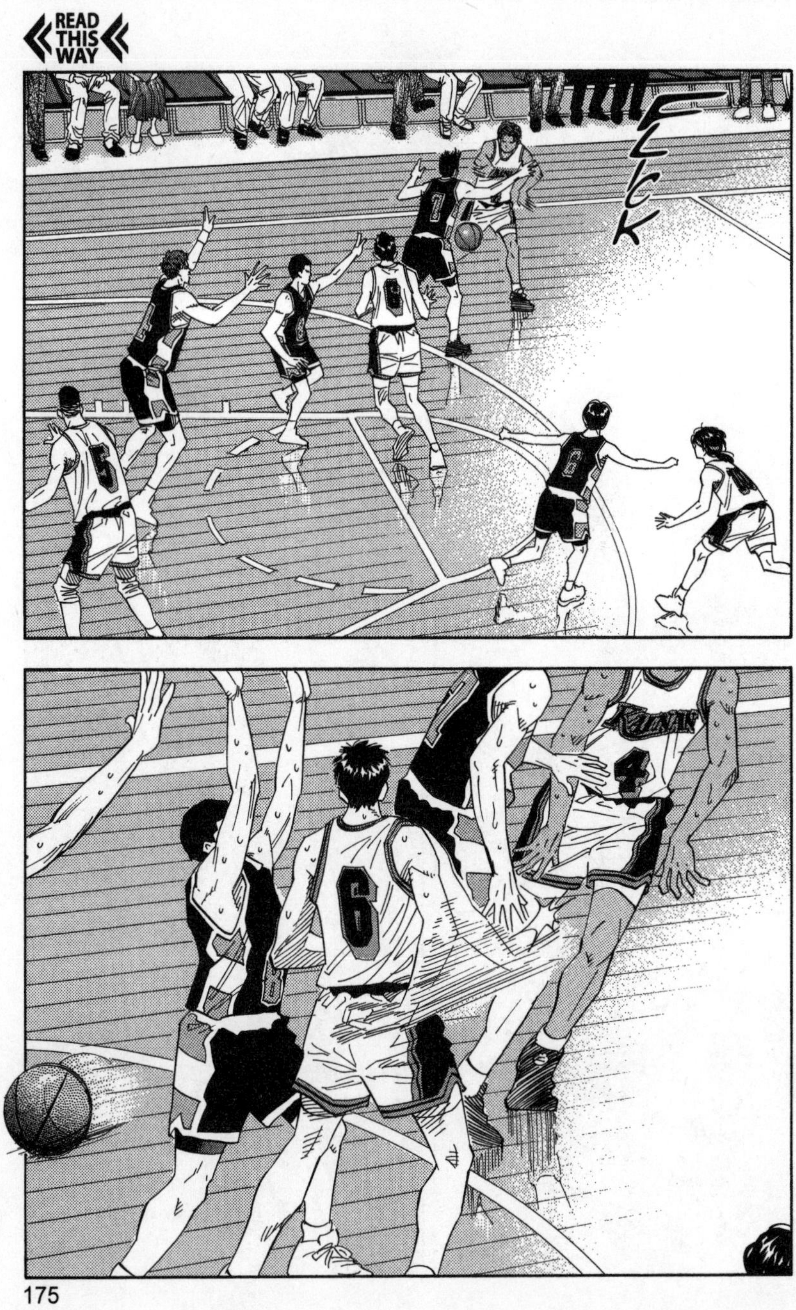
FLICK
KAINAN

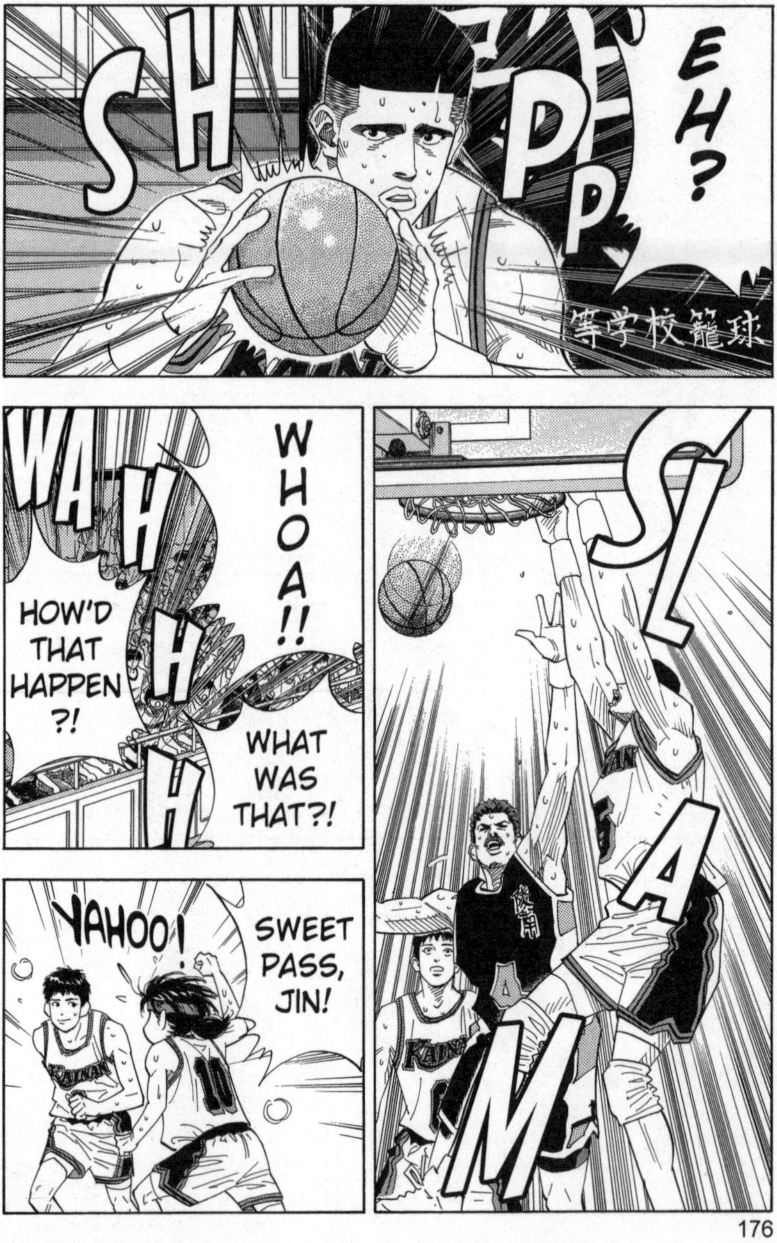
SHPP
EH?
等学校籠球
SLAM
WHOA!!
WAHHHH
WHAT WAS THAT?!
HOW'D THAT HAPPEN?!
SWEET PASS, JIN!
YAHOO!

READ THIS WAY

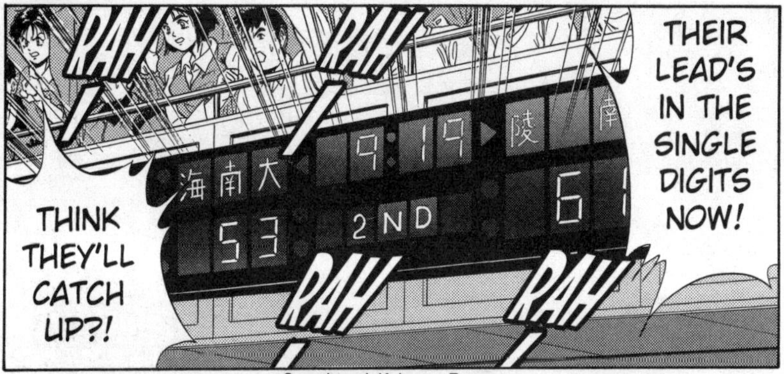
THEIR LEAD'S IN THE SINGLE DIGITS NOW!
RAH
RAH
陵南
61
9:19
2ND
海南大
53
RAH
RAH
THINK THEY'LL CATCH UP?!

Scoreboard: Kainan Ryonan

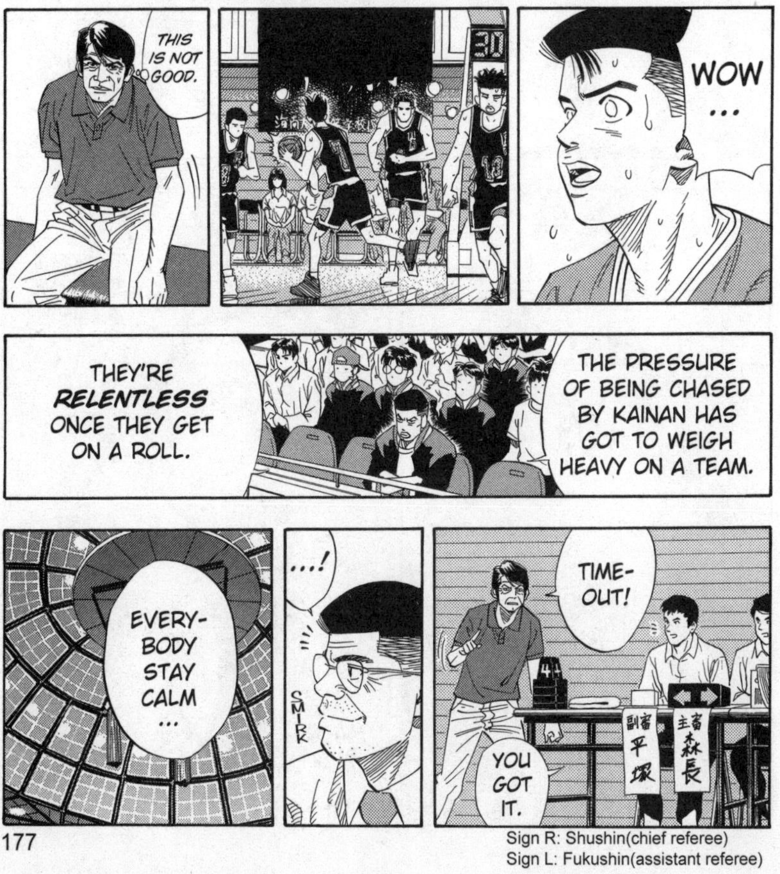
WOW ...
THIS IS NOT GOOD.
THE PRESSURE OF BEING CHASED BY KAINAN HAS GOT TO WEIGH HEAVY ON A TEAM.
THEY'RE ***RELENTLESS*** ONCE THEY GET ON A ROLL.
TIME-OUT!
主審 森長
副審 平塚
YOU GOT IT.
...!
SMIRK
EVERY-BODY STAY CALM ...

Sign R: Shushin(chief referee)
Sign L: Fukushin(assistant referee)

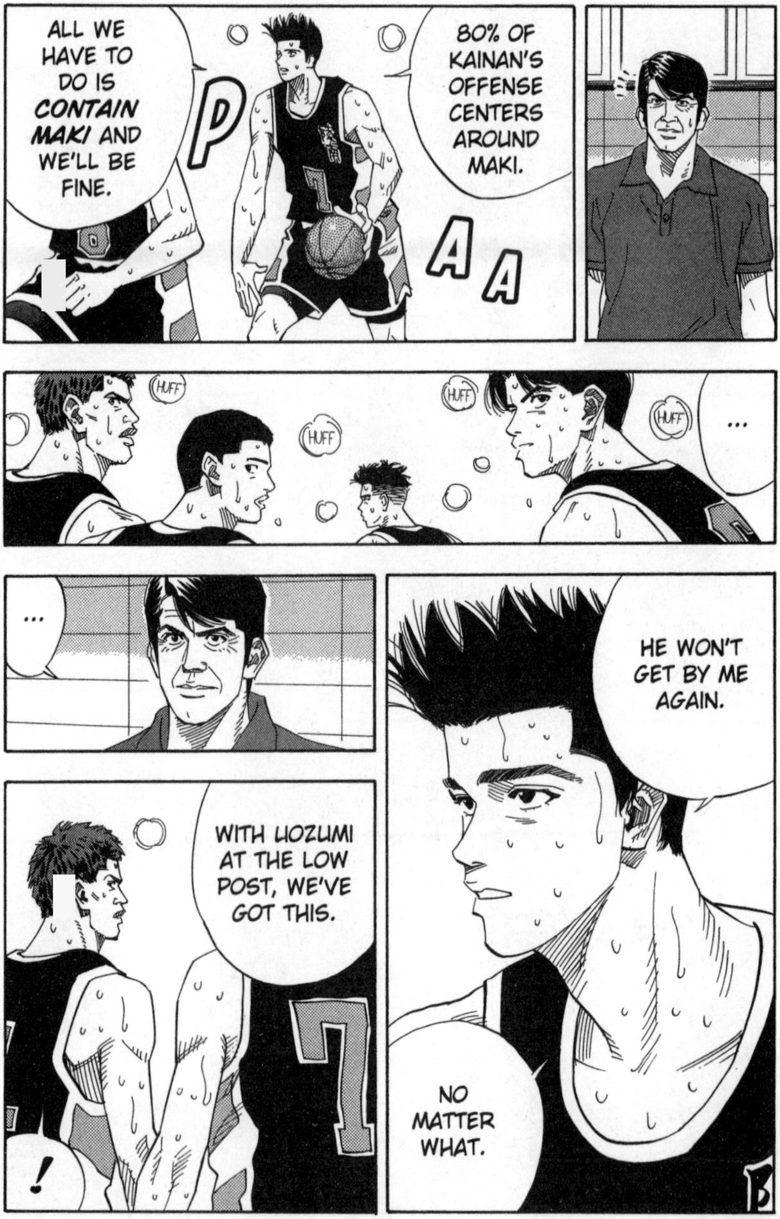
80% OF KAINAN'S OFFENSE CENTERS AROUND MAKI.
ALL WE HAVE TO DO IS CONTAIN MAKI AND WE'LL BE FINE.
PAA
...
HUFF
HUFF
HUFF
HE WON'T GET BY ME AGAIN.
NO MATTER WHAT.
...
WITH UOZUMI AT THE LOW POST, WE'VE GOT THIS.
!

READ THIS WAY

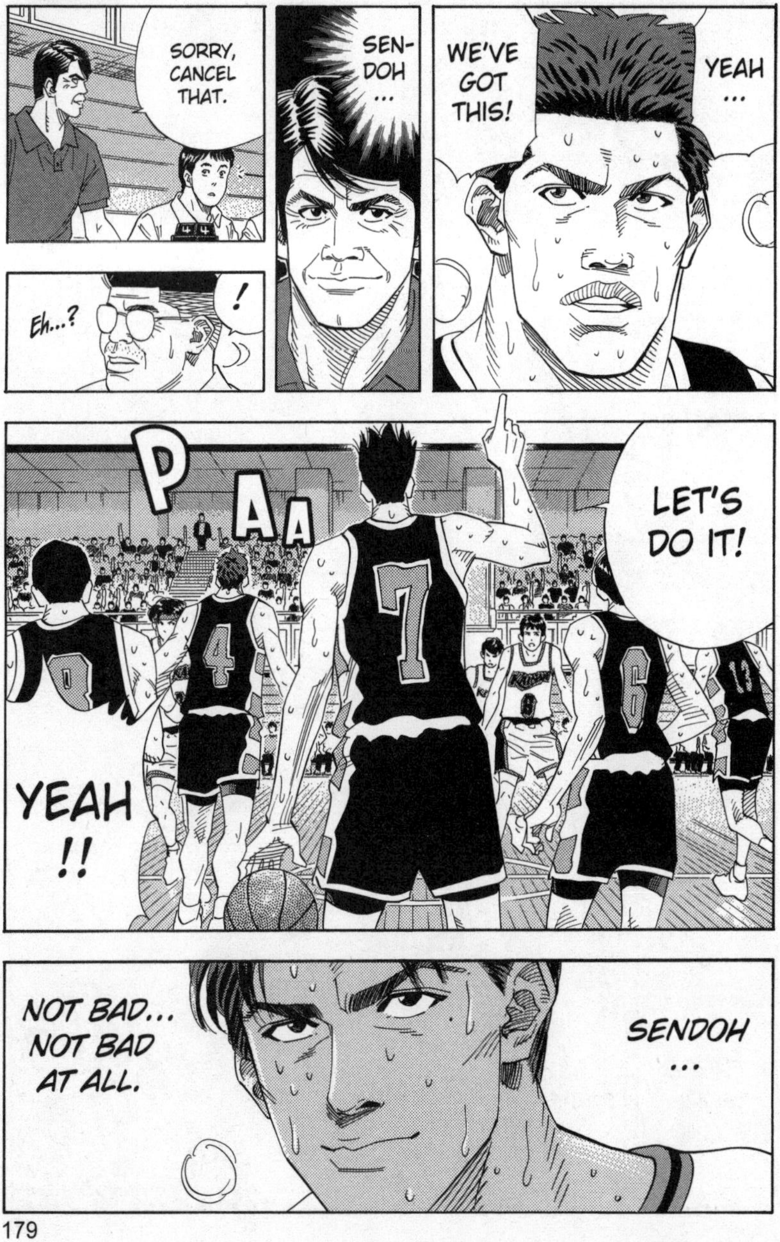
YEAH ...
WE'VE GOT THIS!
SEN-DOH ...
SORRY, CANCEL THAT.
!
Eh...?
LET'S DO IT!
PAA
YEAH !!
SENDOH ...
NOT BAD... NOT BAD AT ALL.

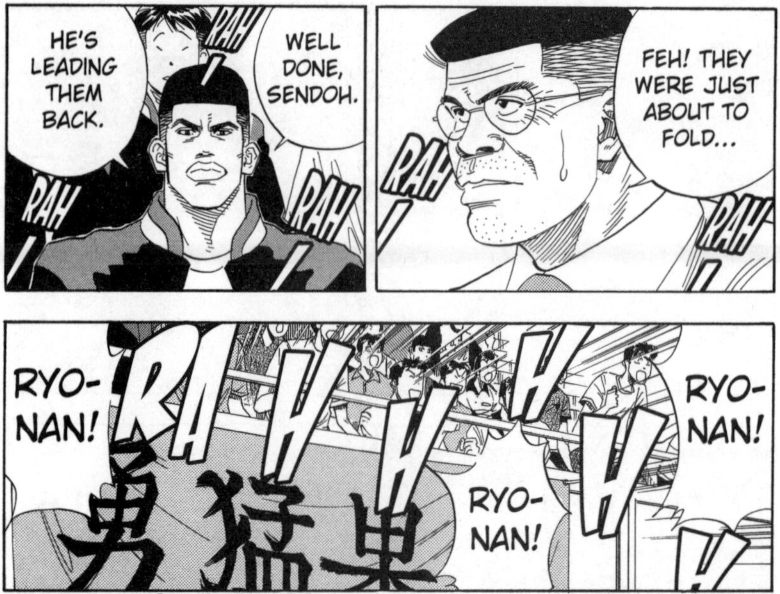
FEH! THEY WERE JUST ABOUT TO FOLD...
RAH!
RAH!
WELL DONE, SENDOH.
HE'S LEADING THEM BACK.
RAH!
RAH!
RAH!
RYO-NAN!
RYO-NAN!
RAHHHHHH!
RYO-NAN!

Banner: *Yumo Kakan* (valiant)
Ryonan High School Basketball Team

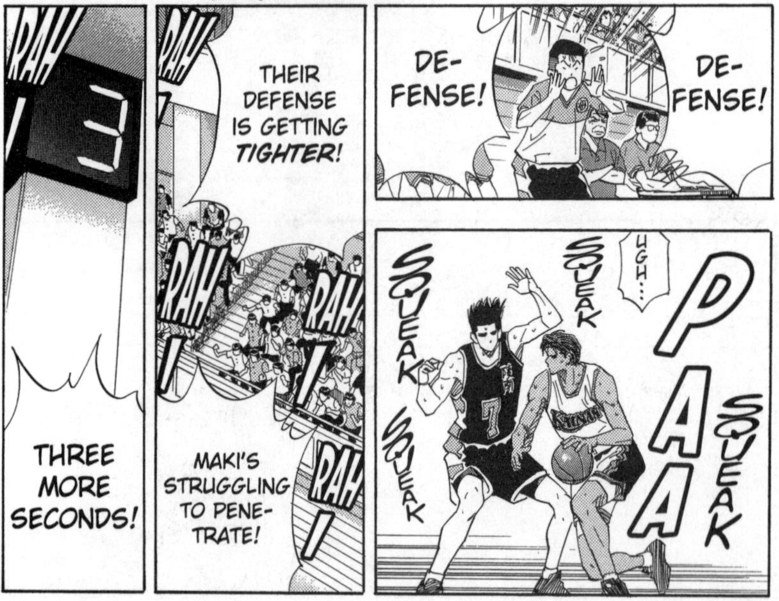
DE-FENSE!
DE-FENSE!
UGH...
PAAA
SQUEAK
SQUEAK
SQUEAK
SQUEAK
THEIR DEFENSE IS GETTING *TIGHTER!*
RAH!
RAH!
RAH!
RAH!
MAKI'S STRUGGLING TO PENE-TRATE!
RAH!
THREE MORE SECONDS!

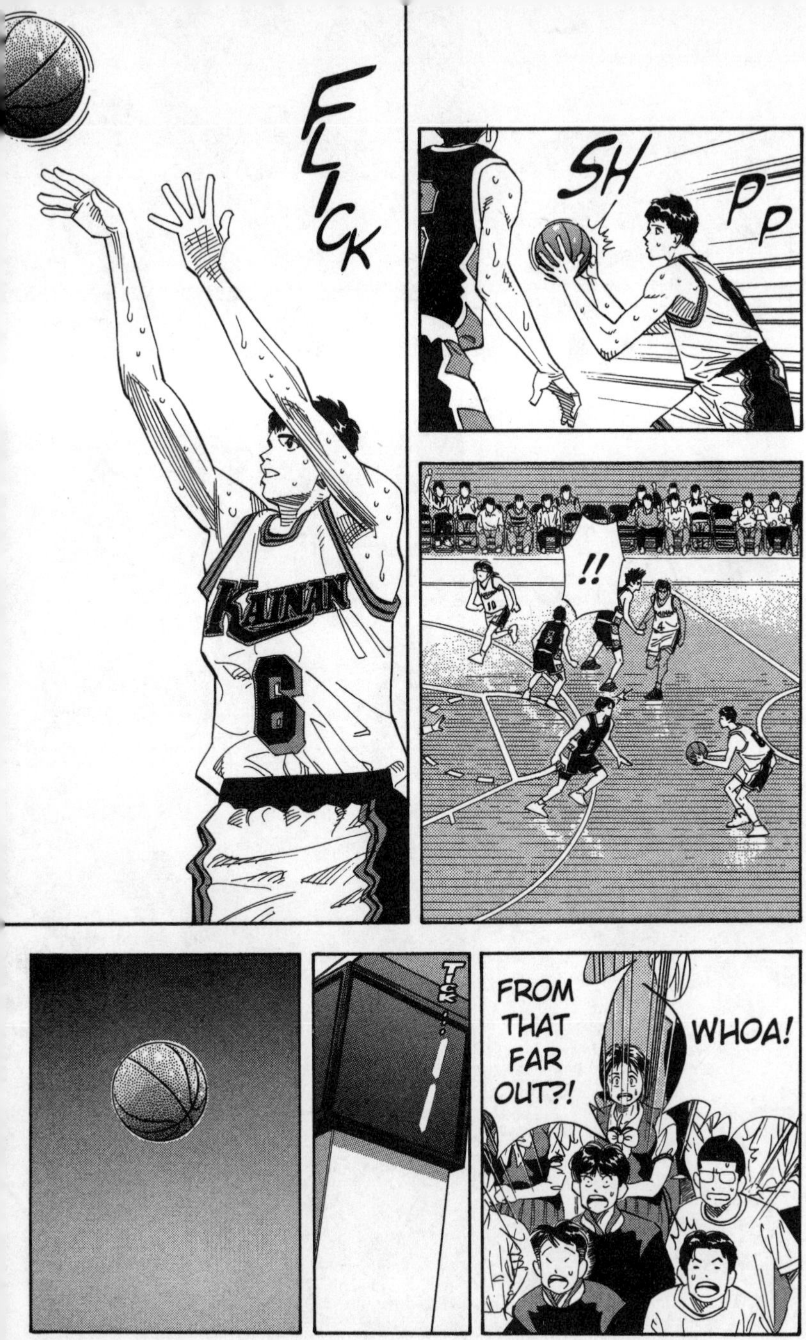
SHPP
!!
FLICK
WHOA!
FROM THAT FAR OUT?!
TICK

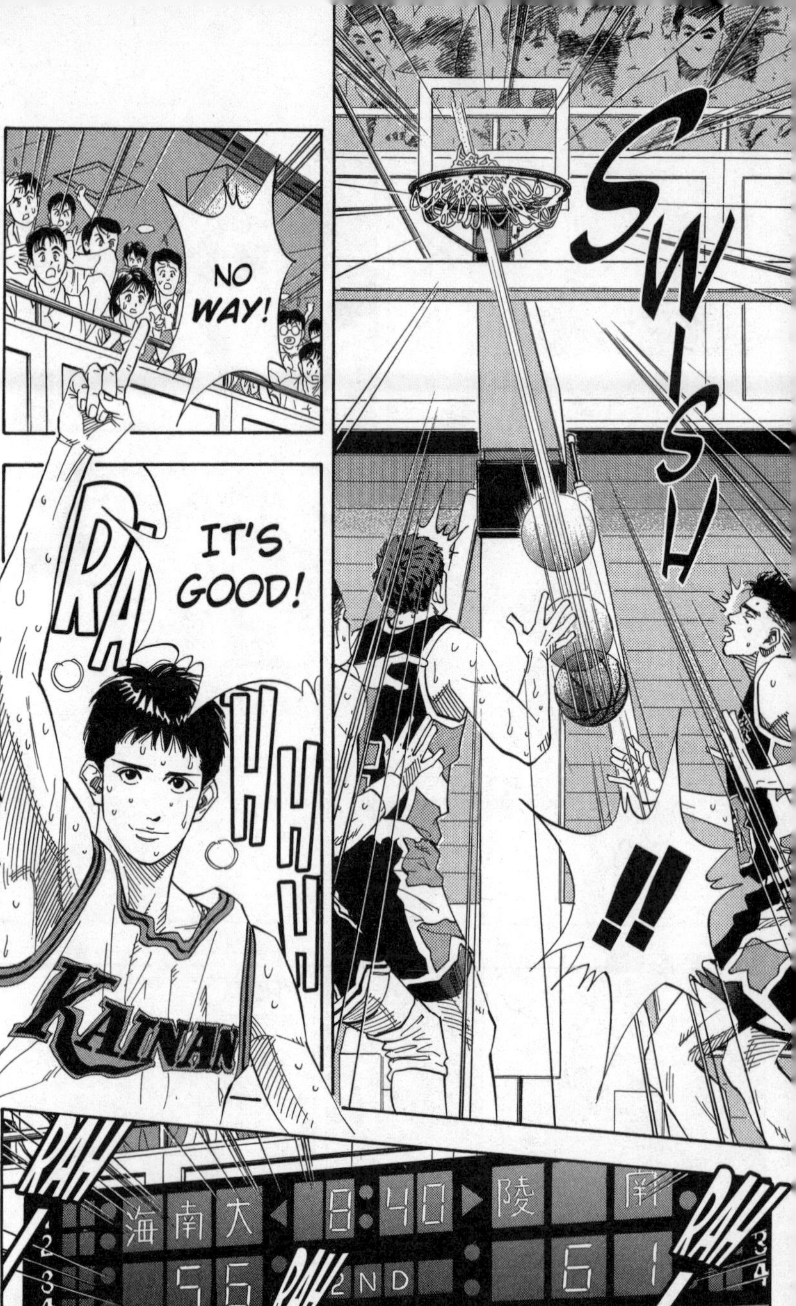
SWISH!
!!
NO WAY!
RAAHHHHH
IT'S GOOD!
RAH
海南大
8:40
陵南
56
2ND
61
RAH
RAH

Scoreboard: Kainan Ryonan

Coming Next Volume

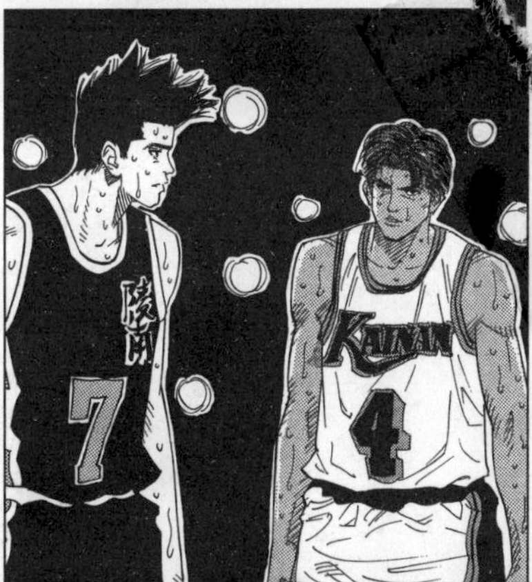
KAINAN

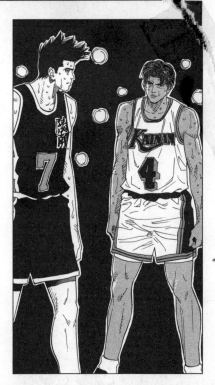

As the boys from Shohoku watch from the sidelines, the much-anticipated game between Ryonan and Kainan continues to heat up. Kainan superstar Maki's stellar playing helps swing the momentum back in his team's direction, aided in no small part by a key player from Ryonan getting into foul trouble. However, Captain Akagi and company leave the game early when they receive an alarming bit of news: Coach Anzai has collapsed and is now in the hospital!

ON SALE NOW

READ THIS WAY

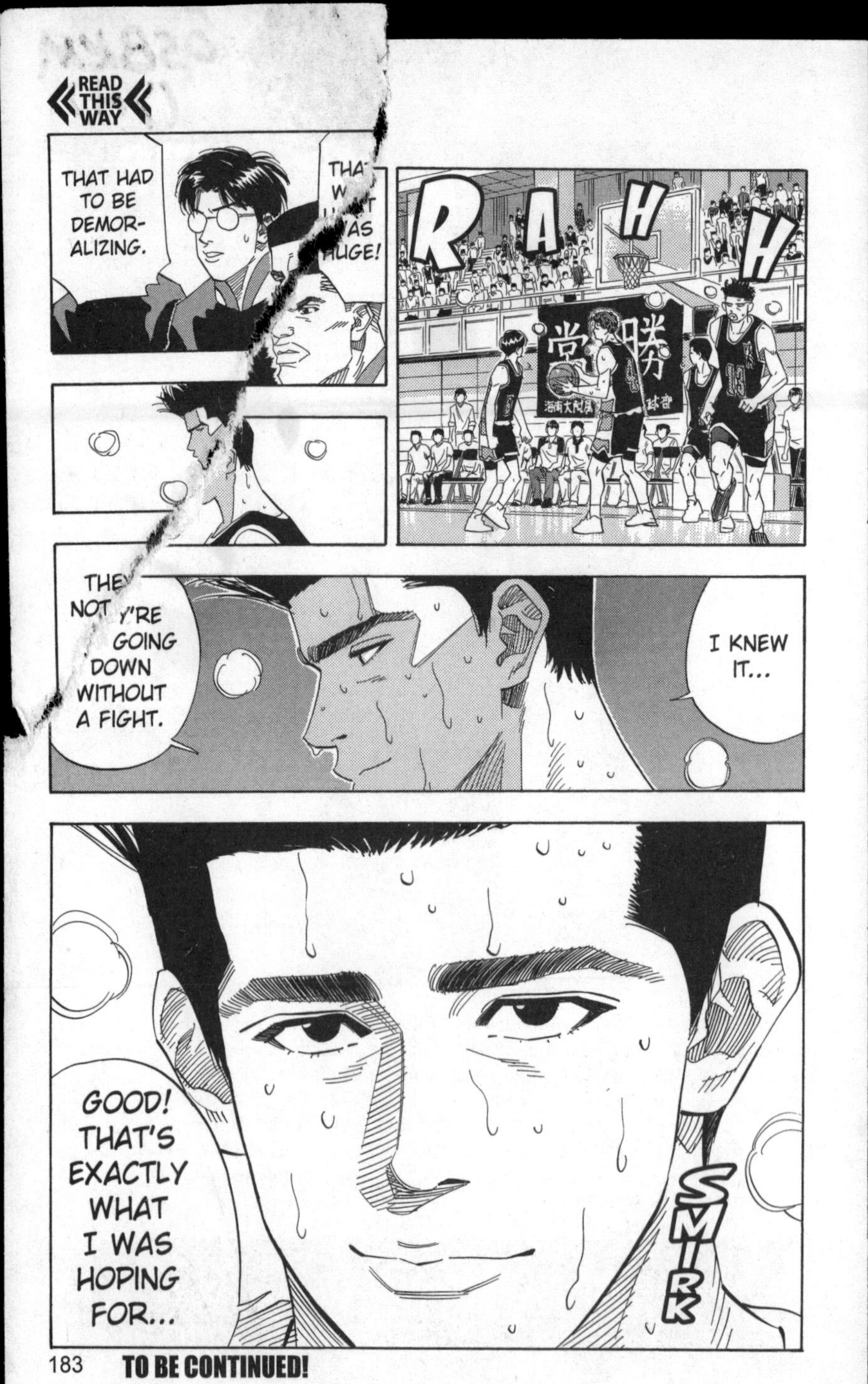
RAHH
THA W T AS HUGE!
THAT HAD TO BE DEMORALIZING.
I KNEW IT...
THE NOT Y'RE GOING DOWN WITHOUT A FIGHT.
SMIRK
GOOD! THAT'S EXACTLY WHAT I WAS HOPING FOR...

TO BE CONTINUED!